JANE AUSTEN'S
COUSIN

FOR MY DAUGHTER

Countess of hearts

JANE AUSTEN'S COUSIN
The Outlandish Countess de Feuillide

GERI WALTON

PEN & SWORD
HISTORY
AN IMPRINT OF PEN & SWORD BOOKS LTD.
YORKSHIRE – PHILADELPHIA

First published in Great Britain in 2021 by
PEN AND SWORD HISTORY
An imprint of
Pen & Sword Books Ltd
Yorkshire – Philadelphia

Copyright © Geri Walton, 2021

ISBN 978 1 52673 463 1

The right of Geri Walton to be identified as Author of this work has been asserted by her in accordance with the Copyright, Designs and Patents Act 1988.

A CIP catalogue record for this book is available from the British Library.

All rights reserved. No part of this book may be reproduced or transmitted in any form or by any means, electronic or mechanical including photocopying, recording or by any information storage and retrieval system, without permission from the Publisher in writing.

Typeset in Times New Roman 11.5/14 by
SJmagic DESIGN SERVICES, India.
Printed and bound by CPI Group (UK) Ltd, Croydon CR0 4YY

Pen & Sword Books Limited incorporates the imprints of Atlas, Archaeology, Aviation, Discovery, Family History, Fiction, History, Maritime, Military, Military Classics, Politics, Select, Transport, True Crime, Air World, Frontline Publishing, Leo Cooper, Remember When, Seaforth Publishing, The Praetorian Press, Wharncliffe Local History, Wharncliffe Transport, Wharncliffe True Crime and White Owl.

For a complete list of Pen & Sword titles please contact
PEN & SWORD BOOKS LIMITED
47 Church Street, Barnsley, South Yorkshire, S70 2AS, England
E-mail: enquiries@pen-and-sword.co.uk
Website: www.pen-and-sword.co.uk

Or
PEN AND SWORD BOOKS
1950 Lawrence Rd, Havertown, PA 19083, USA
E-mail: Uspen-and-sword@casematepublishers.com
Website: www.penandswordbooks.com

Contents

Cast of Characters vii
Author's Notes xi

Chapter 1   Aspirations for a Better Life 1
Chapter 2   Betsy 11
Chapter 3   Back in India 21
Chapter 4   Tysoe Hancock's Last Stand 29
Chapter 5   Paris 37
Chapter 6   Becoming a Countess 48
Chapter 7   Hastings, Jr. 60
Chapter 8   The Year of 1788 73
Chapter 9   The Brink of Revolution 82
Chapter 10 Philadelphia 91
Chapter 11 Reign of Terror 101
Chapter 12 The Count's Fate 108
Chapter 13 Flirtations 116
Chapter 14 Henry 125
Chapter 15 The Re-Married Life 134
Chapter 16 Life Changes 143
Chapter 17 Treaty of Amiens 153
Chapter 18 George Austen's Death 160
Chapter 19 Friendships 167

Chapter 20 A Time to Mourn 174
Chapter 21 Thoughts of a Writer 180

Bibliography 192
Endnotes 196
Index 204

Cast of Characters

Anna Marie Apollonia Chapuset - Common-law wife of Adam Carl von Imhoff, who had an affair with Warren Hastings and married him.

Anne Mathew Austen - First wife of James Austen.

Anne Lefroy - Close neighbour and important friend to Jane Austen, who was older and died unexpectedly in a horse riding accident.

Caroline Austen - Daughter of James Austen and his second wife, Mary Lloyd.

Cassandra Leigh Austen - Wife of George Austen.

Cassandra Elizabeth Austen - Oldest daughter of George and Cassandra Austen and older sister to Jane Austen.

Catherine Knatchbull Knight - Wife of Thomas Knight.

Charles John Austen - Youngest child and son of George and Cassandra Austen.

Clarinda - Housemaid to Philadelphia who returned with the Hancocks to England from India.

Jean-François Capot de Feuillide - Husband of Eliza de Feuillide who styled himself a count.

Edward 'Neddy' Austen Knight - Third child and son of George and Cassandra Austen. He was adopted by the Knights and took their last name.

Elijah Impey - India's first Chief Justice and friend of Warren Hastings, who with Warren Hastings was impeached for crimes in India and the death of Maharaja Nandakumar.

Eliza de Feuillide - Daughter of Tysoe Saul Hancock and Philadelphia Austen, cousin to Jane Austen, and mother to Hastings Jr.

Elizabeth Bridges Austen Knight - Wife of Edward Austen Knight.

Emmanuel Henri Louis Alexandre de Launay, Count d'Antraigues - A French pamphleteer, diplomat, spy and political adventurer during the French Revolution and Napoleonic Wars. He was also a friend of Eliza de Feuillide and was later killed by his servant, Lorenzo Stelli.

Fanny Catherine Austen Knight - Daughter of Edward Austen Knight and Elizabeth Bridges Austen Knight.

Francis 'Frank' Austen - Sixth child and fifth son of George and Cassandra Austen.

Harris Bigg-Wither - He proposed to Jane Austen and although she initially said 'yes', the following morning she had changed her mind and retracted her acceptance.

Hastings-François-Louis-Henri-Eugène de Feuillide - Son of Eliza and the Count de Feuillide who was named for Eliza's godfather, Warren Hastings.

Henry Austen - Fourth son and child of George and Cassandra Austen. He was Eliza de Feuillide's cousin and became her second husband.

James Austen - Oldest son of George and Cassandra Austen. He would marry Anne Mathew and when she died, he married Mary Lloyd.

Jane Austen - Seventh child and second daughter of George and Cassandra Austen. She would become a well-known novelist.

Jane Cholmeley Leigh-Perrot - Sister-in-law of Cassandra Austen. She was arrested in Bath for shoplifting at a milliner's shop but found not guilty by the jury, despite the evidence that she was likely guilty.

CAST OF CHARACTERS

James Leigh-Perrot - Husband of Jane Cholmeley and brother to Cassandra Austen.

John Woodman - He served as Eliza de Feuillide's trustee. Warren Hastings' sister, Ann, was married to him and their son, Thomas, was viewed as a possible future mate for Eliza.

George Austen - Brother to Philadelphia Austen, married to Cassandra Leigh and father to James, George Jr. Edward, Henry, Cassandra Elizabeth, Francis, Jane, and Charles John Austen.

George Austen, Jr. - Second son and child of George and Cassandra Austen. He was disabled, likely deaf, and was sent away to be cared for by Francis Cullum.

Philadelphia Austen Hancock - George Austen's sister, wife to Tysoe Saul Hancock, mother to Eliza de Feuillide, and grandmother of Hastings Jr.

Philadelphia 'Phylly' Walter - Cousin to the Austen clan and Eliza de Feuillide, and the person who Eliza corresponded regularly with, among which there are thirty-six of Eliza's letters that have survived.

Maharaja Nandakumar - Indian tax collector who accused Warren Hastings of bribing him. He was also the first victim hanged in India under British rule.

Margaret Maskelyne Clive - Friend of Philadelphia Austen Hancock's who arrived with her in India aboard the same ship and who married Robert Clive.

Maria Payne - Friend of Eliza's who accompanied her to Cheltenham for a spa visit and who loved pugs.

Mary Gibson - A Ramsgate resident who became the wife of Francis 'Frank' Austen.

Mary Lloyd - Second wife of James Austen and younger sister to Martha Lloyd.

Sir Philip Francis - Irish-born politician, member of the Supreme Council, and opponent of Warren Hastings.

JANE AUSTEN'S COUSIN

Thomas James Twisleton - distant relative of Cassandra Austen who eloped to Gretna Green in 1788 with actress Charlotte-Anne Frances Wattrell creating a scandal. In 1794 they separated and then divorced in 1798, which created more scandal.

Tom Fowle - Fiancé of Cassandra Elizabeth who died of yellow fever in the West Indies.

Thomas Knight - Rich relative of George Austen who adopted Edward 'Neddy' Austen.

Thomas Langlois Lefroy - Nephew of Madame Lefroy who Jane Austen flirted with and is perhaps the model for Austen's character Mr Darcy in *Pride and Prejudice*.

Tysoe Saul Hancock - Husband to Philadelphia Austen and father of Eliza de Feuillide.

Warren Hastings - Eliza de Feuillide's alleged father and named her godfather. He was also first married to Mary Buchanan and after her death married Anna Marie Apollonia Chapuset.

Author's Notes

When I learned that Jane Austen had a cousin who was a countess, I was intrigued. The story of Eliza Hancock, who became the Countess de Feuillide upon marriage, spans some of the most interesting and intense historical periods of the 1700s and 1800s. Her story begins in the mid-1700s during the phase when Britain was dominant in colonial India; covers the horrors of the French Revolution in the late 1700s; and looks at the period when Napoleon Bonaparte reigned supreme as Emperor of France. However, it isn't just these historical events that make Eliza's life interesting.

Eliza led a whirlwind life that led her from exotic India to Georgian Britain, to cosmopolitan Paris and back to Britain. Besides socialising and hobnobbing with Marie Antoinette, French socialites, and the elite of Britain, she also visited the staid English countryside to see her cousin, Jane Austen. Then, as wife to Jane's older brother Henry, Eliza provided inspiration to Jane, who then created fictional characters that today still intrigue readers and spark romantic notions worldwide.

This is Eliza's story.

Chapter 1

Aspirations for a Better Life

> IT LOOKS AS IF ALL THE HOUSES HAD BEEN THROWN UP IN THE AIR.
> JEMIMA KINDERSLEY ON CALCUTTA, INDIA

Certain people possess such a rare force of personality that it fascinates others: songs and stories are written about them, and they become immortalised in the human experience. One such person was Eliza de Feuillide (née Hancock), who inspired some of the most vivid and enduring fictional characters in literary history.

Born to an up-and-coming family in Calcutta, India, Eliza could have reasonably expected to live the life of an English socialite even if she lived far – both geographically and culturally – from the rural English countryside where her mother Philadelphia's birth had taken place on 15 May 1730. At the time, most of the English population embraced a rural life tending animals, ploughing fields, and harvesting crops.

Philadelphia's parents were a not-so-successful Tonbridge surgeon named William Austen and his wife Rebecca Walter (née Hampson). In addition to a son named William Hampson Walter from Rebecca's previous marriage, the Austens also had three other children: Hampson, who was born in 1728 but died in July 1730; George, born in 1731; and Leonora, born a year or so after George. It was this second son, George, who would ultimately be the father of famed novelist Jane Austen.

Sadly, both of Philadelphia's parents died when she and her siblings were young. Rebecca died on Shrove Tuesday, 2 February 1733 and William died a few years later in 1737. As William's second wife would not take on his children, they were left as orphans. Fortunately, William had left a trust for their maintenance, and they were placed under the guardianship of his brother, Francis Austen. Of the children, George and Leonora lived with the Austen clan, whereas 7-year-old Philadelphia was sent to live with wealthy relatives, the Freeman family, who had no time for a young girl.

On Philadelphia's fifteenth birthday, 9 May 1745, she was apprenticed to a milliner named Mrs Cole in Covent Garden on Russell Street in London, with the £45 premium likely paid for by her Uncle Francis. At that time, a milliner was a vendor of all types of fancy wear and articles of apparel, which also included ribbons, gloves, bonnets, and so on. Milliners were also expected to be fine 'needle-women' and 'perfect' connoisseurs of fashion because it was also their job to import the latest 'whims from *Paris*'.

Despite the high degree of skill required to become a milliner, young female apprentices earned a pittance. The majority earned between five and six shillings a week, and out of that they still had to pay for room and board. Low wages were not the only problem these teenage girls faced: according to a 1757 historical account written in *The London Tradesman* (a periodical about the trades, professions, and arts in the cities of London and Westminster), there were many dangers associated with millinery jobs, and parents were forcefully warned not to 'bind their daughters' to such undesirable businesses.

The most dangerous threat was from the 'beaus', 'rakes', and 'coxcombs' who patronised the millinery shops and who exposed the 'young Creatures to many Temptations, and insensibly debauche[d] their Morals before they are capable of Vice.'[1] Moreover, such degenerates threatened the young innocent 'sempstresses' with their barrages of loose talk, rudeness, and ribaldry, all the while forcing the young women because of 'custom and respect' to respond politely and with civility. *The London Tradesman* thus concluded:

> [T]he young Creature is obliged every Day to hear a Language, that by degrees undermines her Virtues, deprives her of that modest Delicacy of Thought ... and makes Vice become familiar to the Ear, from whence there is but a small Transition to the grosser Gratification of the Appetite.[2]

Covent Garden was furthermore not a desirable place to work and had, by the eighteenth century, turned into a red-light district that attracted well-known prostitutes. In fact, by 1757, there was an annual directory of prostitutes published in *Harris's List of Covent Garden Ladies*. The book was distributed for almost twenty years and listed prostitutes who worked in and around the area. Lurid information about these women included such details as Miss L—v—r a 'nymph of fifteen',

Miss R—ch—rds—n and her 'pouting bubbies', and a Miss N—ble who was claimed to revive 'the dead'.

Philadelphia completed her apprenticeship, but she also recognised she did not want to do millinery work all her life. This realisation left her few employment options because, in the eighteenth century, there were only a handful of jobs deemed suitable for women, and those jobs paid but little. Among the jobs she might seek were such occupations as a basket-, button-, coat-, bodice-, tassel-, or cap-maker. Or, she could paint fans, gild metals, or quilt blankets. Moreover, even if she had an occupation, she was still expected to marry and be a housewife, which meant running the household and raising children.

Philadelphia knew that practically the only way a woman could achieve social mobility was through marriage. Still, even if a woman married well, it did not necessarily mean she would have an idle easy life. Some women with big households organised and supervised servants, helped their husbands run their estates, or handled the finances. Moreover, if a woman was married to a travelling merchant, the business often fell to her to manage during his absence.

Women who married poorer, even if they were lucky enough to have a servant or two, also had many responsibilities. These housewives cooked and baked, put up preserves, tended and raised children, cared for anyone sick, and made soap and candles. Besides cleaning the house, beating the rugs, and tending the fire, such women were also responsible for sewing, mending, and washing clothes.

In the countryside, housewives often had all these tasks and more. Out of necessity, country households were expected to be self-sufficient. This meant a farmer's wife often planted and cared for vegetable gardens, milked cows, and fed and looked after the farm animals and chickens. Then, whatever extra goods the country housewife might produce, she sold at market.

Philadelphia was also aware that her beauty and wit were not enough to attract a wealthy husband in England, especially because she had little or no dowry. That was something practically mandatory for marriage at the time. But, in those days, there was a demand for British wives in India.

Many British men were making fortunes in India with the East India Company (EIC). These men arrived in India as poor people, became rich, and began living like royalty. Yet, because there were few British women in India, many of these rich bachelors were taking local Indian women as mistresses. When they began falling in love and marrying some of these Indian women, the EIC was unhappy and viewed such marriages as 'unsuitable'. The EIC therefore decided to import British women, hoping the men would marry them instead. Since there were so few European females in India, lonely Company men were willing to accept women with small or no dowries. This then presented a way for poorer women in England to 'get in on the ground floor' of the *nouveau riche*. In fact, there were so many of these women travelling to India looking for husbands that they became known as 'ship beauties'.

Philadelphia's Uncle Francis knew of these marriage opportunities in India and probably suggested that was her best opportunity. Uncle Francis was also serving as a financial agent to a respectable surgeon, Tysoe Saul Hancock, who worked for the EIC. Hancock had been in India for several years when he decided he wanted a wife. In fact, he had already 'let it be known that he was not particular about a dowry, so long as his bride should be young and of a good family.'[3]

As Philadelphia thus met the criteria, she sailed off to Madras on 18 January 1752 with expectations of marriage. In case it didn't work out or to avoid possible stigma, she told relatives she was visiting friends at Fort St David, a British fort near the town of Cuddalore, a hundred miles south of Madras on the Coromandel Coast of India. She travelled aboard the *HMS Bombay Castle*, a third-rate 74-gun ship funded by the EIC as a contribution to the war effort. She reached her destination almost six months later on 8 August 1752, along with eleven other single women in search of husbands.

Philadelphia's trip proved fruitful because soon, on 22 February 1753, she married Hancock at Cuddalore. He was born in Kent in the village of Sittingbourne in 1723 and was the son of Reverend Thomas Saul Hancock, who served as pastor of Hollingbourne. Hancock had studied medicine in London, completed his apprenticeship, and sailed for India in 1745, after accepting a job with the EIC earning £36 per annum and perhaps imagining that he would get rich.

Hancock might not have been the best match for Philadelphia, a gregarious woman who was full of life. Unlike her, he was a gloomy person who failed frequently in business and was constantly ill. However, he was a loyal man who embraced a strict moral code and was described as kind-hearted, meticulous, and thrifty. If Philadelphia had any complaint about her new husband, it was that his constant illnesses filled him with self-pity, which is perhaps why twenty-first century

Austen historian Deirdre le Faye notes: 'He … seems to have been a melancholy man – unhappy in his medical profession, frequently ill and given to harping upon his fast-approaching decrepitude, even though he was barely seven years Philadelphia's senior.'[4]

Hancock's employer, the EIC, was a global trading company established in the 1600s by several enterprising businessmen. The EIC had achieved stunning success and rose to control a significant part of the global trade, particularly in basic commodities, such as cotton, indigo, silk, spices, saltpetre, opium, tea, and salt. However, in the century following its origin, the EIC's interest switched from trade to acquiring territory because the Mughal Empire was declining, and the French East India Company began to threaten the EIC's monopoly. This resulted in confrontations, and the EIC then established their own military and administrative departments. Before long, they had become an imperial power making decisions, ruling territories, and creating colonies.

After Philadelphia and Hancock's marriage, the couple stayed at Fort St David. Although none of Philadelphia's letters have survived from the period, it is known that Hancock was working as a doctor. Moreover, at that point Philadelphia seemed to have succeeded in her aspirations to find a better life. Rather than waiting on customers and sewing dresses, she was being cared for by some thirty servants, including four personal maidservants (Diana, Silima, Dido, and Clarinda) who served her alone.

Philadelphia and Hancock were not the only ones with numerous servants. Rich merchants in India sometimes had as many as 100 servants. For example, one English lawyer named William Hickey, who described himself as not wealthy, employed sixty-three servants 'including eight whose only duty was to wait at the table, three to cut the grass in the garden, four grooms and one coachman, two bakers, two cooks, a hairdresser and nine valets'.[5]

Fort St David, by 1746, was the British headquarters for southern India, and, in 1756, Robert Clive was appointed its governor. Clive would later be credited with obtaining large swathes of southern Asia for the EIC, which not only made the company wealthy but also made him a multi-millionaire. Clive had been warned about the 'ship beauties' stealing men's hearts but that did not stop him from falling for and marrying Margaret Maskelyne in 1753. She, like Philadelphia, had been aboard the *Bombay Castle* when it sailed to India a year earlier.

In 1759, the Hancocks moved to Fort William, Calcutta, which is in the eastern state of West Bengal and located in eastern India. It was over 1100 miles from Cuddalore and is now called Kolkata. Philadelphia arrived ahead of her husband and stayed with the Clives for several months.

Calcutta was an unkept, unorganised, and undeniably fast-growing European settlement sitting alongside the east bank of the Hooghly River. Clive described it as 'one of the most wicked Places in the Universe. Corruption, Licentiousness and a want of Principle seem to have possess'd the Minds of all the Civil Servants, by frequent bad examples they have grown callous, Rapacious and Luxurious beyond Conception'.[6]

A Mrs Jemima Kindersley, who married Colonel Nathaniel Kindersley of the Bengal Artillery in 1762, had also travelled with her husband to India and described Calcutta as an 'awkward' and 'irregular' place. She noted that Calcutta was continually increasing in size and population. This was due in part to the EIC hiring employees to help with its operations. In fact, she reported that the inhabitants were multiplying so fast that there were never enough houses to accommodate them. Moreover, she stated that Fort William was an 'immence [sic] place' and a 'town within itself'.

Kindersley also reported that despite eighteenth-century Calcutta being large with numerous houses, there was a housing shortage. To solve it, anyone who could afford a plot of land could build a house. Because there were no regulations or rules related to construction projects, people built whatever they liked based on their own personal tastes 'without regard to the beauty or regularity of the town … [making it look like houses] had been thrown up in the air, and fallen down again by accident'.[7]

This lack of zoning laws had created a city that was a mishmash of buildings: a straw hut could be built next to a fine house or a shoddy building next door to a commercial warehouse. It also meant that servants and construction workers, who had nowhere to sleep or live, built for themselves some sort of meagre straw hut often next to the fine house of their master, which according to Kindersley thereby ruined any view the elite homeowner might have wished to achieve.

The interiors of these eighteenth-century Calcutta houses were decidedly different from those found in England. Because of the vermin and heat, both paper and wainscot were deemed improper in India. Walls were usually white and plastered in panels. Floors were also plastered and generally did not have carpets because they added too much to the heat.

Therefore, if a floor was covered it was usually done with a 'fine matt' that was nailed down to hold it in place.

Furnishing and decorating a house in eighteenth-century Calcutta was no easy task either. Furniture was 'exorbitantly dear' as it was difficult to obtain, leaving rooms often sparse. Even when rooms were furnished with couches and chairs, the furniture tended to be a mishmash of varying eras and styles. The most common furnishings for the British were what they could obtain from European ship captains. However, some British citizens did order furniture from China, but by the time such orders appeared, the purchaser was usually returning home to Britain.

The sturdy beds and nicely stuffed mattresses that people used in England were rare in eighteenth-century Calcutta. People generally slept on what was referred to as a cot. These were designed in several pieces so that they could be easily and readily moved because, when people travelled, they took their beds with them. These movable beds were usually covered with either gauze or muslin, and people also slept on thin mattresses or on top of quilts because of the pervasive heat.

Kindersley asserts that the thing most like a street in Calcutta was called the Buzar, a name given to the place where anything and everything was sold from one of the 'shabby-looking shops' that dotted the street. The British rarely entered this area, but if they did and tried to bargain for themselves, they were usually cheated. Therefore, most Englishmen left purchasing at the Buzar to their servants who bought whatever their British master or mistress might desire.

In eighteenth-century Calcutta, there were distinct parts in the city where certain ethnic groups resided. For instance, one section housed the 'Armenians' and those called 'Portuguese' who, according to Kindersley, lived in chimneyless huts built of mud and straw and produced 'disagreeable' cooking odours. The British employed these people.

One activity in Calcutta that many of the British enjoyed was 'taking an airing' or in other words, a daily carriage ride. The participants appeared either at sunset or just before sunrise in an area just outside the city. The spot became popular for airings because it was devoid of smoke and offered clean, fresh air, which the British took advantage of it by driving themselves around a 'sort of ring' that was about two miles long.

In Calcutta, the Hancocks met Warren Hastings, a man who would change their lives. He was a balding, small, thin man born in 1732 at Churchill, Oxfordshire to a poor father and a mother who died soon after his birth. He had joined the EIC in 1750 as a clerk and reached India in August that same year. He quickly became known as a diligent and hardworking employee who spent his free time immersing himself in Indian culture and learning Urdu and Persian. For all his hard work, he won a promotion in 1752 and was sent to Fort William, where he worked for William Watts and gained further experience.

Hastings was also captured for a time when the Bengalese stormed Fort William, a fort that had been founded in 1696 to protect the EIC's trade in Calcutta. The incident occurred in 1756 due to political turmoil arising because the new Bengal ruler, 23-year-old Mirza Muhammad Siraj ud-Daulah, was anti-European and unhappy with the EIC's political interference in his province. He was also upset over the gross abuses in trade privileges by the British that resulted in heavy losses in customs duties for his government. In addition, the British had decided to add reinforcements and strengthen the fort because they were anticipating trouble with Siraj ud-Daulah, but they did so without his permission.

Siraj ud-Daulah then ordered the immediate cessation of reinforcements at Fort William, but the EIC ignored him. Angered, he then launched an attack against the British. To avoid a massacre, the British quickly surrendered. The number of captives taken in Calcutta has been debated, but supposedly Hastings was among those detained on 20 June 1756 and eventually locked in the fort's prison, called the 'Black Hole'.

The Black Hole allegedly measured about 14 feet by 18 feet, far too small for all the captured prisoners. It thus resulted in a catastrophe, and it was reported:

> [The] dungeon of the fortress, [was] a strongly barred room, ... and never intended for the confinement of more than two or three men at a time. There were only two windows, both opening toward the west, whence under the circumstances, but little air could enter. Add to this that a projecting verandah outside, and thick iron bars within, materially impeded the ventilation there might be, while conflagrations raging in different parts of the fort gave the atmosphere an oppressiveness unusual even in that sultry climate, ... exhausted with previous fatigue, and packed so tightly in their prison that it was with difficulty the door could be closed. A few moments sufficed to throw them into a profuse perspiration, the natural consequence of

which was a raging thirst. They stripped off their clothes to gain more room, sat down on the floor that the air might circulate more freely, and when every expedient failed, sought by the bitterest insults to provoke the guards to fire on them. One of the soldiers stationed in the verandah was offered 1,000 rupees to have them removed to a larger room. He went away, but returned saying it was impossible. The bribe was then doubled, and he made a second attempt with a like result; the nabob was asleep, and no one durst wake him. By 9 o'clock several had died, and many more were delirious. A frantic cry for water now became general, and one of the guards, more compassionate than his fellows, caused some [water] to be brought to the bars ... and two or three ... received it in their hats, and passed it on to the men behind. In their impatience to secure it nearly all was spilt, and the little they drank seemed only to increase their thirst. Self-control was soon lost; those in remote parts of the room struggled to reach the window, and a fearful tumult ensued, in which the weakest were trampled or pressed to death. They raved, fought, prayed, blasphemed, and many then fell exhausted on the floor, where suffocation put an end to their torments. The Indian soldiers, meanwhile, crowded around the windows, and even brought lights that they might entertain themselves with the dreadful spectacle. The odor which filled the dungeon became more deadly every moment, and about 11 o'clock the prisoners began to drop off fast. At length, at 6 in the morning, [Siraj ud-Daulah] awoke, and ordered the door to be opened. Of the 146 only 23 ... remained alive, and they were either stupefied or raving.[8]

Some historians claim the story of the Black Hole is a myth invented to conceal the EIC's oppressive empire-building and numerous scandals. Others claim the story is true but question whether the deaths were intentional, the specific number of captives incarcerated, and the exact number who died in the Black Hole. There are also those who claim Hastings was not among those captured, but regardless it is indisputable that Hastings ultimately escaped to the island of Fulta, along with other refugees from Calcutta. There, he met and married Mary Buchanan, mother of two daughters by a lieutenant, who had reputedly been trampled to death in the Black Hole. Soon after Hastings and Buchanan married, a British expedition from Madras under Robert Clive arrived to rescue them.

Hastings went on to serve as a volunteer in Clive's forces that retook Calcutta in January 1757, and the Black Hole allegedly became the reason that the British decided to take over all of India. Hastings greatly impressed Clive and arrangements were soon made for Hastings to return to Kasimbazar and resume his pre-war activities. Then at Clive's instigation, Hastings became the British Resident in the Bengali capital of Murshidabad where he demonstrated great sympathy for the Indian rulers who were ordered about by the EIC. Hastings therefore tried to establish understanding relationships with them and their people, and this in turn allowed him to mediate between the two sides and resulted in him being appointed to the Calcutta Council.

During this time, Hastings' wife Mary gave birth to two children: George, born in December 1757, and Elizabeth, born in October 1758. Unfortunately, baby Elizabeth died about three weeks after her birth. Mary and Philadelphia had been good friends back in London, and Philadelphia probably comforted Mary over the death of Elizabeth as they had renewed their friendship.

Then another tragedy struck. It happened while Hastings was away on a business trip. Mary became deathly ill, and Philadelphia stepped in to care for her. Despite Philadelphia's care, Mary died on 11 July 1759. Philadelphia then took care of the children, and Hastings was so grateful for all she had done that he gave her a rosewood Indian writing desk inlaid with ivory.

Some people surmise that it was after the death of Mary that the lonely and handsome Hastings began having an affair with Philadelphia. She would have been close to Hastings' own age, and although her husband was affectionate, Hancock was probably not as interesting or exciting as Hastings. Hancock also did not possess the same drive and intelligence that would cause Hastings to succeed in India. Moreover, if Philadelphia and Hastings did have an affair, tacit consent may have been given by Hancock because he refused to look too closely at their relationship. Perhaps he feared ruining his business relationship with Hastings or perhaps he would not allow his pride to think that a suddenly pregnant Philadelphia could be having anyone's child but his.

Chapter 2

Betsy

> MAKE NO CHANGE IN THE PLAN YOU HAVE ALREADY LAID DOWN.
> WARREN HASTINGS ON ELIZA'S FUTURE

Eliza Hancock, called 'Betsy' for her first few years, was born on 22 December 1761, some twenty months after the death of Mary Hastings. Even before Eliza was born, rumours swirled that Hastings was her biological father. These rumours were encouraged by the fact that Philadelphia had been married for eight years without any children when she suddenly became pregnant, and her pregnancy happened during a time when the Hancocks were friendly with Hastings.

Some of the allegations came from the correspondence between Robert Clive and his wife. The Clives had left India in February 1760, before Eliza's birth, with a fortune of about £300,000 (worth over £60,000,000 today). They also had Robert's *jagir*, a type of land grant that enabled him to collect tax revenues from appointed territories. After they left, Mrs Clive kept in touch through sporadic letters with Philadelphia and with another friend, Major John Carnac. The mail was slow as it had to the cross the sea, and therefore it usually took six months for letters to arrive. Staying abreast of the latest news was therefore difficult, but on 19 November 1761 Carnac wrote Mrs Clive a note containing tidbits from the rumour mill in Calcutta: 'Would You believe it, Madam, Mrs Hancock is pregnant. The scandalous chronicle gives the credit thereof to Hastings.'[1]

Although Carnac implied Eliza was Hastings' child, some biographies and historians dispute it. They allege the rumour was started by a backbiting woman named Jane 'Jenny' Kelsall, who was first married to Captain Thomas Latham and then later married Clive's secretary, Sir Henry Strachey, 1st Baronet. Supposedly, she or Strachey may have been upset about a favour that Hastings did for Hancock, which is why she began to slander Philadelphia.

Jenny had also never been a fan of Hancock, despite the good doctor once using his medical skills to save her life. Apparently, she had shown him nothing but 'ingratitude', and after the Hancocks returned to England, Hancock alleged that while they had lived in India, Jenny had behaved with 'contempt' and 'coolness' towards Philadelphia. What further fanned the flames of rumour about Philadelphia and Hastings was what Clive wrote to his wife in the summer of 1765:

> In no circumstances whatever keep company with Mrs Hancock for it is beyond a doubt that she abandoned herself to Mr Hastings, indeed, I would rather you had no acquaintance with the ladies who have been in India, they stand in such little esteem in England that their company cannot be of credit to Lady Clive.[2]

Eliza lived her first four years in Calcutta. A month after her birth, she was baptised, and Mrs Clive was named her godmother and Hastings her godfather. Furthermore, she was named for Hastings' dead daughter Elizabeth.

Eliza was pretty with tiny delicate facial features on a large moon-shaped face. Samuel Staveley, called 'Old Rattle,' provided glimpses of what life was like for young Eliza in Calcutta, where she was often the centre of attention, which may have shaped her personality and interest in performing. Festivities, baptisms, and pleasant evenings were mentioned as well as children, who were of particular interest because according to author Le Faye, 'The English children were evidently the plaything of the whole group, news of their health being anxiously sought and transmitted whenever any member of the community was away'.[3] Such news about those living in India was regularly transmitted in letters to the people back home in Britain. For instance, one mention by Staveley of those in Calcutta stated:

> Mrs Hancock sup'd last night at ye Gardens ... Mrs Hancock & Miss Ironside sup at the Gardens to Night ... George and Bob [Vansittart] are both very well & Miss Betsy Hancock. ... Little Betsy is [also] very fond of Miss Ironside & her Guitar. ... I was last Night at a tete a tete with Mrs Hancock.[4]

During Hancock's time in India, he was busy making and saving money, just like Hastings. This was the same goal embraced by many of the British EIC men who travelled to India. They wanted to earn a fortune and then return to their homeland to live out their lives in comfort and to be reunited with their families and friends.

By this time, Betsy was four. Her parents and Hastings both believed they had amassed sufficient wealth and investments in India to set themselves up nicely in England. So, both families left India in January 1765 on the ship of war, the *HMS Medway*, with 'the passage … presumably granted as an act of grace; but Hancock mentions that he had to pay £1500 for the transport of his own and his wife's possessions, so that the naval officer of the day was not averse from making an honest penny out of his guests'.[5] Also on board was Clarinda, Philadelphia's most beloved maidservant.

The ship docked in London in the summer of 1765. Their arrival happened a little over a year after Philadelphia's brother George Austen married Cassandra Leigh at the Walcot Church in Bath on 26 April 1764. The bride was married in her travelling dress and she needed it because the newlyweds immediately left for Deane, a village in the county of Hampshire, England about sixty-seven miles away from Bath.

In 1761, before the Austens' marriage, a friend of Hastings had taken Hastings' son George back to England so that he could be educated there, a custom that was common at the time. Soon the young boy was living with the Leighs in Bath, and then he was sent to George and Cassandra Austen in Deane for an education. Unfortunately, sometime in the autumn of 1764, he developed putrid sore throat (diphtheria), and died. 'Mrs. Austen had become so much attached to him that she always declared that his death had been as great a grief to her as if he had been a child of her own'.[6]

As it took six months for news to reach India, George Austen's letter about the boy's death had not reached Hastings, who was by then on a ship sailing back to England. Thus, it was the first thing Hastings learned when he landed on England's shores. The news must have been devastating as Hastings loved his son dearly. Still he did not blame the Austens or the Leighs as they had provided good care for his son, and so he submitted reluctantly to the will of 'providence'.

After arriving in London, Hastings and the Hancocks found residences near each other and new acquaintances were also made. The Hancocks met Hastings' sister Ann and her husband John Woodman, who lived on Cleveland Row, St James. A friendship quickly developed between the Hancocks and the Woodmans, and the couples became so close that Hastings once remarked the two families were like one. Hastings even sent joint letters to them. Moreover, the Woodman's son Thomas was near the age of Eliza, and for some time there was great hope between the families that their children might someday marry.

Meanwhile, rumours continued to circulate about the Hastings and Philadelphia affair that supposedly produced Eliza. If true, Mrs Clive ignored the fact and wrote several more letters to Carnac without mentioning the scandal. Eventually, however, she indirectly referred to the situation in a letter dated 15 December 1765 where she stated:

> For my part I see nothing but the utmost propriety ... I have seen Mr and Mrs Hancock several times, but his indisposition makes them dislike meeting much company ... I find my little god-daughter a wonderful fine child, & am much pleased with her.[7]

Mrs Clive's husband Robert was unhappy about his wife's friendship with Philadelphia. In fact, he sent explicit instructions to her in May 1766 telling her to stop fraternising with Philadelphia. Mrs Clive then wrote to Carnac and stated of Philadelphia and Hancock:

> I am concerned to see a particular paragraph in your & Lord Clive's letter, I mean that which relates to an acquaintance of mine, now in England. Her outward deportment is so strictly proper, that I hope if anything has been amiss, she has only the punishment of remembering it, I mean that nobody here thinks any harm of her ... She is going to retire into the country with her husband, & one of the prettiest sensible children in the world. ... My Lord's injunctions are so positive not to keep up the acquaintance, that I shall not seek for occasions of meeting. Her husband is prodigiously fat, but in a very bad way I think.[8]

By 1768, if the rumours and innuendoes were not bad enough, the Hancocks were struggling financially. Everyone knew that life in

London was expensive. Salaries were 'not lavish' and incomes varied greatly among English residents:

> A wealthy man like the duke of Newcastle would be worth £40,000 a year ... the average income among the aristocracy might be closer to £10,000, with many "poor" peers receiving £3,000-£4,000. A bishopric such as Oxford or Bristol would be worth about £300 a year; the bishoprics of Winchester, Durham, or London, perhaps ten times that much. Members of the squirarchy might make anywhere from £200-£5,000 per year.[9]

Prices for goods also varied greatly. Higher prices might be charged at shops located in fashionable districts or at quality stores that catered to an exclusive clientele. Charges also varied at dining establishments with popular or modish spots charging more. Of this variance in prices, Professor Richard B. Schwartz notes that in London in the 1760s:

> The fees which one rank of people paid would, with the services received, be largely unknown to another rank. ... A doctor might charge 10s. or more for a visit; a famous one ... would charge more. ... Four doses of Dr James's famous fever powder would cost 2s. 6d. ... To educate your child at a grammar school would only cost a few guineas a year, because of the endowments. A private boarding school might cost as much as £30-£40 per year; ... A good saddle horse might cost 15 guineas ... A hunting horse could cost as much as 50 guineas. A good pair of hunting hounds ... 50 guineas. The cottages of the poor, past which the horses and hounds would run, might cost £15-£20 ... a two-bedroom cottage would cost £40-50. ... To see Johnson's play Irene at Drury Lane cost the following: box seat, 5s.; pit, 3s.; first gallery, 2s.; upper gallery, 1s. ... Coal cost 25s-32s. per chaldron (26-27 cwt) at the beginning of the century, and 36s-38s at the end, but the prices fluctuated depending on location: the bushel of coal that cost 5s in London at the end of the century might cost 10d in Bath.[10]

To further demonstrate how expensive London was, James Boswell, a Scottish biographer and diarist, wrote *Scheme of Living* wherein he provided his annual budget. He enjoyed a yearly allowance of £200 but complained that he had difficulty living within his means. Taking a brief look at his expenditures shows what it was like to survive in London in 1762 and 1763. This single gentleman was spending £157 annually for such items as lodging, food, candles, coal, clothes, shoes, stockings, and laundry and shoe cleaning, and he still needed the other £43 for coach travel, entertainment, and tavern diversions.

London living caused Hancock real financial problems. His expenses were £1,500 annually, a sum twice his income. He recognised the need for frugality, but nothing could induce Philadelphia to reduce her spending. She had no head for accounting, did not embrace economy, and failed to understand thrift. Yet it was not just Philadelphia's overspending that was causing the Hancocks' financial woes:

> Hancock's pecuniary troubles were in part due, like those of his friend [Hastings], to the failure of his Indian investments, and in part to the fact that he had come home ill, and left many of his affairs outstanding. He had also underestimated the sum necessary to secure a competence in England. In one of his ... letters to his wife he points out that his expenses at home, including a compassionate allowance to a sister, amounted to £1534 a year, needing an invested capital of £44,000 to defray them, and investing money in India was something like gambling. When an Anglo-Indian returned home, he appointed two or three of his friends his attorneys. They were not necessarily or even usually lawyers, but rather what we now call trustees, placing his money out in various enterprises, and remitting him the proceeds when these were successful, and apologies and regrets when they were not. This was the ideal procedure; but both Hastings and Hancock complained bitterly that whereas when in England they could get no accounts from their Indian attorneys, on their return to India they received none from those they had appointed in England.[11]

Hancock came to the realisation that to solve his financial crisis, he needed to make more money, and the only way to do that was to go back to India. Hastings reached a similar conclusion, having also overspent. In fact, Hastings likely recognised he had to return to India earlier than Hancock because, like the Hancocks, he too had been living at the most fashionable addresses and spending far beyond his means.

The men's decision to return to India was not an easy one. They had resigned their positions when they came back to England, and the EIC system had no allowance for leave or for military or civil furloughs when EIC men left India. Thus, when men wanted to return, they did so of their own accord and at their own expense. Once in India, jobs through the EIC were not easily obtained unless the returnee pestered powerful acquaintances to appoint them to some profitable position. Moreover, the man who found it necessary to sail back to India usually remained there until he made a fortune or died. So, it was also a scary proposition for Hastings and Hancock to consider.

Hastings had the good fortune to be appointed as deputy ruler at Madras, even though his initial application was rejected. The rejection happened because Hastings had made political enemies, and he would not have got the appointment if he had not appealed to Robert Clive, who then intervened. Yet, Hancock was not as lucky.

He knew that he would have no steady employment when he arrived in India, and, moreover, he could barely afford his passage. In fact, his finances were such that to ensure his wife and daughter could continue to live in comfort during his absence, he was forced to acquire a bond, but it had to be secured. That is when Hastings, although impoverished himself, helped by providing the security for it.

Hancock also had no desire to work again as a surgeon in India. He had given up doctoring a month before Eliza was born to pursue a partnership with Hastings. Their business involved dealing in merchandise that they thought would be profitable. Goods included timber, carpets, salt, rice, and Bihar opium. The plan this time was for Hancock to survive by obtaining a *dustuck* that gave permission to privately trade in Bengal without paying customs or transit duties, something that of course became a cause of disagreement with Bengal's native authorities.

At sea, Hancock, who left several months ahead of Hastings, could not help but wish he was home. He thought about his daughter and his wife, and he regularly reminded himself of Philadelphia's appearance by looking at a small oval miniature of her, painted by John Smart. The miniature was encircled by twenty-seven diamonds and showed a thin, sophisticated woman with dark upswept hair dressed in a turquoise gown and wearing a pearl necklace. Later, in 1774, when Hancock made out his will, he ensured that this miniature would go to Eliza.

After Hancock arrived in India, his concerns about his daughter prompted him to write a gloomy and fretful letter to Hastings. He had fears about Eliza's education and alarm over her future. Still, he hoped that he might be able to provide his daughter with a sufficient dowry for her to have a better life and not be forced to marry a 'Tradesman' or 'any Man' just because that was the only way she could be supported. In addition, because Hancock had not heard from Hastings, he expressed his fears about his prospects in India and concerns over their joint business venture. He also noted that his future financial future appeared 'precarious'.

When Hancock wrote home to Philadelphia and his daughter, he made sure to keep a duplicate of each letter, which he placed in his letter-book because sometimes letters got lost or shipwrecks happened. One of his first letters to Philadelphia indicated his concern for his daughter. One worry was that Eliza would forget him as he knew that he would be gone at least three years, if not longer. There was also his continual worry about his daughter receiving a proper education.

Both he and Philadelphia had already decided Eliza should be educated in France, but in his next letter to his wife, he wavered. This time, he wrote that he might not be able to provide the fortune necessary for Eliza to obtain a station in life equal to her education. He therefore suggested that it might be more prudent for her to be educated in a humbler fashion. He reasoned that if she had fewer options, she would be more willing to 'Submit' to less and not be disappointed.

Amidst all his concerns about Eliza's education, Hastings arrived in India. Hastings then sent an upbeat and encouraging reply to Hancock. He wanted his friend to concentrate on business, and his letter was filled with gentle urgings that Hancock have no fear about his daughter or the future:

> Make no Change in the Plan you have already laid down. Neither French nor Dancing will disqualify a Woman for filling the Duties of any Sphere in Life. Her own natural Understanding & gentle Disposition improved by the Precepts of such a Mother as few Children are blest with

will fit her Mind to be satisfied with any Lot that she may meet with & to become it. But God forbid she should be disqualified for a better Way of Life because it is Possible she may not have a Fortune equal to it. A frugal Style of, and an early Practice in Economy will be sufficient Precaution. – I cannot say all I will upon this Subject. My own Prospects and my Life are precarious, and it will require some years for me to get much above the world, but if I live & meet with the success which I have a Right to hope for, she shall not be under the necessity of marrying a Tradesman, or any Man for her Support. I would not say thus much, but that I wish in every respect to dispel your Apprehensions.[12]

Hastings' reassurance was enough for Hancock to be hopeful. This was evident in his next letter home. He now wrote that Eliza's education was a priority and that his prospects were better than he imagined. Hancock also noted that if his daughter's education was interrupted at this point, she would never obtain any 'Degree of Perfection' as he maintained it could only be achieved in a child's early years, so therefore they should continue the educational course they had planned. In addition, he noted:

I hope soon to amend our Situation so much that you shall not have Occasion to deny yourself anything which may be agreeable to you. It is true this in a great measure Depends on the Existence of a very infirm Old Man: but the Care I take & the Reliance I have on Providence make me hope that I may live long enough to provide for you & my Dear Betsy.[13]

Despite all Hancock's hopes and Hastings' urgings that the future was bright, Hancock had left various debts behind in India when he left in January 1765. These debts were now haunting him as a suit was brought by a man named Drake whom Hancock described as a 'dirty fellow'. In addition, when arrested for the debt, Hancock was being plagued by ill health. It might have been worse if a friend had not intervened and rescued Hancock from jail much to 'his lasting gratitude'.

Things did not improve for Hancock when he reached Calcutta. The EIC had issued an order that for people to be granted a *dustuck* they needed to be at least a factor, which was a type of trader who received and sold goods on commission. Hancock could not yet fulfil that requirement, so he looked for something else to support himself and followed General Richard Smith's advice to accept the post of Surgeon Extraordinary to the Calcutta garrison. However, Hancock was unhappy in the position as he did not want to be a doctor. He wrote to Philadelphia stating: 'You know ... how much I hate the practice of Physick, yet I am obliged to take it up again. Nothing could have induced me to do so, but the hopes of thereby providing for my family.'[14]

Although his position was intended to be a sinecure, Hancock found himself constantly working and claimed that his continual labour was 'perfect slavery' and 'without profit', partly because he had to keep a carriage to visit his patients, most of whom lived in the countryside. Furthermore, he was not as confident in his medical skills as his patients were. If that was not depressing enough, a famine swept through Bengal making life miserable and causing him to state:

> The deceases [sic] which have been and continue to be very fatal here are chiefly owing to putrefaction, occasioned by the prodigious number of dead bodies lying in the streets and all places adjacent ... This mortality is the effect of the most terrible famine, which has half depopulated Bengal.'[15]

Modern historians say the famine was caused by the EIC's harmful practices that involved maximising profits by creating exorbitant land taxes and destroying food crops in order to cultivate fields of opium poppy. But Hancock had a slightly different opinion. He claimed that the famine was exacerbated by English residents, who monopolised the grain in their own districts. Because of these monopolies even when good harvests happened, he maintained that grain prices were never reduced. He also observed that he found the costs of necessities 'enhanced', provisions doubled, and manufactured native goods altered for the worse.

Chapter 3

Back in India

> IMAGINATION CAN SCARCELY FORM AN IDEA OF A MORE DISMAL PLACE.
> TYSOE HANCOCK IN A LETTER HOME ABOUT INDIA

Hastings had set sail from Dover in March 1769 aboard the *Duke of Grafton*. His first wife Mary had been dead ten years by then, and during the sea trip, Hastings met a German Baron named Adam Carl von Imhoff and his common-law wife, Anna Marie Apollonia Chapuset. Von Imhoff was a miniaturist and portrait painter who had moved to London because he could earn more for his artwork there than in Germany. Unfortunately, despite earning more, the cost of living in London was also higher, and von Imhoff found, like Hancock and Hastings, that he was unable to afford to live there. He then sought new opportunities and was lucky enough to obtain a position as a cadet in the army of the EIC, despite not being English.

When Hastings met the couple, he was immediately intrigued by Chapuset, a woman that Hancock described upon meeting as 'twenty-six years old, with a good figure and the remains of beauty ... sensible, lively, and needing only to be a great mistress of the English language to prove that she has a great share of wit.'[1] If he had cuckolded Hancock, Hastings would do it to another man because, by the time the ship docked in Madras, Hastings and Chapuset were having an affair.

Furthermore, when the three arrived in India, von Imhoff and Chapuset lived with Hastings while von Imhoff drummed up business and did some miniatures in the local area. How Hastings was able to maintain a friendship with the husbands of the women with whom he had affairs remains a mystery. Yet he did, and in fact, Hastings now wrote to Hancock and asked that von Imhoff be removed from Madras to Calcutta, supposedly so that Hastings could be alone with Chapuset:

> In my last I desired you to take the trouble to enquire for a lodging for Mr Imhoff, who proposes to try his fortune as

a miniature painter in Bengal. Mr Imhoff is a shipmate of mine, and officer of some rank in the German service, sent hither with great expectations as a cadet with a family, to seek a livelihood in more profitable employment. He has had some success here, having taken off the heads of half the settlement, but he must soon be aground.[2]

Meanwhile, Hancock's general unhappiness in India probably got a brief respite due to an amusing incident that happened to his wife and daughter after they had journeyed to Steventon in Hampshire to see their Austen relatives. In comparison to Calcutta, Steventon was a rural village situated seven miles south-west of the town of Basingstoke and lying between the villages of Overton, Oakley, and North Waltham. It couldn't have been more opposite from the bustling and fast-growing city of Calcutta because in Steventon, residents all knew one another.

Philadelphia and Eliza travelled to this cosy village in August 1770. In comparison to her brother George, Philadelphia was rich, and she probably wanted to flaunt her wealth and make sure her brother and sister-in-law knew. Philadelphia was also impulsive and liked to take holidays on her terms, which she often initiated without much planning. Typical of this characteristic was this trip that Mrs Austen later recounted in a letter to her sister-in-law, Susanna Walter:

> Sister Hancock staid with us only a few days, she had more Courage than you had and set out in a Post Chaise with only her little Bessy, for she brought neither Clarinda or Peter [Indian servants] with her, but believe she sincerely repented, before she got to her Journey's end, for in the middle of Bagshot heath the Postillion discover'd She had dropped the Trunk from off the Chaise. She immediately sent him back with the Horses to find it, intending to sit in the Chaise till he return'd, but was soon out of patience and began to be pretty much frightened, so began her Walk to the Gold Farmer about two miles off, where she arrived half dead with fatigue, it being in the middle of a very hot day. When she was a little recover'd she recollected she had left all the rest of her things (amongst which were a large parcel of India Letters, which she had received the night before, and some

of them she had not read) in the Chaise with the Door wide open – She sent a man directly after them and got them all safe and after some considerable time the Driver came with the Trunk, and without any more misfortune got to Bolton Street about Nine o'clock – she is now settled in the Cottage, her direction is at Byfleet, near Cobham, Surrey.[3]

Apart from taking holidays, Philadelphia was receiving exotic presents from her husband. Some of these gifts from India were delivered through one of Hastings' subordinates, a trusted albeit somewhat odd man named David Anderson. Early in 1773, Hastings sent him to the Woodmans in England, carrying dispatches along with expensive scents from Hancock to his wife. Hancock noted that Anderson was so devoted to Hastings that there was no one he loved more, but he also warned Philadelphia that the young man often greatly embellished his stories and the characters in them.

Hancock also regularly sent other things to Philadelphia that she loved. Among these items were Indian foods like pickled mangoes, hot chillies, pickled limes, curry leaves, and cassoondy sauce. He also sent 'shawl handkerchiefs', which some sources suggested are silk or crêpe-fringed squares with printed patterns.

Hastings later described the shawl handkerchiefs as being inferior to the Kashmir shawls that bore the scent of patchouli made from kashmire wool, called cashmere by the British. These shawls became fashionable during the French campaign in Egypt (1779–1802) after one was sent to Paris. Every woman who saw one wanted it, and the sensation for the shawls was so great that immediate plans were laid to manufacture them in France. However, although the French were able to imitate the shawl's fabric, they could not imitate the smell. When at last the secret scent was found to be patchouli, the French began applying it to their shawls, which they then proclaimed as the real thing. Charles Dickens noted this in the mid-1800s:

> We all remember the rage there was for this scent a short time ago; and how the whole world was delighted with patchouli in essence and patchouli in powder, patchouli sachets and patchouli bouquets, till one grew almost to loath the very name of the sweet scent … and the test of the real Indian shawl used to be this strange odour, which had not then found its way into the Western world. The shawl

could be imitated, but not the perfume; so that all knowing purchasers of true Cashmeres judged by the sense of smell as well as by those of touch and sight. And they could not be deceived in this.[4]

Despite managing to send gifts to his family, life in India was difficult for Hancock. He was often ill, which probably contributed to his pessimistic outlook. Among the illnesses that he suffered was gravel, which today is known as kidney stones. It is a disease that involves small stones forming in the kidneys that then pass through the ureters to the bladder and are expelled in urine.

Hancock also had gout, a Georgian era disease suffered by many well-known individuals at the time. One famous sufferer was Great Britain's Prime Minister, Frederick North. In fact, there is a humorous story about North and his gout. He suffered so severely that he eventually purchased 'large gouty shoes' to reduce the uncomfortable pain. One time when he felt a gout attack coming on, he sent his servant John to get his gouty shoes, but his servant looked in all the usual spots and could not locate them. Unhappily he notified Lord North that the shoes had been stolen and then mightily cursed the wretched thief. Lord North seeming to be very grave about the loss remarked, 'Poh ... how can you be so ill-natured John? Now all the harm I wish the poor rogue is, *that my shoes may fit him*.'[5]

Besides being frequently ill, Hancock had constant financial worries and was always short of cash. He believed there were schemes afoot to obstruct his plans to obtain money and plots to defraud him. Moreover, even though he obtained a contract with a partner to supply salt to the EIC, he found it was fraught with problems and involved him making surprise visits to ensure that his workmen did not steal. The salt was obtained in the Sundarbans, the name given for the tidal swamp forest formed by the estuary of the Ganges, which he described in a letter home:

> Imagination ... can scarcely form an idea of a more dismal place than the Sunderbunds [sic]. They begin just below Culpee, and extend southerly to the sea; to the eastward they are terminated by Luckypore; so that their extent is greater than all of England. The whole is divided by a prodigious number of rivers into islands, some large and some small; all entirely covered with jungles so thick that

you cannot see ten feet into them, except in some few places where the salt-makers have cleared the ground for the space of fifty or a hundred yards. Throughout all the woods, there is no fresh water but at two places. The only animals are the rhinoceros, tygers of a very large size, deer and wild hogs. The rivers abound with fish. In the Sunderbunds are neither houses nor hutts, therefore the people who are employed in making salt or chunam are obliged before sunset to remove in their boats from the shore into the middle of the rivers; where they are not perfectly safe, for the tygers sometimes swim off and take them out of their boats. We have unfortunately lost eight men by these terrible beasts.[6]

Despite all his trials and tribulations, Hancock continued to regularly send letters to Philadelphia. Many were depressing, and some contained the travails that befell some of the young women who had come to India, just like Philadelphia had in search of a husband. Hancock mentioned one such woman who had been planning to marry a Major Blair, but, unfortunately, on the day she arrived, the major died:

> The girl said Blair had "promised to leave her a thousand rupees, but that she had got nothing but two or three old trunks with some old clothes worthy very little". The consequence was easy to guess. On Christmas Day, sick with fever, she had come to Hancock and begged him to give her money. "I did so," he wrote; "but I am sorry to find that she has got with a set of people who, I believe, intend to make a market of her." The girl, he said "seemed not pleased at my enquiring so strictly into her situation".[7]

Between letters of Hancock's ill-health and sad tales, he remained committed to ensuring that his daughter had the best education and upbringing, which Philadelphia honoured by keeping her daughter busy learning French, practising music, and studying 'Arithmetick'. Philadelphia also devoted herself to finding Eliza marvellous tutors and obtaining for her the 'best Writing Master.' In addition, while Hancock was saving money and living frugally, Eliza was surrounded by the best, the most expensive, or the highly prized. This included a harpsichord for her music lessons that Hancock stated should be of supreme quality without thought of its price.

During his absence, Hancock also fretted over Eliza forgetting him and wrote to his wife to keep his daughter's 'recollection' of him alive. However, to ensure that he would know what his growing daughter looked like, Philadelphia also sent him a portrait of the 9-year-old. He acknowledged that he received it on 13 March 1771, stating:

> I have received Betsy's Picture – Why should I, who hitherto never had hid my Sentiments from you, hide them now? On looking at it I was greatly disappointed indeed. I will tell You its faults – the drawing is so very bad that the Face is broader than the Breast and the head bigger than the upper part of the Body; the Face is also very full, and the Features are those of a Child not more than four Years old. I am sure that Betsy was remarkably well-proportioned when I left England. Another great defect is owing I believe to the materials of which the Picture is Composed. For being made of small Clippings of hair stuck on by Gum, it is impossible there can be any shading & consequently the Face must want Expression, without which there can not be a good Picture or a good Likeness. I am not Singular in my Opinion, for every one to whom I have shewn it dislikes the Picture, tho' ignorant of what are the Faults. I intend sending it to Mr Hastings for his Opinion. Do not imagine from what I have said that I am the less obliged to You for your kind intention in sending the Picture.[8]

Meanwhile, Hastings was having considerably better luck on his return to India. He was steadily rising in the ranks and would eventually be appointed Governor-General. Part of the reason for this appointment was that he initiated trading practice reforms that benefited both the EIC and Indian workers; improved the efficiency of land revenues collections; consolidated British control over Indian authorities; launched a crackdown against bandits operating in the Bengal area; and restored order to the judicial system in the provinces. Although Hancock was happy for Hastings and the success he was having, he noted that his friend had been 'much harassed' by court martials and other 'disagreeable business' in Madras. He added that 'This Government will prove to him a crown of thorns.'[9] Little did Hancock realise that his sorrowful prophecy for Hastings would eventually come true.

While Hastings was advancing in his career, Hancock continued to suffer with little success. Part of his problem was that he was frequently ill and unable to attend to business. Still he could not refuse his daughter anything, including a request for a horse, which he agreed to buy her in November 1771 telling Philadelphia to purchase the 'best little horse' for Betsy that she could afford.

Around this time, Philadelphia learned about the Hastings-Chapuset affair. Soon after, in the summer of 1772, Hancock received a letter from his wife proposing to bring Eliza to India so that Hastings would continue to hold both her and Eliza in his affections. This, of course, adds credence to the argument that Eliza was Hastings' daughter as it appears that Philadelphia was concerned about Chapuset being involved with Hastings.

From the start, Hancock opposed the suggested visit from Philadelphia and Eliza. He replied to his wife in a letter adding comments between 23 September and 7 November, and firmly insisting that his daughter should never return:

> You say She will be so well accomplished at twelve as many are at fifteen Years of age; I believe she will; but let me ask you if it be possible she should have any Degree of Judgement at that Tender Age. Her Arrival Here would be at the Period of Life when she will naturally form to Herself false Notions of Happiness, most probably very Romantick, the Disappointment of which may greatly embitter the rest of her Days. You know very well that no Girl, tho' but fourteen Years Old, can arrive in India without attracting the Notice of every coxcomb in the Place, of whom there is very great Plenty at Calcutta, with very good Persons & no other Recommendation. You Yourself know how impossible it is for a young Girl to avoid being attached to a Young Handsome Man whose address is agreeable to Her. Debauchery under the polite name of Gallantry is the Reigning Vice of the Settlement. I scarcely know to whom I would wish my Daughter Married were she of a proper

age; which she will not be for some Years, as I am certain nothing Shortens a Woman's days as much as her being Married when too Young.[10]

The above comments by Hancock also seem to imply that Philadelphia had become 'attached to a Young Handsome Man' and provides more evidence to support the idea that Hastings was Eliza's father. However, even if that was not the case, Hancock seemed adamant that he did not want Eliza in India and continued by arguing that an accident might happen en route. He then noted that he couldn't imagine the horror he would feel if that were the case.

Hancock also stated that even if his wife and daughter arrived safely, there was always the danger of Eliza catching some ailment because of the 'unfriendly' climate, and he remarked that the once-prevalent hospitality had disappeared. Moreover, he said that few people lived 'decently' except for those in high positions and ended his letter urging his wife against any voyage to India as he thought it 'Highly improper' and Bengal a 'lewd' place. Hancock may also have had another reason for not wanting Philadelphia and Eliza to visit. He may have been worried that they would be disappointed in him.

As Hancock laboured, Hastings continued to ascend, reaping the benefits of his hard work. Fortunately, Hastings' prosperity allowed him to be generous and help his old friend, and around this time, he gave Eliza a gift that amounted to 40,000 rupees or £5,000. Today that amount would be worth over £757,000. Of this generosity, Hancock wrote to Philadelphia from Calcutta on 11 December 1772 and made a point of noting the secrecy surrounding Hastings' gift stating:

> What I am going to tell you will, I am sure, make you very Happy: A few days ago Mr Hastings, under the polite Term of making his God daughter a present, made over to me a Respondentia Bond for forty thousand Rupees to be paid in China; I have given directions for the Amount, which will be five thousand Pounds, to be immediately remitted home to my Attorneys. Let me caution you not to acquaint even the Dearest Friend you have with this Circumstance; tell Betsy only that her Godfather has made a great Present, but not the particulars; let Her write a proper Letter on the Occasion.[11]

Chapter 4

Tysoe Hancock's Last Stand

I BELIEVE NO MAN EVER LIVED MORE GENERALLY BELOVED.
PHILIP DORMER STANHOPE ON TYSOE HANCOCK

By 1772, Tysoe Hancock was in dire straits. His quest to secure wealth in India and live an upper-class life in England with his beloved wife and beautiful young daughter was slipping away. Even as he strove to keep his personal expenses low and managed to secure a bond for Eliza from Hastings, his health was failing, and Philadelphia continued outspending his income by double. In fact, the day after Hancock wrote his letter explaining the bond from Hastings, Philadelphia rented an expensive house in Hertford Street. Their letters probably crossed in the mail, although Philadelphia's letter did apologise for the expense of the new rental.

Philadelphia and Betsy travelled to Steventon during the December 1772 holiday season, this time without misplacing any baggage along the route. The primary goal of their trip was for Philadelphia to help her sister-in-law, who was nearly ready to give birth. Cassandra did so on Saturday, 9 January 1773, and after four boys – James, George Jr., Edward, and Henry – the Austens welcomed a girl, Cassandra Elizabeth.

The day after Cassandra Elizabeth's birth, Philadelphia wrote a letter to her husband telling him the joyous news of his niece's arrival. Hancock was not necessarily happy about it as he had been concerned about the growing family for some time. His worry stemmed in part from the realisation that his godson, the Austens' second child, George Jr., had numerous physical difficulties. He had been born in 1766 and began having fits when he started teething. Moreover, George Jr. had other issues, such as the fact that he could not speak and may have been deaf. Hancock's anxieties caused him to write back to his wife stating:

> That my brother and sister Austen are well, I heartily rejoice ... but I cannot say that the News of the violently

rapid increase of their family gives me so much pleasure ... especially when I consider the case of my godson who must be provided with the least hope of his being able to assist himself.[1]

Along with the worries about hereditary maladies in his brother-in-law's family, Hancock was still thinking about his daughter's request for a horse. Hancock seemed to send mixed messages to Philadelphia. At times, he complained about her expenditures, while at other times he urged spending, such as buying a horse for Eliza. It took a while for her to obtain it, and although he wrote in April 1772 that he hoped by now she had a good saddle-horse, he did not mention its acquisition until 22 June 1773. He then wrote that he had agreed to it more for health reasons than for his daughter's pleasure as he believed horseback riding was 'wholesome Exercise'.

Not everyone thought horse-riding was healthy for girls. In a well-known case around the same time, the Austrian diplomat, Count of Mercy-Argenteau, objected to the future French queen, Marie Antoinette, having a horse. She had proposed the idea to French King Louis XV, perhaps thinking it would be a good way to spend more time with her new husband, his grandson Louis, who loved to hunt.

Mercy-Argenteau, who had been influential in arranging Marie Antoinette's marriage, had appointed himself as a spy for Marie Antoinette's mother, Empress of Austria Maria Theresa. In this way, he sought to gain favour with the Empress by revealing everything her daughter was doing, thinking, or feeling. Then, he used his influence with Marie Antoinette to get her to do the things her mother wanted.

Objecting to Marie Antoinette's aspirations to ride horses, he wrote to her mother and asserted moderation was the key to good health and riding was 'violent exercise'. The Empress agreed with his assessment, 'thinking it ruinous to the complexion, injurious to the shape, and not to be safely indulged in under thirty years of age.'[2] So, under the guise of being helpful, Mercy-Argenteau stated to King Louis XV that Marie Antoinette was too young and that he feared that she would be hurt if she rode horses. When Marie Antoinette insisted, the King finally relented but only if she agreed to ride donkeys, which upon her agreement resulted in a nationwide search to find sweet, gentle ones.

On the other hand, Hancock did not fear dangers associated with horseback riding and rather believed it would be healthy for his young daughter. Eliza had suffered a few illnesses, and her father believed that if she became fond enough of horseback riding, she would do it regularly, which would help her maintain good health. That was something that he was clearly without and the main reason he gave for being unable to earn a proper living.

In November 1773, the news he sent home was gloomy. He complained that it was hard to continue living as he was 'too old' and 'too infirmed'. He was also probably unhappy about his absent wife, his daughter not knowing him, and being stuck alone in India. In addition, his thrifty and frugal attitude to save money by refusing to visit others had backfired. People came to think of him as an unfriendly loner and it made his life in India that much more difficult: 'I was given to understand that I was looked upon as one whose misfortunes had sour'd his temper and made him unsociable; accordingly I was shunned by almost everybody. This had a bad effect on my affairs'.[3]

Back in London, the Christmas holiday season was a time of merriment. As usual, the Hancocks and Woodmans celebrated Hastings' birthday on 17 December and Eliza's on 22 December. Of these celebratory times, Woodman wrote a letter to Hastings noting that he had seen the Hancock women over the holidays and that Eliza was turning into a 'fine Girl' whom he found to be accomplished and agreeable.

Philadelphia still hoped that her husband might get his finances in order and return home. After two years of constant written assurances from her that she was doing whatever she could to reduce her expenses and spending, her husband finally acknowledged that he believed her and that he did not think her extravagant. He also claimed that he was not trying to stop her from living like a 'gentlewoman'. However, he maintained in a letter written from Calcutta on 16 January 1774 that he had come to the realisation that his return was an impossible task:

> To further your Enquiries I can only Answer, that what I can leave you, should I dye soon, tho' my all, will not do more than purchase a tolerable Annuity for your Life: this ought to be your Resolution, as Betsy is provided for: I am not certain but that I may direct it to be so disposed of in my Will.

> My present Expences including Yours (tho' I never see Company) are twice the Amount of my present Gains; from this judge the probability of my returning to England.[4]

Hancock seemed to have few wants for himself, but he did write to his wife about his daughter's picture. Apparently, the climate had spoiled it and the crayons used for it had 'mouldered into Dust'. Hancock was also displeased or rather 'chagrined' as that was the word he used when he learned that Eliza's horse had been given away. He therefore implored Philadelphia to acquire another one as quickly as possible.

Hastings was by then serving as the Governor-General of India, and although Philadelphia and Eliza did not realise the seriousness of Hancock's ongoing health problems, Hastings did. He knew that Hancock was probably near death. Therefore, he kindly increased the original bond of £5,000 to £10,000, a generous gift that today would amount to well over £1,500,000. It was to be invested in a trust fund, with Hastings' brother-in-law Woodman and George Austen acting as trustees.

Hancock informed Philadelphia about the money and told her that when the papers reached England, her brother George was to sign and seal them and that she was to pay for his expenses for the trip. The interest derived was to be paid to Philadelphia and Hancock, but once they died, the balance would go to Eliza. Moreover, Hancock reported that the interest should amount to nearly £400 annually and that meant that Eliza would have a nice fortune.

With the £10,000 bond from Hastings, the financial future of Hancock's wife and daughter now seemed secure, and so Hancock admitted to his wife that he was chronically ill and dying. He did so in a letter dated 25 March 1775. He also stated that he thought Woodman and Austen would serve as good trustees. A day later, he wrote his last letter to his daughter:

> My Dear Child, I have received your two little Letters, greatly pleased that you seem to be at the Time of writing them in good Health & Spirits. Your Writing is so much amended that I have Hopes you will daily improve; You can not please me more than by giving the greatest Attention to Writing and Arithmetick, as they will be most useful to you hereafter.

As your Horse did not suit You I have desired your mama to buy you another, not only to please You but for the sake of your Health because I think your good Behaviour deserves Encouragement.

The Governor, your Godfather, desired me to send a very fine white Persian Cat of mine to you as a present from Him, which I would have done with Pleasure, but your Cousin Stanhope having quarrelled with the Gentleman who lived at an House next to mine & the Cat having straied into His House, this Gentleman or some of his People shot Her; ... If I should be so fortunate as to procure another I will send it next Year.[5]

One of Hancock's last letters to his wife was dated a few months later in May. In it he mentioned four sets of string pearls that were 'exceedingly even' being sent as a gift to Eliza from a Mrs Bowers, who had been friendly with the Hancocks since Eliza was born. Bowers kept a 'House of Entertainment' in Madras that Hancock made sure to mention to Philadelphia was not a house of 'Ill Fame'.

On 5 November 1775, at the age of 51, Hancock died in Calcutta. He would never return to England, not even in death. He was buried in the Great Burying-ground at Chowringhee with a gravestone that misspelled his name as Tyso and erroneously stated his age as 64, perhaps because of his haggard well-worn looks.

In his will, everything was left to Philadelphia, except for a miniature given to Eliza of her mother. Hancock requested that Eliza keep it to remind her of her mother's 'vertues'. Like Eliza's picture, Philadelphia's portrait had been likewise injured by India's climate, but Hancock had it sent home and without consideration for the costs had it 'put right'.

When it came to Hancock's estate, though, he would have little left after his debts were paid. Philadelphia did receive £3,500 from Woodman and the EIC settled Hancock's estate in India for the sum of £4,800. Ennos acknowledges in his book that the final money from Hastings that was put into the trust was likely considered to be the 'final pay off' by Hastings, as he was involved with Chapuset and had no intention of seeing Philadelphia again, nor did he have any intention of declaring Eliza his daughter if that was the case.

News of Hancock's death was also slow to reach London as the mail had to cross the seas. In the meantime, in India, there was just one young man who grieved Hancock's demise. He was Philadelphia's cousin, Philip Dormer Stanhope of Chesterfield. He saw Hancock's death as a severe 'misfortune' noting:

> 'I have sustained a loss which requires all my philosophy to support, and the death of Mr Hancock has deprived me of a sincere friend and generous benefactor. I believe no man ever lived more generally beloved, or died more universally regretted. He was the patron of the widow and the fatherless, and I pay but a just tribute to his memory, which I say that in unaffected charity and real integrity of heart he was not inferior to Mr Hastings.'[6]

Unaware of his death, life went on without concern in London. Eliza attended a ball at Mr de Latouche's in Winchester the same month her father died. Like most balls, the room where it was held was likely overwhelmingly hot because it was crowded with people and lit by candles. Moreover, like most balls at the time, it was probably a polite affair that involved participants who needed to maintain rigid and exacting behaviour. Dances were physically demanding and involved complicated steps that required much practice to be performed properly. Fortunately, 14-year-old Betsy's allemande (a court dance developed in France from a German folk dance) was claimed to be the 'most applauded' at the event.

Within six weeks of Hancock's death, Mrs Austen gave birth for the seventh time on Saturday, 16 December 1775. After Cassandra Elizabeth's birth, there had been another boy, Francis William, dubbed Frank, born in April 1774 and now another girl joined the family. Her birth did not generate any undue excitement at the rectory beyond the fact that Mr and Mrs Austen were happy she had finally arrived. She had been long expected, as explained by George Austen in a letter to his sister-in-law:

> You have doubtless been for some time in expectation of hearing from Hampshire, and perhaps wondered a little we were in our old age grown such bad reckoners but so it was

for Cassy certainly expected to have been brought to bed a month ago. However, last night the time came, and without a great deal of warning, everything was soon happily over. We have now another girl, a present plaything for her sister Cassy and a future companion. She is to be Jenny.[7]

If the Austens had known that their little Jenny would become the famous novelist Jane Austen, they might have celebrated rather than obligingly returning to the drudgeries of home life. Jane was privately baptised the day after her birth in Steventon but because the winter of 1775–1776 was severe, roads were blocked, and she did not receive her formal baptism and christening until Good Friday in April 1776.

News of Hancock's death finally reached Philadelphia on 7 June, coming in a letter from Mrs Bowers. Fortunately, Mr and Mrs Austen were staying with Philadelphia in London when she learned of her husband's passing. Less than two weeks later, Hastings confirmed it. With his confirmation he also mentioned Hancock's debts.

Philadelphia was worried. Snobs abounded in London and they often viewed money earned in India as low-class unless some amazing fortune had been amassed. That was clearly not the case with Hancock. Moreover, Philadelphia and her husband had never fitted in with London society as they did not have the requisite old money, nor some illustrious heritage or relative to brag about.

Some months later, in December, George Vansittart, who had made his fortune as a merchant in India and was uncle to Hastings' son, called on Philadelphia. Part of the reason for his visit was to deliver a small package sent to her by Hastings. Vansittart reported on this visit to Hastings and mentioned that Philadelphia did not look healthy, perhaps because she was so worried about the financial future of her and her daughter.

It took a year for all the financial aspects to be disentangled and for Philadelphia to understand that she and Betsy were left with an annual income of £600, roughly £90,000 in today's money. Rough diamonds sold on her behalf would also net her approximately £3940 in mid-March 1777 and in early April, she opened an account with Hoare's Bank, the opening credit stating £3483.13s.6d.

George Austen probably thought his sister possessed a fortune, partly because his financial situation was not good and, in fact, he would eventually borrow money from nearly all his relatives including his sister Philadelphia. Moreover, he had a growing family and his yearly income from tithes was only about £210. He initially supplemented it by selling produce from his farm and then began in around 1773 to take in male pupils, running his boys' school more like a large family than an educational institute.

Although the amount Philadelphia was living on was about three times that of her brother, she considered herself nearly a pauper. It was not nearly enough for her and her daughter to live fashionably in expensive London. Therefore, the only thing Philadelphia could think to do was leave. She believed that she and her daughter could live more elegantly and for less money anywhere else, so around late 1777, they and their servant Clarinda departed. Betsy, though, was now having everyone call her 'Eliza', having decided to use a diminutive that she felt more age-appropriate and sophisticated for a 15-year-old girl.

Chapter 5

Paris

> THE QUEEN IS A VERY FINE WOMAN.
> ELIZA ON MARIE ANTOINETTE

Tysoe Hancock's brutal sacrifice in India had secured two important things for his family. Firstly, they had a modest, reliable income, and, secondly, Eliza was well-educated. Her education was not, however, intended for her to earn money by pursuing a career. Rather, Eliza had become quite skilful at fitting in with upper-class society and being perceived as a suitable wife for a wealthy man. Not only was she attractive, she was smart, played music, and danced extremely well. She spoke multiple languages and could hold a lively conversation. This was the kind of education needed for a woman of her day to secure an upper-class lifestyle, as surely Philadelphia was all too aware from her own struggles. Thus, armed with Eliza's education and some letters of introduction and credit, Philadelphia and Eliza set off with Clarinda in tow to find a new home and social circle.

They first visited Germany and then Belgium, reaching Brussels in the summer of 1778. About the same time, some 125 miles away in Amsterdam, there were some important French visitors. The Princess de Lamballe, who had married one of the richest heirs in France and who became Superintendent of the Household to Queen Marie Antoinette, was travelling incognito with her sister-in-law, the Duchess of Chartres. They were using the names Countess of Joinville and Countess of Lisigny, respectively. Moreover, they were accompanied for a few days by the gout-ridden Benjamin Franklin, who had written a dialogue between himself and the painful disease.

Although Philadelphia and Eliza never met the illustrious princess, the duchess, or Franklin on this trip, they did later find themselves in France and came face-to-face with the Princess de Lamballe and the fashionable French Queen, Marie Antoinette. In the meantime, Philadelphia stayed busy writing to relatives and friends about her travels and perhaps she and Eliza even visited the new Brussels square, called at the time Saint Michael's Square, that was laid out in a uniform neoclassical style according to the design of Claude Fisco.

By October 1779, Philadelphia and Eliza were settled in Paris and adapting to the change. The French people were also adjusting to change. They had a new king, Louis XVI, who began his reign on 10 May 1774 after his grandfather, King Louis XV, died from smallpox. The King's death had been unexpected and rather sudden. He had begun to feel unwell on 26 April and left the Palace of Versailles for Petit Trianon with an entourage that included his mistress, Madame du Barry. Although he hunted the next day, he continued to complain of feeling unwell and his doctor insisted he return to Versailles, which he did along with Madame du Barry.

When he failed to improve, doctors decided to bleed him and did so three different times. Nonetheless, there was still no improvement. Soon they realised the king had broken out in red eruptions they diagnosed as smallpox. It was a dangerous disease to which there was no immunity, and so to ensure the safety of the future Louis XVI, he and his bride Marie Antoinette were asked to leave the palace.

> Although the smallpox vaccine had been around for some time, the French people were generally suspicious of it. They had heard about inoculations going wrong, and they thought it crazy to put a healthy person at risk on the basis that it might somehow protect a person. Even the French medical community considered the practice of inoculation risky because it required injecting a small amount of pus from a smallpox sufferer under a healthy patient's skin.
>
> [Yet, when] Marie Antoinette urged ... her husband to get a smallpox inoculation, [he agreed because he was] more fearful of the disease than inoculation. He received his inoculation on 18 June 1774, and his brothers followed suit the same day. Those who feared inoculation blamed Marie Antoinette for encouraging the king and his brothers to undertake such a radical step. However, fashionable ladies soon got smallpox inoculations, and the idea of inoculation

became such a fad women "wore in their hair a miniature rising sun and olive tree entwined by a serpent supporting a club, the pouf à l'inoculation" which advertised the idea of inoculation and caused inoculation to spread like wildfire among the French populace.[1]

Despite Louis XVI, his brothers, and other fashionable people getting a smallpox inoculation, Louis XV's daughters were not willing, nor were they inclined to leave their father's bedside. A visitor who saw the king around this time reported that the small bumpy eruptions that covered his face were like a 'mask of bronze' and by 3 May, he himself realised the seriousness of his situation. Four days later, he summoned his confessor, last rites were given, and 64-year-old Louis XV died at 3.15 am on 10 May.

His grandson, Louis-Auguste, was not supposed to become Louis XVI. People generally assumed that position would have fallen first to his father and then to his older brother, Louis-Joseph Xavier, Duke of Burgundy. Unfortunately, Louis-Auguste's brother died prematurely on 22 March 1761 from extra-pulmonary tuberculosis and this unexpected event was followed on 20 December 1765 by the death of their father, and so when Louis XV died, Louis-Auguste became Louis XVI.

Even though he was a King, Louis XVI remained notoriously unconfident, famously unloved, and decidedly uncertain. This was partially due to his parents having favoured his older brother. In addition, the traits that might have made his older brother ideal for accession to the throne appeared to be absent in him. His passions were more common and included reading, hunting, and shooting.

Louis XVI also had a distinctly unroyal appearance. He was painfully clumsy and waddled across the floor, unlike his Austrian wife who glided. Furthermore, his voice was harsh, his manners abrupt, and if that was not unkingly enough, his haphazard appearance did not fit in with the powdered and ruffled royals who surrounded him. He was untidy, and despite having his hair expertly coiffed it 'was generally in such wild disorder, from continually passing his hands through it, that it looked as if it were constantly the sport of the four winds of heaven'.[2]

If Philadelphia or Eliza noticed these things about France's new king, they did not mention them. They were probably too busy surveying their new surroundings. Sir John Lambert, who acted as a contact for many English travellers, probably introduced them into French society and helped them find their accommodations located in a fashionable part of Paris.

Eliza quickly sent off a letter to her cousin, who had been named for Philadelphia, the 'shy country-mouse' Philadelphia 'Phylly' Walter. She was living at Ightham parsonage in the county of Kent, about four miles east of Sevenoaks and six miles north of Tonbridge. The parish church dated from the twelfth century and Ightham itself was famous for growing a species of hazel nuts called Kentish cob nuts.

In contrast to Phylly's staid country life, Eliza was staying in an international city full of sophisticated and modish people who patronised amusements and who promenaded along the boulevards. Thus, it was probably no surprise to Phylly when Eliza's letter proclaimed all the wonders that a young girl of the eighteenth century might see in Paris:

> The country is pretty & I do not doubt spending some time agreeably, besides I shall not be sorry to quit for a little while the dissipations of the Town, & to enjoy a little quiet. Paris is however the city in the world best calculated to spend the whole Year in, it is not like London, where the summer months are insupportable. The walks and rides here, The amusement which continue the whole year round, The almost continual residence of people of Fashion, all these Things render it at all times agreable. ... There is perhaps no place in the world where dress is so well understood & carried to so great a perfection ... Powder is universally worn, & in very large quantities, no one would dare to appear in public without it, The Heads in general look as if they had been dipped in meal tub; Hats likewise (which are called English but which do not bear the least resemblance to those of our nation) are much the fashion. The hair is cut in shades, not worn high at all. It was with reluctance, I conformed to the mode in this article, as my hair was very long on my arrival, & I was obliged to have it cut to half its length; but what will not All powerful Fashion effect.[3]

Of course, Eliza and her mother made a visit to see the French Queen, of whom they had heard so much. They attended a ceremony called

Grand Couvert when 'the good honest people from the country, after visiting the menageries to see the lions, tigers, and monkeys ... hastened to the palace to see the king and queen take their soup'.[4] To accomplish this, the room where the royals dined was railed off and spectators filed past one by one. Almost no one was refused admission, so throngs of people poured through the royal apartments, such that 'those in the advance [were] crowded slowly along by those in the rear, and all eyes riveted upon the royal feeders.'[5]

Although the Queen hated Grand Couvert because she felt as if she were on public display, Eliza loved it. She wanted to ensure she shared every detail with Phylly, including every element she noticed about Marie Antoinette. Thus, Eliza's fine penmanship with its small flourishes of delicate legibility covered the page from margin to margin:

> The Queen is a very fine Woman, She has a most beautiful complexion, & is indeed exceedingly handsome; She was most elegantly dressed, She had on a corset & Petticoat of pale green Lutestring, covered with a transparent silver gauze, The petticoat & sleeves puckered & confined in different places with large bunches of roses an amazing large bouquet of White Lilac, The same flower, together with gauze, Feathers, ribbon & diamonds intermixed with her hair. Her neck was entirely uncovered & ornamented by a most beautiful chain of diamonds, of which She had likewise very fine bracelets; She was without gloves, I supposed to shew her hands, & arms, which are without exception the whitest & most beautiful I ever beheld.[6]

Eliza found there were plenty of other attractions in Paris in 1779. Fashion was, of course, fashionable, and the Queen's dressmaker Rose Bertin became so well-known she capitalised on her fame and opened a dress shop called the *Grand Mogol* in 1773. It catered to wealthy fashion-conscious clients and was located on the Faubourg rue Saint-Honoré. Furthermore, because fashion was so important, a specialised press provided illustrations of the latest styles with the first Parisian fashion journal *Le Journal des Dames* appearing in 1774, followed in 1778 by the *Galerie des Modes et du Costume Française*.

One of the chief entertainments of Parisians was to promenade, but in the early 1700s, people only had the wide bridge called Pont Neuf for this activity, as the narrow streets of Paris were crammed with carts, coaches, and animals. Fortunately, as the century advanced, new boulevards were created along with the Champs-Élysées. It turned into a fashionable avenue with trees on either side sporadically forming rectangular groves. There were also three gardens easily accessible to the public by the 1770s. They were the Tuileries Gardens, the Jardin des Plantes, and the somewhat neglected Luxembourg Garden. In addition, the boulevards and gardens attracted street entertainers and performers like acrobats, musicians, and animal acts.

The late eighteenth century was also a time of significant scientific discoveries, and these new technologies changed Parisian industries forever. For instance, between 1778 and 1782, large steam engines installed at Chaillot and Gros-Caillou allowed drinking water to be pumped from the Seine. There were also major changes in chemical manufacturing beginning in 1770. That was the year the first chemical factories were built relying on the work of French chemist Antoine Lavoisier, considered 'the father of modern chemistry' because he changed science from qualitative to quantitative.

Waxworks had long been common in England, but this attraction had only recently become popular in the French capital. The most trendy of these waxworks were those created by Dr Philippe Mathé Curtius, mentor of the soon-to-be famous wax modeller Madame Tussaud. He owned the Salon de Cire (House of Wax) where visitors could see wax models that were sometimes arranged in scenes. One of these scenes was in fact a representation of the Grand Couvert, apparently for those who couldn't or didn't want to make the twenty-mile trek to see the actual event. The wax museum's version was nearly as good as the real thing. It cost spectators just a few sous to gawk continually at the wax replicas of the king and queen dining, and the wax figures would not glare back.

While Eliza did seem to enjoy seeing new things and interacting with people, she began to show signs that she herself longed for home and had little interest in marriage – the very goal of her top-quality education. In a letter, she told Phylly that she thought it highly unlikely that she and her mother would permanently settle abroad and noted that she had not left any part of her heart in Germany or France. In fact, she maintained that her heart was so filled with friendship that no other sentiment, such as love, could invade it.

As mistress of her heart entirely, she stated that she believed that both she and Phylly's hearts could not be engaged any time soon by any 'male *creature breathing*'. Perhaps having grown up getting whatever she wanted, Eliza did not feel pressure to secure a man for financial support, and without a father figure during her teenage years, she perhaps did not have a good role model for marriage. At any rate, she reassured Phylly that there was no one she'd rather see than her cousin.

As Eliza waxed on about her and her cousin's lack of interest in love, Philadelphia was trying to figure out how to solve difficulties related to her servant Clarinda. For months, Clarinda had been suffering from a damaged hand. This meant Philadelphia found herself responsible for paying Clarinda's medical bills. Philadelphia hoped that Clarinda might be able to pay her own way as Clarinda had entrusted Hastings with her savings. Therefore, Philadelphia wrote to him on 3 March 1780 hoping he would help solve her Clarinda dilemma.

Contact with Hastings now seemed legitimate to Philadelphia, even though he had made it perfectly clear some time ago that everything was settled with Hancock's estate and that he did not welcome any further correspondence from her. In addition, he was now married to Chapuset, who according to gossip had acquired a sizeable fortune in India by being avaricious and accepting presents. The rumours about her greed seemed to crystallise into facts when she returned to England in 1784 and made 'lavishly bejewelled appearances' that poets mentioned in clever ditties:

> Tis Mrs Hastings' self brings up the rear!
> Gods! how her diamonds flock
> On each unpowdered lock!
> On every membrance see a topaz clings!
> Behold! – her joints are fewer than her rings![7]

Perhaps rumours of Chapuset's wealth encouraged Philadelphia to think that Hastings might be willing to give her financial aid, even if she was living (as usual) above her means. She also now felt that the once generous trust fund set up for Eliza was not sufficiently large, and she didn't care that Hastings might have considered it a final settlement when she was having to worry about every penny she spent. She thought he might change his mind if she wrote and therefore, she took the chance and plainly expressed her woes:

> After a silence of so many years on your part nothing shd. have prevailed on me to have troubled you with another Letter but my earnest desire to have some information concerning Mr Hancock's affairs, and to whom can I apply but you? ... I wish also much to know if anything is secured for Clarinda, whose demand I enclosed to you, be that as it may I take it on myself that She shall not be a sufferer in her little Fortune. Alas! She has but too severely suffered in her Health and perhaps may not live to want it – it is now more than five Months that She has been quite helpless and that from so small a beginning as a whitlow on her left thumb which notwithstanding all possible assistance and after six operations performed threatened the loss of her Hand & even her life & before those wounds were healed the humour conveyed itself to her right Shoulder where She has already had three severe operations performed & threatened with a fourth without some extraordinary change in her favour. She has been attended by three Surgeons one of them the first in Paris and a Physician; the latter still attends her and one of the Surgeons dresses her Arm twice a Day ... This has been a most unfortunate affair on all accounts & has cost me more anxiety than I can describe – the expence too has been and is still very heavy, it could not have happened at a worse time, but of that I shan't complain if the poor faithful creature can be restored to me.
>
> I once thought to have confined this Letter to Business but knowing your Heart as I know it and being convinced that in spite of appearances it is not changed for your Friends, I cannot refuse you the satisfaction of knowing my Daughter ... is in perfect Health & joins me in every good Wish for your Happiness – you may be surrounded by those who are happy in frequent opportunities of shewing their attachment to you, but I will venture to say no one among them who can boast a more disinterested steady & unshaken Friendship for you than that wch. for so many years has animated and will ever continue to animate the Breast of.[8]

Although Philadelphia may have been thinking about securing more funding from Hastings, 19-year-old Eliza was thinking about her Austen relatives and as it had been some time since they had seen her, she sent a miniature portrait addressed to 'my Uncle G. Austen' depicting her 'native brown' complexion, dark eyes, and snub nose. She probably wanted to ensure that the Austens were aware of what she looked like as an older and sophisticated continental traveller, who was powdered and beribboned. She also made a point of noting that she was wearing what she usually wore, the latest and most fashionable outfit she could buy in Paris.

> Mr Austen, though, was rather less impressed by the receipt of this miniature than his niece might have hoped. For all the affectation of sophistication, what he saw was a small, pointed girlish face with large dark eyes and a sad mouth. Blue ribbons trimmed her dress and were entwined among her artfully dishevelled curls. Yet the bare neck and slender shoulders seemed to him more waif-like than alluring.[9]

In May, when mother and daughter got tired of the hustle and bustle in Paris, they left for the tranquil countryside of Comblaville, a commune in the south-eastern suburbs of Paris near Fontainebleau. It was an area cultivated since Roman times and had a rich heritage of farming. They stayed at the house of a friend, the Countess of Tournon. There Eliza noted that she amused herself with ordinary things like taking amiable walks, reading, and playing musical pieces on an instrument that she claimed was the most fashionable at the time, the harpsichord.

While there, Eliza sent a letter at the end of June she termed *si griffonée* because her usual elegant legibility was missing. The letter was long and filled with interesting tidbits. She talked at length about dancing and balls and remarked that whereas in England, you might not dance with the person you wanted, in France it was different. Partners were changed every dance and she noted that she herself had more opportunities and partners than a person could imagine. Apparently, she found herself engaged for more than fifteen dances on the same evening and even had scheduled eight to ten dances for her next ball.

Eliza's likely appeal with the gentlemen was not only due to being pretty but also because she could dance extremely well. At the time, children from the gentry classes were expected to dance with style and grace, and to ensure boys and girls danced properly, dancing masters were often hired to teach them. Therefore, it is also no surprise that nearly all of Jane Austen's characters could dance. This included Mr Darcy from *Pride and Prejudice* and Mr Knightley from *Emma,* who just like Eliza, danced exceedingly well.

In Paris, Eliza also reported on cosmetics and again noted the beauty of Marie Antoinette's complexion. Single ladies, she revealed, generally did not wear rouge, and, in fact, to do so was often met with great disapproval. However, once a woman was married, she observed that many women made 'ample amends', sporting cheeks so red it made up for any denial they had experienced while single. However, she also reported that her married friend, the Countess of Tournon, never wore any rouge.

Eliza also shared the latest fashion news because she thought such Parisian trends would amuse Phylly:

> The hind hair instead of being turned up or plaited as usual is curled at the ends, fastened with a small comb, & suffered to wave over the shoulders in three or four large curls. The hair in general is worn exceedingly low before, young people who have good hair in an undress go without a cushion or any thing to raise it. Hats of all sorts are worn, chip in particular of all colours something in the form the English gentlemen wear them of a morning. Large gold earrings, that is to say a ring with a single drop in the form of a pearl are much the ton, they are not at all like what I have seen in England, in short was I to give you an account of all the different modes. I should never have done. They have more taste & more whims in this country than in any other.[10]

There was other news. She mentioned that the portrait she sent her Uncle George had been received and she hoped Phylly might see it and decide if she thought Eliza remained as she remembered her. Eliza also mentioned a nun from Paris. She had befriended her, exchanged portraits, and wrote to her weekly. However, over the course of her lifetime, Eliza would have many friends and although she mentioned the nun at this time, she didn't mention her again in any of her letters and so it's doubtful their friendship lasted.

Eliza did share many stories of her continental life with her country cousin Phylly, probably because the two women were close in age, rather than that they had a lot in common. Eliza seemed to want to show how exciting her life was, but also may have believed her tales could broaden Phylly's staid, rural, and boring existence. Yet, although Eliza seemed to be open with Phylly and present her feelings frankly, Phylly always seemed somewhat critical of Eliza's lifestyle and choices.

Eliza also once again mentioned Clarinda. Although she continued to improve, Eliza noted that she remained 'entirely helpless,' something that Philadelphia probably found frustrating. Furthermore, Clarinda's recovery did not seem to last because this was one of the last mentions Eliza made of her, and so it is possible that she died from some complication soon after.

In Eliza's letter, she stated that she had acquired many French friends who were encouraging her to stay in France, and that even if she and her mother decided to settle there, she would always return for visits to England. Eliza also maintained that she still had no serious thoughts of marrying. Yes, perhaps, by now Philadelphia was hinting to her daughter that marriage was the proper thing to do and that a Frenchman might make a good match, but if she was, Eliza was not on the same page. Eliza had further told Phylly that she had never had any 'tender sentiments' towards any man and that she doubted she would ever feel for a gentleman anything more than loyal 'friendship'. Therefore, she stated, it was practically impossible that she would ever return to England with a new last name.

Chapter 6

Becoming a Countess

> IT IS A TRUTH UNIVERSALLY ACKNOWLEDGED, THAT A SINGLE MAN IN POSSESSION OF A GOOD FORTUNE, MUST BE IN WANT OF A WIFE.
> JANE AUSTEN FROM *PRIDE AND PREJUDICE*

Despite having moved to Paris to save money, Philadelphia and Eliza still lived above their means. Perhaps the need for money, plus Philadelphia's urging and Eliza's desire to please her mother, may have convinced Eliza to change her mind about marriage. Whatever the exact reasons, she soon became involved in a courtship with the Count Jean-François Capot de Feuillide.

The Count was an impressive man who probably seemed to be the ideal husband for Eliza. Contemporaries described him as bold, captivating, and one of the handsomest men of his time. He owned an estate of 5,000 acres near the village of Gabarret, close to Nérac, and he was a captain of the Queen's Regiment of Dragoons, where he had established himself as one of the dragoon's finest officers.

To attract such a man, Eliza was introduced to him as an heiress of immeasurable wealth. Her mother had supplemented this story by letting it be known throughout Paris that they were connected to 'la famille du fameux lord Hastings, ancien gouverneur de l'Inde.'[1] This connection was also mentioned in a letter, MS. Eng. misc. e. 250, found in the Bodleian Library archives. Although the letter writer has never been identified, he noted that he dined with Philadelphia, her 'fille' Eliza, and others at the dinner table of 76-year-old Thomas Prattle, a one-eyed man who had been an EIC director in India. The anonymous writer also stated that a doctor told him Eliza was Hastings' daughter. Of course, any connection to Hastings would have led people to believe the Hancocks would receive more money from Hastings, and that Philadelphia and Eliza had to be wealthy.

The promising start soon took an ironic twist as it turned out that the Hancocks were not the only ones embellishing their circumstances. So was de Feuillide, who like George Louis Leclerc, simply began calling himself a count. In Leclerc's case he styled himself the Count of Buffon, despite being the son of a minor local official. De Feuillide also decided to style himself a count because like Leclerc, de Feuillide's father did not have a feudal title and was just a provincial lawyer who had served as the mayor of Nérac.

Not only was de Feuillide not a real count, the estate he owned was useless swamp land. He had acquired it because of his father's position in the forestry and marshland department. To be of any value, it needed to be drained and converted to farmland, and the Count did not have the money necessary to accomplish the task. He perhaps believed that marriage to a wealthy Englishwoman would solve this problem.

Interest in each other's perceived wealth was probably the initial attraction for both. However, by the time marriage was proposed, the truth was out. When Eliza's trustees learned of the upcoming nuptials, Woodman sent a letter to Hastings making his and George Austen's position clear. The letter was dated 7 August 1781:

> Mrs & Miss Hancock are yet in France & likely to continue there the young Lady being on the point of Marriage with a French Officer which Mrs Hancock writes is of good family with expectation of good Fortune, but at present but little. Her Letter was to Mr Austen & Self on the Subject and she seems inclined to give up to them the Sum which was settled on her for Life, and wants the Money to be transferred into the French Funds which we have thought prudent for her sake to decline and Mr Austen is much concerned at the connection which he says is giving up all their friends, their Country, and he fears their Religion.[2]

George Austen also thought Eliza was behaving rashly and suffering from 'romantic foolishness'. Nonetheless, her marriage to the Count de Feuillide had nothing to do with love, as she would later state. Understanding her motivation for getting engaged required looking no further than her mother, Philadelphia.

Eliza loved her mother, wanted to obey, and as a young girl of nineteen she would have looked to her for guidance. Philadelphia probably believed that the Count de Feuillide's aristocratic title, even if it was not real, was too enticing to pass up, and perhaps more than that, she likely believed a title would increase their social standing and allow them to continue to hobnob with the French court and Parisian elite.

Eliza being engaged to the Count also entitled mother and daughter to entertainments they might not have otherwise enjoyed. One example was their attendance at various celebrations surrounding the birth of the Dauphin, Louis Joseph of France, born on 22 October 1781. His appearance sent Frenchmen into flurries of excitement and resulted in many festivities and assemblages that included fireworks, illuminations and balls. Eliza and her mother were privileged to appear at some of these 'exceedingly fine' balls, including one attended by the King and Queen.

Although the French court was said to be always brilliant, Eliza noted that one celebration for the Dauphin's birth was 'beyond conception'. It was held in a saloon filled with irreplaceable paintings and priceless sculptures illuminated by 8,000 lights. The most beautiful and the most fashionable attended and everywhere Eliza looked she found herself dazzled by the sparkle of wealth in the silver, gold, and diamond jewellery attendees wore.

The King appeared adorned in a 'gold grounded coat' embroidered thick with jewels and the Queen's dress was even more costly. She appeared in what Eliza termed a beautiful 'Turkish dress' created from silver silk with hints of blue and trimmed in glittering jewels. Its puffed sleeves had an occasional diamond and a dazzling diamond sash was tied around her waist. The Queen's hair was also adorned with an intermix of costly and precious jewels, flowers, and white feather plumes.

Whatever happiness Eliza experienced socialising and celebrating the Dauphin's birth was probably crushed when she received word of her uncle's rejection to her marrying de Feuillide. Her uncle found it imperative to look after her long-term interests, no matter what impulsive harebrained scheme his sister Philadelphia might devise. Eliza could plainly see how her uncle felt about her marrying the Count as his refusal to give her the trust fund money to help with the de Feuillide's swamplands made it all too clear.

Nonetheless, Eliza still felt that she must offer some explanation as to her motives for marrying the Count in late December 1781. She did so in a letter to Phylly dated 27 March 1782:

As you know the affection you have borne me, I doubt not but you will expect & wish I should give you some account of myself. My Uncle Austen acquainted you with my marriage soon after its taking place. This event, the most important one of my life, was you may imagine the effect of a mature deliberation, & as it was a step I took much less from my own judgement than that of those whose councils & opinions I am the most bound to follow, I trust I shall never have any reason to repent it; on the contrary, if I may be allowed to judge of the future from the past & present I must esteem myself the most fortunate of my sex. The man to whom I have given my hand is everyways amiable both in mind & person. It is too little to say he loves me, since he literally adores me; entirely devoted to me, & making my inclinations the guide of all his actions, the whole study of his life seems to be to contribute to the happiness of mine.

My situation is everyways agreeable, certain of never being separated from my dear Mama whose presence enhanced every other blessing I enjoy, equally sure of my husband's affections, mistress of an easy fortune with the prospects of a very ample one, add to these the advantage of rank & title, & a numerous & brilliant acquaintance, amongst whom I can flatter myself I have some sincere friends, & you will unite with me in saying, I have reason to be thankful to Providence of the lot fallen to my share; the only thing which can make me uneasy is the distance I am from my relations ... & country, but this is what I trust I shall not have always to complain of, as the Comte has the greatest desire to see England, & even to make it his residence a part of the year.[3]

After Eliza's marriage, life remained a series of fun-filled entertainments for her and her mother. Yet, despite the sociality and pleasantness of Paris, de Feuillide continued to think of his swamplands in Nérac. Draining the marshland was a huge undertaking and an even bigger expense. Although he could not touch Eliza's trust fund, he soon devised a way to circumvent Eliza's trustees. He obtained a loan of £6,000 from Eliza's mother, an amount which would never be repaid.

Around this time, de Feuillide also obtained the license from the king that he desperately needed to finalise his ownership of the swamplands and drain them. As that was happening, Woodman remained opposed to Eliza's marriage. He was unhappy about the funds the Count de Feuillide had obtained, suggested that he was a good-for-nothing fortune hunter, and wrote of his fears to Hastings:

> I wrote Mrs Hancock ... who is in France, where I believe she intends to end her days, having married her daughter ... to a gentleman of that country, I am afraid not very advantageously, although she says it is entirely to her satisfaction. ... Her uncle Mr Austen, and brother, don't approve of the match, the latter is much concern'd at it; they seem already desirous of draining the mother of every shilling she has.[4]

With the money and license, the Count could now proceed with his project to create a profitable farm and so he returned to Nérac, leaving Eliza and her mother behind in Paris. The 5,000 acres would remain tax-free if drained and turned into productive agricultural farmland. He was anxious to do so because he needed to start turning a profit. He therefore quickly put local labourers to work, digging dikes while Eliza and Philadelphia continued to enjoy the varying social activities that Paris so richly offered.

Life also continued uninterrupted for the Austen family. In 1782, Cassandra Elizabeth was old enough to be sent away to school with her cousin Jane Cooper. The Austens' Jane was now seven years old and she wanted to go with her older sister and supposedly begged her mother to agree. Even though she was too young, Mrs Austen gave in and allowed it. All three girls were then sent to school at Mrs Cawley's in Oxford, but a measles outbreak happened shortly after their arrival.

To ensure the students were safe, Cawley moved her school from Oxford to Southampton. However, the move didn't prevent the girls from getting sick because when troops returned to the port of Southampton, they brought typhus with them. In lieu of catching measles, all three girls caught typhus instead. In early September 1783 Jane Cooper sent a letter to her parents informing them of their illness. Mrs Cooper told

Mrs Austen and they both went and collected their daughters. Although all the girls recovered, Mrs Cooper caught typhus and died in October.

Back in Paris, Eliza continued her life of endless fêtes and social activities. In May 1783, she wrote another letter to Phylly that discussed what winter was like in Paris. Her letter in part stated that numerous private balls had been held and that a new Opera House had been built at the Palais-Royal.

Like the first Opera House that had burnt down in 1763, so did the second one in 1781. It happened during a performance of *Orpheus* when a piece of stage scenery caught fire. Smoke soon engulfed the building and the audience members and performers poured into the streets as coloured flames licked to heights of 200 feet. Fortunately, it was not a windy night and a slight rainstorm helped confine the fire so that just the Opera House burnt to the ground.

The third Opera House was constructed on the same site, but according to Eliza, Parisians were dissatisfied with it. She reported that because Parisians were so hard to please, the Tuileries Palace was being 'fitted up' with a theatre. Eliza thought a theatre at the Tuileries was better because between acts, audience members could 'take the air' in the fine gardens that surrounded the palace.

She also mentioned Holy Week and vespers. According to her, vanity now replaced devotion because although people went to the Abbey of Longchamps west of Paris, that was situated in the fine, thick woods of Bois de Boulogne, they never entered the monastery to say their prayers. Rather the reason for their trip was to be seen parading in 'fine cloaths' and riding in 'fine Equipages'.

Although the French might appear at Longchamps in magnificent carriages with the finest horses just like elite people did at Hyde Park, Eliza remarked the French equipages were much more stylish and glorious than any seen in London. According to Eliza, Frenchmen owned the latest and most elegant carriages; pulled them with four or six premium strutting horses; and outfitted them with up to eight lackeys. Frequently they also had numerous splendid, liveried footmen trotting alongside.

Anyone who was anybody could be seen at Longchamps, and Eliza mentioned observing some single French gentlemen, whom she called 'Elegants', riding in open carriages or on horseback. The Royal Family was also there to contribute to what Eliza termed the 'Shew'. She noted that she saw several princesses riding in open calashes with six prancing horses, and that among the most notable and elegant of these was the one that held the Princess de Lamballe and her sister-in-law, the Duchess of Chartres.

Everyone parading at Longchamps was of course decked out in their best finery and while Eliza seemed impressed by many of the Parisian styles, she could not help but mention some 'fashionable follies'. One was that Parisians had begun calling everything *à la Marlborough,* a term that was based on General John Churchill, 1st Duke of Marlborough. He was an English soldier and general who had fought against France under King Louis XIV.

Marlborough had died years earlier in 1722 after suffering a stroke while living at Windsor Lodge. Eliza mentioned that the great general would probably have been shocked to discover his name was so much in vogue. She claimed it all began because the Dauphin's nurse was singing an old ballad named *Death of Marlborough* to put the baby to sleep. Marie Antoinette overheard it, began singing it herself, and the next day, the whole court had it memorised.

The court's example spread and before long, the term was embraced by the public in clever pantomimes and skilful verses. This also resulted in *à la Marlborough* being applied to every 'frippery of Dress' and every fashionable finery. *À la Marlborough* was also linked to every popular ribbon and fashionable silk. Even the prevailing colour, a fine, deep, intense black, was called *la mort de Marlborough* (the death of Marlborough).

The fad of *à la Marlborough* was not the only interesting tidbit Eliza reported to Phylly. There was also the invention of balloons noted by Eliza in one of her next letters. The first known flight of any balloon was a hot air balloon flown by the Montgolfier brothers – Joseph-Michel and Jacques-Étienne – on 14 December 1782. However, the first public demonstration with their hot air balloon did not happen until 4 June 1783 in Annoay, France. It was then that a group of dignitaries from the *États particuliers* watched the Montgolfiers' balloon ascend.

When word spread about the incredible feat of balloon flight, Frenchmen went wild. Two and a half months later, the first manless hydrogen balloon ascent happened on 26 August. Jacques Charles and two engineering brothers – Anne-Jean and Nicolas-Louis Robert – known collectively as Les Frères Robert (Robert brothers) conducted the flight. The balloon rose successfully and travelled until it landed in a Gonesse village. At the time, many people had no idea about balloons and villagers were so terrified when they saw something huge coming out of the sky, they attacked it with their hoes, picks, and shovels, believing it to be some sort of monster.

Like the French monarchy and the French public, Eliza was caught up in the excitement of balloon ascents from the moment she heard about them. It seemed astonishing that it was possible to leave the earth, float through the heavenly clouds, and land safely without incident. Even a year later in 1784, Eliza was still amazed about balloon flight and mentioned it in another letter to her cousin.

This time, it was about a discovery made by Jean-Pierre Blanchard, a French inventor and balloon flight pioneer. He claimed to be able to control the course and direction of a balloon using wings and a rudder. Beneath the 26-foot balloon built for this occasion was an umbrella-shaped sail, so that if for any reason the balloon burst, the sail would act as a sort of parachute for the car beneath that held the travellers and had wings, oars, and a rudder.

A demonstration of this steerable balloon was slated for 2 March 1784 and it was agreed that Blanchard and a Benedictine monk would ascend together and 'row' northeast to La Villette. However, once the balloon began to rise, the monk was struck by fear, turned deathly pale, and crossed himself. He did not have much to fear because fortunately for him, at about that same moment, a leak was discovered in the balloon and it returned to the ground.

After the necessary repairs were completed, Blanchard decided to ascend alone to the relief of the monk. However, moments after Blanchard seated himself inside the car, a brash military student named Dupont de Chambon decided that he should accompany Blanchard. He jumped in and demanded that he be included in the flight. When Blanchard refused, de Chambon began to slash at the balloon's mooring ropes with his sword.

A violent scuffle ensued as Blanchard tried to stop de Chambon but not before he damaged and destroyed the wings and oars. The crowd was by now impatient and further upset that de Chambon had delayed Blanchard's ascent. So, a bystander grabbed de Chambon by the scruff of the neck and roughly pulled him out of the balloon.

With de Chambon now under control, Blanchard could finally give the crowd what they wanted and with broken wings and other damage, he ascended alone in his balloon. As he rose to 1500 fathoms, word spread that he was undertaking a dangerous flight and Parisians were gripped with fear believing that at any moment, Blanchard and his balloon would plummet from the sky. Instead it headed off in the direction opposite to its planned route, having been pushed by the wind. According to Eliza, after travelling to Billancourt he then returned to his starting point and landed safely to the astonishment of most spectators.

Although travelling in the sky now seemed possible, in May 1785 Eliza and her mother were planning a trip the old-fashioned way. They were taking a carriage to de Feuillide's estate where they would reunite with him. The 450-mile trip took them to an isolated area in Landes called Gabarret that was described by author Claire Tomalin as possessing a 'few aristocratic families within driving distance to be called on, otherwise only a sparse population of peasants speaking an unintelligible patois and living in conditions so primitive they seemed almost another species'.[5] The commune's population was under 1,000 and the nearest town twenty miles away offered nothing like the hubbub and activity of Paris.

Upon their arrival, Eliza's husband installed them temporarily in the rented Château de Jourdan, where they met his widowed mother and his two sisters. The charming country château with dormer windows stood atop a hill, surrounded by woodlands and wildlife with a serene lake below and flat land around it. It was located on the edge of Sainte Meille near the small village of Gabarret, an isolated but beautiful spot. In the meantime, the Count continued to build a new 'square, unromantic' château that once finished would allow him and his family to move into it. Despite not having nearly enough funds to build his new château, he remained busy erecting stables, cottages, and even a house for his absent brother, Jean-Gabriel, who was away in the West Indies.

Life in the French countryside involved quiet days and nearly noiseless nights. Any entertainment or excitement that Eliza and her mother enjoyed was created from their own ingenuity. The women likely spent their free time reading books and writing letters. Perhaps Eliza also focused on improving her French language skills with her mother-in-law, as it would be noted later that she spoke flawless French.

Eliza also proved to be a reliable helpmate and wife. She had good reason to want her husband to succeed with his marshland project because, if he did, their fortune would be secure and they could enjoy the luxuries that France had to offer. Therefore, Eliza became almost as involved as her husband in trying to help him tame the swampy wilderness and she could be found regularly aiding him in some way.

Long before Eliza and her mother settled in at the Château de Jourand, the Knights, a wealthy couple who had a connection to the Austens, set off from England on 24 September 1784 on a continental tour. Thomas Knight was an English politician who sat in the House of Commons and was a rich relative of George Austen's. Knight had visited the Austen clan with his new wife, Catherine Knatchbull of Chilham in Kent, during their wedding tour in May 1779. The newlyweds were delighted by the Austens' third son, 11-year-old Edward, affectionately called Neddy. In fact, they were so pleased they asked that he be allowed to accompany them on the remainder of their honeymoon.

After the honeymoon trip ended, Neddy settled back into life at the rectory and a few months later, the Austens' eighth and last child, Charles John Austen, was publicly christened at Steventon on Friday, 30 July. In the meantime, the Knights did not forget Neddy. The next summer they asked George Austen that Neddy be allowed to spend the holidays with them. Supposedly George worried that his son might fall behind in his studies, but Mrs Austen was insistent he should go, and so it was not long before Neddy was off once again with the well-to-do Knights.

If anyone was jealous of the partiality that Neddy received from the Knights, it was his younger precocious brother Henry. There was about a three and a half year age difference between the two boys and Henry could not understand why Neddy was the lucky one who got to live like a noble and visit the Knights at the palatial estate of Godmersham Park with its summerhouses and a Hermitage that belonged to Knight's father, Thomas Brodnax-May-Knight.

Despite his wealth, the younger Knight and his wife Catherine remained childless, which was also one reason they continued to maintain a deep interest in Neddy. Eventually they asked the Austens that they be allowed to adopt him, which happened in 1783, the same year he was designated their legal heir. To commemorate the handover, a silhouette by London artist William Wellings was also commissioned showing the 16-year-old welcoming his new parents with open arms.

Now the Knights were taking a continental tour. They had also allowed Neddy and his brother Henry to travel with them as far as Calais. From there, the boys returned to Dover in a French packet boat and the

Knights travelled to Rheims, Châlons-sur-Marne, Dijon, Mâcon, and Lyons before taking a leisurely boat ride down the Rhône and reaching Avignon on 28 October. On 9 November they rented a house in Nice and knowing that would be near to where Philadelphia, Eliza, and the Count were living, they sent a letter to Philadelphia suggesting that they might visit her in Gabarret. However, in April 1785 when they arrived at Agen, they were still forty miles away and the distance made a visit impossible.

As Eliza and her mother were adjusting to life in the French countryside and as the Knights were thinking about visiting them, Hastings left India on 2 February 1785 aboard the *Berrington*. He had resigned in 1784 and had been succeeded as acting Governor-General by Sir John Macpherson. Unfortunately for Hastings, he did not embrace a new life of leisure upon landing in England in June 1785 because he was impeached for the death of Maharaja Nandakumar.

Nandakumar had been appointed by the EIC to be a tax collector. In 1773, he accused Hastings of bribing him with more than one-third of a million rupees and claimed that he had proof against Hastings in the form of a letter. In the meantime, the EIC had established the Supreme Council of Bengal. It was the highest executive authority under the EIC and subordinate only to the EIC's court of directors and the British Crown.

The council consisted of five members, including the Governor-General Hastings. Three of the council members – Sir Philip Francis (an Irish-born British politician); John Clavering (an English army officer and diplomat); and a Baron Monson, who came from a family of politicians – joined together and were constantly at odds with Hastings, probably due to personal petty motives. Thus, when Nandakumar charged Hastings with bribery, the three men agreed to entertain his allegations and soon they began to accuse Hastings of corruption.

Hastings had the ultimate decision on the Supreme Council and could overrule any decision made by council members. Therefore, in 1775 he brought charges of fraud against Nandakumar and accused him of forging a bond to deprive a widow of more than half of her inheritance. Nandakumar was then tried under Elijah Impey, who was appointed to serve as India's first Chief Justice in 1773. Impey also happened to be a friend of Hastings, which then made some people suspicious when Impey found Nandakumar guilty and ordered him executed on 5 August 1775.

BECOMING A COUNTESS

Monson died in 1776 and Clavering passed away in 1777. This allowed Hastings to dominate in the Supreme Council as Francis no longer had a majority, even though he remained embittered towards Hastings. Everything came to a head between Francis and Hastings when Hastings stated in council meeting minutes what is considered by some people to be the worst indictment brought by any man against another:

> I judge of his [Sir Francis] public conduct by my experience of his private, which I have found void of truth and honour. This is a severe charge, but temperately and deliberately made, from the firm persuasion that I owe this justice to the public and to myself.[6]

When Francis read the minutes, the message was clear. Warren Hastings was referring to a scandalous affair Francis had with a married woman named Catherine Noël Grand. Francis had no choice but to issue a challenge with the date of the confrontation fixed for 17 August 1780. The duel resulted in Francis being severely wounded, but he fortunately recovered completely and soon after, left India for England.

With Nandakumar's death, Hastings thought everything was settled and that he would face no problems when he returned to England. He soon learned otherwise. Nandakumar's case had gained notice in Britain because he was the first victim hanged in India under British rule. In addition, Francis still had an axe to grind with Hastings because of the duel and what Hastings said of him. Francis now encouraged the Irish statesman Edmund Burke to do something about Hastings and Impey, whom he claimed had committed judicial murder of Nandakumar.

The House of Commons then decided to impeach Hastings and Impey for crimes and misdemeanours alleged to have been committed during their tenure in India. The charges took Burke two full days to read. Moreover, the case against the two men then dragged on for seven painful years.

Chapter 7

Hastings, Jr.

> YOUR OUTLANDISH COUSIN'S HEALTH & GOOD LOOKS ARE
> PERFECTLY RESTORED.
> ELIZA TO HER COUSIN PHYLLY WALTER ABOUT HERSELF

In July 1785, while Hastings faced charges in England, the de Feuillides would find both joy and heartache in their lives. Months of sweat and toil on their property were at last showing results. The drainage canals the Count built on their estate had allowed the land to be converted to a fertile productive plain. But the work had taken a toll. De Feuillide, who was ten years older than Eliza, had been experiencing poor health and then caught a fever. Eliza was also suffering disappointment because of a recent miscarriage. Thus, when de Feuillide's doctor suggested the waters of Bagnères-de-Bigorre to restore the Count's health, the couple made plans for a trip.

It had also been a harsh and cold winter in the French countryside. Although this extreme weather was no fault of the French monarchy, it caused hardship which agitated the forces seeking to remove the monarchy from power. The bitter winter was in large part due to the Laki eruption in Iceland along with the nearby Grímsvötn volcano. The Laki eruption began on 8 June 1783 and ended eight months later while the Grímsvötn volcano erupted over a two-year period from 1783 until 1785. The lava produced ultimately covered a huge area in southern Iceland and its ash and accompanying poisonous gas blanketed Europe. The 'Laki haze', as it was called, caused thousands of deaths in 1783 and 1784.

The eruption also resulted in a general cooling effect in Great Britain and France between 1783 and 1785, which was later claimed to have been partly caused by a higher atmospheric aerosol content. With a colder than usual winter, everyone was stuck indoors at the

Château de Jourdan, and it was probably no surprise that once one person caught 'the fever', almost everyone else in the household did too. In fact, Eliza's mother-in-law never recovered and died suddenly about mid-June 1785.

As the Count lay ill trying to recuperate while mourning his mother's death, he showed no awareness of the looming signs of social upheaval. Rather, he and his wife planned for rest and recovery in Bagnères, a town that was some seventy-five miles away and situated amid the Pyrenees partly in the valley of the Adour, some eleven miles southeast of Tarbes and nine miles east of Lourdes. The town was well-known for its healing spring waters, and in the late 1700s, Bagnères was embracing the latest popular trend of hydropathy, also called the water cure, and still later hydrotherapy. It involved using water for medical treatment and pain relief and was viewed by most patients as being a type of spiritual and natural healing.

The local landscape of Bagnères was also stunning. Charming villages dotted the countryside and visitors could see cultivated and fertile sections awash in green foliage alongside the majestic Pyrenees that offered 'eternal snows'. Such picturesque scenery was further enhanced by the clearest, bluest crystal springs imaginable. In fact, Eliza claimed the springs were so stunning, she could not believe they existed even in the minds of the greatest poets.

The town of Bagnères was not in the mountains nor in the country. Instead it was situated and embraced by a slope. When entering it, you could see a few spires and steeples peeping over red roofs and as Eliza stated, it presented 'no inelegant appearance'. That was partly because glistening marble had been used extensively in its construction as it was readily available in the area.

Like other spa towns, Bagnères offered activities other than healing waters or health cures. For instance, among the 'public Diversions' was those offered by a convent that had been transformed in 1775 into a gambling establishment called the Vaux-Hall, which featured dining and dancing. Visitors could also enjoy the daily plays presented at the local theatre or attend any of the frequent balls given. These activities were probably why fifteen English families were already present when de Feuillide, Eliza, and her mother arrived.

The spa vacation proved to be exactly what the Count and Eliza needed: he came away vigorously cured, and she came away pregnant, much to her delight. She mentioned the successful trip in a letter to Phylly sent from the Château de Jourdan, dated 17 January 1786:

> I flatter myself You will partake my Satisfaction in being able to inform You that the purpose of the abovementioned Journey has been entirely answered, & your outlandish Cousin's Health & good Looks perfectly restored indeed I have every reason to be pleased with my excursion which has brought me acquainted with one of the most beautiful Spots in the World. ...
>
> 'It is now in agitation whether I shall or shall not set out for England next June; my husband votes for the affirmative but I am not myself quite determined from some reasons which You will be a better judge of, when I have let You into a little piece of my family history, namely My Dear Friend, that [it] is now two months since I have had a prospect of giving you an additional relation, should a Son be *in store* for M. de Feuillide he greatly wishes him to be a native of England for he pays me the Compliment of being very partial to my Country; but I own I have repugnance to undertaking so long a journey in a situation so unfit for travelling. This important question must be determined in the course of a few months, I am the more impatient for its decision.[1]

She also wrote to Phylly that she was thinking of returning to England for a visit around the first of June, and if she gave birth to a boy while there, it would automatically fulfill her husband's desire that their son be a 'native of England'. Of course, undertaking such a trip when she was pregnant was something she referred to as 'repugnant'. Still she noted that her decision to travel in such a delicate condition need not be made for several months.

Eliza also mentioned the potential arrival at the Château de Jourdan of George and Cassandra Austen's oldest son, her 21-year-old cousin James Austen. Born on 13 February 1765, he was four years younger than Eliza. Described as a gentle, sweet child, he became his mother's favourite and by the time his sister Jane was born, he was ten years old. However, this big age difference between the two did not mean that they had a distant relationship.

From a young age, James excelled at writing and poetry. In fact, even though Jane became the famous author of the Austen family, it was James who was always considered the most talented writer. He was also intellectual, studious, and ambitious. Thus, George and Cassandra had big plans for him. They wanted him to become an Anglican minister just like his father; therefore, at the age of fourteen, he was sent to his father's alma mater at Oxford and matriculated at St. John's College.

James always enjoyed Eliza's visits and wanted to visit her so he suggested that he spend the spring months with her and her family. She was still deciding if she would make the trip to England and was unsure because the first few months of her pregnancy had proved difficult as she was constantly suffering from morning sickness. Fortunately, however, by May she was feeling better and thus decided to undertake the journey to England. Plans were then made for her and her mother to leave at the end of the month, and as the Count remained busy with his reclamation project, he was not accompanying them.

Leaving in May seemed to ensure that the expected baby would be born in England. The plan was for the women to arrive in London by early July, a month or so ahead of the expected date of the baby's arrival. However, either because of miscalculation or a too strenuous journey, Eliza delivered the baby early in Calais on 25 June 1786.

The very fat, very fair, and very pretty boy was quickly given five impressive names: Hastings-François-Louis-Henri-Eugène. His first name was, of course, a tribute to Eliza's godfather, Warren Hastings. Naming the baby Hastings seemed to confirm the suspicions many people had long held that Eliza was indeed Hastings' child. Whether true or not, Eliza decided to delay Hastings Jr.'s baptism, and the baby was not baptised until 1 June 1787 after they reached London.

After Hastings Jr.'s birth, Eliza took time to recover before they headed off to England. They did not arrive in London until 24 July 1786 and when they did, they learned that about a week earlier, Neddy had set off on a four-year Grand Tour that allowed privileged young Englishmen to travel with their tutors throughout Europe. It was a rite of passage with trips lasting between two and four years. Such tours allowed travellers to see historical and cultural places, and, moreover, young men lucky enough to experience the Grand Tour came back refined, polished, and knowledgeable gentlemen.

In the meantime, Eliza and her mother found accommodation on Albermarle Street at Lothian's Hotel, cited as one of the first hotels providing 'elegant accommodations' and noted in 1802 to be one of seventeen hotels designated as accommodating 'recently arrived' families in London. The women also quickly embraced the sociality of the city by undertaking a whirlwind of social calls to friends in and around London, including visits to many longstanding acquaintances from Philadelphia's time in India.

In addition, they received visitors because the day after their arrival, Hastings and his wife, Chapuset, called on them. The Hastings in return invited Philadelphia and Eliza to visit at their newly purchased Beaumont Lodge, described as 'a very pleasant little estate of ninety-one acres,'[2] located on the outskirts of Windsor Forest. The women obliged and left London in August to spend three weeks with the Hastings in the Berkshire countryside.

Hastings reported that he took a phaeton to Hounslow on 4 August to meet them, but they were not there because apparently they had been detained as Eliza was 'indisposed'. The women arrived at Beaumont Lodge later that day about 1 pm. Unfortunately, during their visit Eliza and Philadelphia noticed that Hastings seemed to have little time to enjoy Beaumont's 'recreations'. He was busy worrying about the Nandakumar incident and what would happen because of his involvement. As to Chapuset, she had been sick but suddenly seemed brimming with health.

By October, Philadelphia and Eliza were in Surrey visiting the Woodmans at their country farm in Ewell, and in early November, Eliza probably heard news that her Austen cousin Neddy was in Switzerland, and that James Austen had set off to visit her husband in the south of France. James was going even though Eliza was in England. Unfortunately for him, he found himself wind-bound in Jersey, and his arrival in France was delayed by almost a month.

The day before Eliza turned 25, she and her mother arrived at Steventon. Eliza had not been there since about 1776, and her arrival this time was anything but quiet and sedate. The difference between the countrified people of Steventon and Eliza, fresh from cosmopolitan Paris, had to be a stark contrast for both parties. To those at Steventon, Eliza probably glittered like a brilliantly-lit chandelier at Versailles. She also must have created a flutter of exotic intrigue wearing the latest French fashions and speaking impeccable French.

Eleven-year-old Jane had surely never met anyone as fascinating as her. All she knew of her sophisticated, worldly, and mysterious cousin was what she had heard from her letters. She probably imagined Eliza living in exotic India, attending elegant Parisian balls, and being romantically courted by a handsome and worldly French count. Although Jane knew what Eliza looked like, having seen the miniature she sent when she was nineteen, she soon found that Eliza was full of exciting tales. Thus, Eliza's outlandishness had to be noticed by her cousins as the definition of the word means bizarre, unfamiliar, or foreign.

Eliza was also a witty, flirtatious and vivacious extrovert who exuded elegance, style, and grace. At the same time, she was also willing to laugh at herself and offered a breath of fresh air whenever she appeared. When she entered a room, people noticed. Mrs Austen certainly did and, in fact, the flurry of excitement generated by Eliza and Philadelphia's arrival prompted her to write to her niece Phylly:

> We are now happy in the company of our Sister Hancock Madame de Feuillide & the little Boy; they came to us last Thursday Sennet [21 December] & will stay with us till the end of next Month. They all look & seem to be remarkably well, the little Boy grows very fat, he is very fair & very pretty; I don't think your Aunt at all alter'd in any respect, Madame is grown quite lively, when a child we used to think her too grave. We have borrowed a Piano-Forte, and she plays to us every day; on Tuesday we are to have a very snug little dance in our parlour, just our children, nephew & nieces ... quite a family party; I wish my third niece could be here also; but indeed, I begin to suspect your Mother never intends to gratify that wish. ... Five of my children are now at home, Henry, Frank, Charles & my two Girls, who have now quite left school; Frank returns to Portsmouth in a few days, he has but short holidays at Christmas. Edward is well & happy in Switzerland. James set out for La Guienne, on a visit to the Count de Feuillide, near Eight weeks ago, I hope he is got there by this time and am impatient for a Letter; ... Every one of our Fireside join in Love, & Duty as due and in wishing a happy 87 to our dear Friends at Seal.[3]

Eliza and Jane shared the same birth month of December and over the years they would learn that they shared even more. Jane would find her bubbly, lively, and story-telling cousin, who so impressed her as a child, was also a friend. Further, Eliza's exciting experiences would spark Jane's imagination in a way no one else did and she would incorporate Eliza's outlandish characteristics and stories into her novels.

Eliza had always been willing to join in all the Austen holiday fun and this year was no exception. Her tales were more like fascinating novels and her musical abilities on the pianoforte likely inspired Jane to improve her own piano-playing, because it resulted in the Austen family acquiring their own instrument and Jane taking regular lessons until 1796. During these gatherings, Eliza got to know the then 16-year-old Henry. She found him witty and charming; similarly, he was immediately drawn to her and danced with her often. Of course, Eliza always craved attention and having an admirer boosted her ego. But their bond was much deeper than a casual flirtation.

The year 1786 was also the year that Jane would develop one of her most important friendships. It was with the intelligent conversationalist Anne Lefroy born in 1749, who because of her generosity and acts of kindness became known as Madam Lefroy. She had married the Reverend Isaac Peter George Lefroy in 1778, and as they lived in Ashe, they became the Austen family's closest neighbours. Jane had likely been invited to play with Madam Lefroy's oldest child and only daughter, Jemima Lucy Lefroy, 'but [Jane's] quick wits and literary interests had evidently soon endeared her to Mrs. Lefroy as a personal, even if very youthful, friend'.[4] Of course, a young Jane could not have been more flattered that Madam Lefroy found her interesting and intelligent.

At the end of January, Eliza and her family swept out of Steventon just as they had swept in and returned to London. Eliza was focused on rejoining the *haute ton* of London and it was made easier when she rented a fashionable residence on the north side of London on Orchard Street. Her life then became a whirlwind of non-stop activities and constant parties. For instance, she appeared in a single day at three exclusive events: a daytime reception held at the palace of St. James, a party hosted by the Duchess of Cumberland, and an exclusive ball held at the social club Almack's. This whirlwind of activity resulted in her calling herself the 'greatest rake imaginable' and complaining about wearing a heavy hoop that was fatiguing because it was of 'no inconsiderable weight'.

During this time, Eliza invited the infatuated Henry to visit her in London for the month of April, and, according to family gossip, the two apparently devised a scheme for him to accompany her back to France the following year. Unfortunately for Henry, that trip would never come to fruition. One of the fellows at Oxford either died or married (Henry was unsure which), and he was obliged to fill the vacancy and had to cancel the trip.

Although Eliza may have seemed light-hearted when she arrived in England, a year later she realised her young son was not developing as expected. Like George Jr., Eliza's son would show similar problems that became more pronounced as he grew: at two years old, he had convulsive fits, squinty abnormal eyes, and could not stand or speak.

In 1779, the Austens had decided to send their disabled 13-year-old son away to live with his Uncle Thomas Leigh, who had also exhibited problems and who had been placed under the care of Francis Cullum in Monk Sherborne years earlier. Cullum would also take in George Jr. and he would continue to care for him until Cullum's death in 1834. After that, Cullum's son (also named George) became responsible for George Jr.

Eliza, though, could not send Hastings Jr. away. She was very loyal and cared deeply for him, as she did her family. Perhaps she was also naturally optimistic and believed the future might bring an improvement. Possibly she worried that, because of her previous miscarriage, Hastings Jr. might be her only child.

Whatever the reason, Eliza chose home care. She then provided Hastings Jr. with a rich, stimulating environment for learning and did everything possible to encourage his improvement. In fact, no matter how tiny his accomplishment, her reports on his progress glowed with optimism and good news.

It is unclear when Eliza told her husband about their son's abnormal eyes, fits, and lack of improvement, but she did not have Hastings Jr. baptised until almost a year after his birth. It happened at London's St. George's Hanover Square Church, with its elegant portico of Corinthian order and handsome bell tower. The baptism also made Hastings Jr. an Anglican member like his mother, rather than Catholic like his father.

While adjusting to her new responsibilities to care for a developmentally disabled child, Eliza continued to build her relationship with her cousin Phylly. Between 7 and 16 September 1787, they travelled with Eliza's mother to the spa town of Tunbridge Wells in western Kent, located in a sandy bottom surrounded by steep hills. It was allegedly discovered by Dudley, Lord North during the reign of James I and is the oldest watering place next to Bath. It offered pure air and medicinal waters of the chalybeate type that were claimed to be beneficial for digestion, circulation, and nervous female complaints. Supposedly the waters also aided anyone in a delicate or weakened state.

One year before Eliza visited Tunbridge Wells, a description of the area appeared in an eighteenth-century guidebook that stated:

> Tunbridge Wells ... is partly built in Tunbridge parish, partly in Frant Parish, and partly in Speldhurst parish; and consists of four little villages named *Mount-Ephraim, Mount-Pleasant, Mount-Sion,* and the *Wells;* which, all united together, form a considerable town; whole boundaries are *Tunbridge* on the north, *Lamberhurst* on the east, a large and partly uncultivated *Forest* on the south, and *East-Grinstead* on the west.[5]

The Wells, as it was called, was the centre for all the action because the chapel, assembly rooms, markets, and medicinal waters were all located there. There was also a prominent public parade that consisted of an Upper Walk that was nicely paved and raised about four steps above the Lower Walk, which was unpaved and used primarily by 'country people' and local servants. In addition, alongside the Upper Walk on the left side was a row of trees and in the middle was a gallery for music that was separated from the Lower Walk by a palisade. The parade also had a portico supported by Tuscan pillars that extended its whole length; the shade it provided extended to the right-hand side of the Upper Walk where visitors could patronise the millinery shops, toy shops, Tunbridge ware shops, a library, a coffee house, and the assembly rooms.

Trade conducted in this spa town was said to resemble that found in German spa towns because the most popular items sold were wooden toys. These included tea chests, dressing boxes, snuff boxes, punch ladles, and numerous other little articles of the same type. Great quantities of these wooden items were sold during the summertime to visitors just before they left as it was customary for travellers to take some trinkets home to their family and friends.

Visitors also benefited from the three principal taverns – Sussex, the Kentish, and the New Inn Tavern – that were 'pleasantly situated'. They were known to provide great 'conveniences' and 'good accommodations'. These three taverns were also constantly improving and upgrading their buildings. In fact, in 1786, the Sussex had undergone recent development that resulted in the creation of new apartments, both for dining and sleeping.

The Tunbridge Wells area was attractive to visitors in other ways. Besides the fresh air, the healthy waters, and shopping, it also had easy access, a large variety of activities, and a daily schedule that allowed Eliza, her mother, and other visitors great freedom. In fact, Tunbridge Wells was considered the perfect rendezvous spot in the summer for 'gaiety and politeness'. It was also stated that because this spa town was only thirty-six miles from London, a daily post was established, a stagecoach arrived regularly every afternoon, and newspapers appeared twice daily.

First-time visitors to the area initially visited the well. There they tasted the water and paid a customary fee, known as a 'welcome penny' to the dippers and then dependent upon the amount of water taken, they paid another fee upon leaving. From there, tourists often proceeded to visit other public places where according to their rank they might pay a crown or more at the assembly rooms. Coffee houses were also available for gentlemen, and both female and male guests could also take to their lodgings any books that they desired to read from a library; this consisted of several thousand volumes and was said to be constantly enlarging because of the receipt of the latest publications.

Besides these activities, visitors were greeted by a musical band that performed three times daily and made its appearance in the orchestra on the public walks or at the balls supported by subscription. Guests could also promenade and if the weather was 'fine', music might 'attend' them the whole time they walked.

Daily schedules were usually similar among travellers. For instance, promenading generally happened between seven and eight o'clock in the morning and usually lasted for an hour or two before visitors went to eat breakfast. This morning meal was generally accomplished by everyone joining together in 'public rooms' or for simpler breakfasts, people could eat at the coffee houses.

Once breakfast was finished, there were several activities that guests might enjoy. For instance, it was fashionable to attend the chapel for morning services, during which all music ceased playing outside and did not start up again until the services were complete. Those who chose not to attend services might take a coach airing or a horseback ride as others whiled away their time playing at the billiard tables, taking a rural walk, or visiting the local bookseller.

Also around this time, visitors of different ranks and circumstances began to once again fill the walks, forming thick crowds on the parade and engaging in conversations 'that an attentive listener to the several parties would ... fancy himself at the Royal-Exchange, and the next at the Palace; now at an India factory, or an American plantation'.[6] Travellers could also shop, and shoppers could be found filling the toy shops, milliners, or jewellers that dotted the local streets.

Having spent daytime hours in this fashion, dinner was served and afterwards the band again struck up and the crowds once again returned to the walk. The difference this time was that the visitors' morning wear had been laid aside and everyone was dressed in fine attire intended to impress and described as 'full and splendid'. Moreover, 'the general desire of all is to see and be seen, till the hour of tea-drinking, when they assembly together, as in the morning, commonly at the public rooms, or at the coffee-house rooms.'[7]

Yet, that was not the end of the day for guests at Tunbridge Wells. The evening hours were also filled with numerous activities. There was dancing, theatre productions, gambling, and more:

> [C]ards succeed in the great rooms, which are supplied with a proper number of tables, and all necessary accommodations, and where the greatest order and regularity is observed ... Twice in a week there are public balls in the Great Assembly Room – on *Tuesdays* at the Room on the Walk, and *Fridays* at the Lower Rooms; every other night in the week (*Sundays* excepted, when the company in general meet to drink tea at the Great Room on the Walk) are card-assemblies at each of the public-rooms alternately.[8]

As the popularity of the spa town increased, so too did patronage by the wealthier classes. It drew some of the most famous people of the eighteenth century including such individuals as writer Dr Samuel Johnson, actor and theatre manager David Garrick, and the writer and printer Samuel Richardson. Eliza's appearance at Tunbridge Wells also likely caused much excitement as everyone was agog when her magnificent coach-and-four rolled in, or when they witnessed her daily flurry of extravagant shopping bedecked in the finest and richest of Parisian fashions.

Eliza's cheerful frivolity and unrepentant extravagance was almost too much for her sedate cousin Phylly, who a day after her return home wrote a letter full of details to her older brother James about her time at Tunbridge Wells. She noted that she had just spent ten days with her Aunt and cousin and that a 'gayer life' she had never experienced before. Every hour of every day was apparently filled with some sort of engagement. It was too overwhelming for her and she stated she couldn't have been more 'miserable' and that she would have given anything to have escaped. However, because her Aunt and Eliza showered so much kindness, affection, and attention on her, she reported that she reconciled herself to embracing their 'dissipated life'.

Phylly then recounted more about the trip. She stated that from the moment of their arrival in their elegant coach-and-four, a round of breathless activity ensued. They first listened to two Italian singers, which was then followed by dancing that lasted well past midnight. The next day involved shopping at all sorts of milliners to find Phylly the perfect hat, which when discovered she wore behind her hair and off to one side. The night brought another rousing evening of dancing that kept her up well past two in the morning.

Over the next eight days the non-stop activities continued. There was horse racing, visiting the chapel, an airing, card-playing, an evening at the tea rooms, dining, visits to the theatre to see *Which is the Man?*, *Bon Ton*, *Percy*, and *The Maid of the Oaks*, a visit to the High Rocks, an evening ball, more dining, more airings, and more plays, this time *The Drummer* and *Robinson Crusoe*. The continual activities seemed as if they would never stop.

Having provided details of her time there, Phylly then concluded her letter by summing up her thoughts on her Aunt Philadelphia and her outlandish cousin Eliza:

> To begin with my Aunt, I do not know a fault she has so strictly just and honourable in all her dealings, so kind and

obliging to all her friends and acquaintance, so religious in all her actions, in short I do not know a person that has more the appearance of perfection. The Countess has many amiable qualities, such as the highest duty, love and respect for her mother; for whom there is not any sacrifice she would not make, and certainly contributes entirely to her happiness; for her husband she professes a large share of respect, esteem and the highest opinion of his merits, but confesses that Love is not of the number on her side, tho' still very violent of his; ... Her dissipated life she was brought up to, therefore it cannot be wondered at, but her religion is not changed. Her partiality to me was very great. I do not believe she has a thought she would wish to keep from me, tho' I took the liberty of differing in opinion on many subjects; we often kept up a dispute for some time. They were very desirous of keeping me longer with them, and as they had some thought of going for a week to Brighton wished me to be of that party, but I declined it upon my mother's account.[9]

Chapter 8

The Year of 1788

> THE TROUBLES IN FRANCE ARE NOW HASTENING TO A CONCLUSION.
> NORFOLK CHRONICLE

While Eliza was in Steventon for the Christmas season of 1787–1788, she was encouraged by her Austen cousins to participate in their Christmas theatricals. Cousin James had returned from France, and he and his siblings wanted the theatricals to be better than the previous season. To ensure that happened, their father agreed to allow them to turn the barn into a theatre with painted scenery.

Theatricals may have provided Eliza with an effective escape from thinking about Hastings Jr.'s difficulties. She again mentioned that he was having problems in a November letter to Phylly while still in London at Orchard Street. Although she did not provide any specific details, he had apparently 'suffered incredibly' during the two months prior and there was no better way for Eliza to forget her son's disabilities than by performing on stage.

She knew acting would be an uplifting experience as the play's participants were bound to gain greater enjoyment from the productions than their audience. So, Eliza was as eager as the Austen clan for the theatricals to take place and had, in fact, joined in amateur dramatics in France in 1786. Now she wanted to re-experience the same fun at Steventon and she wanted her cousin Phylly to participate, hoping that Hastings Jr. would be 'quite stout again' by the time she arrived. Eliza therefore refused to let Phylly forget her request to participate and mentioned that Phylly's assistance would make the theatricals a 'vast deal better':

> You may remember when you was at Tunbridge my expressing a very earnest & a very natural wish to have you with me

during the approaching festival, & on finding there were two unengaged parts I immediately thought of you, & am particularly commissioned by My Aunt Austen & her whole Family to make the earliest application possible, & assure you how very happy you will make them as well as myself if you could be prevailed on to undertake these parts …
I assure you we shall have a most brilliant party & great deal of amusement, the House full of Company & frequent Balls. You cannot possibly resist so many temptations, especially when I tell you your old Friend James is returned from France & is to be of the acting party.[1]

Although Eliza might have wanted Phylly there, Phylly did not want to participate. She bowed out gracefully using her well-worn excuse that she couldn't leave her mother. Thus, the theatricals went on without her, even if she did mention to her brother that the Austen barn was to be 'fitted up' and that all the 'young folk' were excited and planned to participate.

Two of the chosen plays had been suggested by Eliza and were ones that she and Phylly had seen at Tunbridge Wells. They were *Which is the Man?*, a popular comedy written by Hannah Parkhouse Crowley in 1782, and *Bon Ton*, a two-act comedy by Garrick. However, despite the intention of putting on these two plays, they were not performed. Instead an old romantic comedy popular since 1714 called *The Wonder – a Woman Keeps a Secret* was performed twice, the first time on 26 December.

A week or so later, a new production was performed. It was *The Chances* and was a play adapted by Garrick from the original that first appeared in 1647 by John Fletcher. This romantic comedy involved confusion, jealousy, and misidentification of a town beauty that was ultimately straightened out in the end.

James was tasked with organising the theatricals and writing the epilogues and prologues. These tasks he viewed as fun because it allowed his creative writing juices to freely flow. Eliza was to perform the starring female roles, play the pianoforte, and present James's prologue, which she did with all the fervour and enthusiasm she could muster.

James had become smitten with Eliza like his little brother Henry, even though both brothers knew that they had no chance with their married cousin. Still they remained fascinated and intrigued by her. Performing emotionally-charged dialogue together and working on romantic lines only increased their adoration for her. They found the pretty Eliza an enticing flirt, 'clever ... and highly accomplished, after the French rather than the English mode',[2] and they apparently did not care that she liked to maintain the upper hand when it came to the male sex.

After great success with the Christmas theatricals, Eliza returned to London. Hastings' trial was set to begin on Wednesday, 13 February 1788 and was to be held at Westminster Hall. Two days before it began, accommodations for those wishing to view the trial were summarised by the examining clerk who 'stated that besides the accommodations [reserved] for the Lords, and the Members of the House of Commons, there were places provided for eleven hundred persons more, allowing eighteen inches to each'.[3]

In the meantime, Eliza asked Phylly to come and stay with her at Orchard Street. Phylly obliged, appearing around 1 April. Of course, she was quickly exhausted by all their social activities just as she had been overwhelmed in Tunbridge Wells. After being there three weeks, she again sent off a letter to her brother James detailing her various complaints:

> I never experienced so thorough a racketing life and had no idea that it cou'd be equal to what I now find it. ... Our mornings are spent in ridiculous sort of calls from one door to another without ever being let in, shopping and by way of treat to me sometimes a walk in Kensington Gardens. ... My dear friends are all affectionate kindness to me, and do everything for my pleasure. I have even the coach with a coronet always at my command, but when able to find my way I prefer walking ... The opera we went in style to, as we sat in Mrs. Hasting's box. I have had the pleasure of seeing a great deal of the Hastings. ... I have drunk tea at his house in St. James' Place ... I have once been to the Trial, which, because an uncommon sight, we fancied worth going to, and sat from 10 till 4 o'clock, compleatly tired, but I had the satisfaction of hearing all the celebrated orators, viz. Sheridan, Burke & Fox. The first was so low we cd. not hear him, the 2nd so hot and hasty, we cd. not understand, & the 3rd was highly superior to either as we cd. distinguish every word, but not to our satisfaction as he is so much against Mr. Hastings whom we all here wish so well.[4]

Whereas Phylly found the trial fatiguing, it was of indirect benefit to 12-year-old Jane Austen, as noted by author Park Honan:

> Since the keynote of Warren Hastings's accusers was their emphasis on morality, ethics, above-board politics and responsibility, and since his defenders cited his probity and ethics, the spirit of the time favoured the "ethical search". People talked about ethics. And during the seven years of the trial Jane was encouraged to give more and more "sense", depth and moral point to her own juvenile joke-writing or *Jeux d'esprit.*[5]

The outcome of the trial held special interest for Eliza and Philadelphia, who unconditionally supported Hastings. So did the Austens, and all of them could not wait to hear every excruciating detail of the trial. As to the public's perception, they saw the Hastings affair as a form of intriguing entertainment and were fascinated by the catalogue of crimes attributed to him. Thus, long queues of people formed early every morning for admittance into Westminster Hall.

Around the end of May, Eliza and Philadelphia took Phylly home to Seal in Kent. They then travelled to Tunbridge Wells because Hastings Jr. was once again suffering from convulsions, and Eliza hoped that the healthy waters there would resolve his issues. From there, they journeyed to the great seaside town of Ramsgate where they had access to its seawater, also thought to contain curative properties.

Seawater's popularity began in the 1740s when British physician Richard Russell began to encourage his patients to imbibe and bathe in the salty water. He also published a dissertation in Latin that was translated into English and became known as *Glandular Diseases, or a Dissertation on the Use of Sea Water in the Affections of the Glands*. In his book Russell claimed seawater had medicinal properties. Other doctors soon supported his views and began to advocate the use of it to improve health.

Ramsgate had initially been a poor fishing village but like other seaside towns, it started to gain popularity once physicians lauded sea bathing and drinking seawater as a health cure. In fact, seawater treatments became so popular that seaside towns began to vie with one another for the top position. Indicative of this is in 1764,

Ramsgate boatmen could be hired to row gentlemen bathers out to deep water and female bathers could undress and change in one of two sheds while waiting to use vacant bathing machines. Ramsgate continued to be fashionable for bathing in 1824 when it was described in the following fashion:

> The bathing-place lies in front of a long line of high chalky rocks at the back of the pier, and is composed of reddish sand, soft and pleasant to the feet ... The rooms for the accommodation of bathers are commodious ... [and included] four warm salt-water baths, also a plunging and shower bath ... attached [to] convenient waiting and dressing rooms.[6]

Around the end of July 1788 as Eliza and her family were returning to London, Phylly wrote another letter to her brother. It was dated 23 July and provided gloomy news about Hastings Jr.'s outlook for becoming a normal child. Phylly called him 'Poor little Hastings' and remarked on his most recent fit. She noted the similarities he demonstrated to those of George Jr. such as a weak head and unusual eyes. In addition, although she mentioned that Hastings Jr. appeared to be healthy, he was unable to walk in the slightest and the only talk he made was continual guttural-like noises.

Hastings Jr.'s prospects weren't the only worry Eliza was facing. Around this same time, news reached her about various disturbances in France. These troubles had been sparked due to economic fears that the country might go bankrupt. Tensions had also been building throughout France because of the high cost of bread and the outlook worsened when another poor harvest was forecast after an epic hailstorm hit on 13 July 1788.

The storm rained down in torrents from Rouen in the north to Toulouse in the south. Thomas Blaikie, a Scottish gardener, witnessed it and provided a bleak assessment. He gave the following details on the carnage wrought by the giant hailstones:

> [The] hail which fell in rather large peices of ice and had cut down branches of trees and killed hares patriges and many other things; there was the peices of ice to put the

wine in, not Melted after 24 hours in the Month of Jully ! ... tiles of the houses with the rafters were broken and people all in consternation; ... even the Potatoes was dug out of the ground by the ice and hashed to Pieces and crops intirely destroyed and the poor people crying and saying that the day before they had the prospect of abundance and at present they could not find a hand full of grass in many places to give to a Cow or ass.[7]

If everyone thought it was poor harvests that would incite the people, they were wrong. Rather it was a riot in Grenoble, that became known as the 'Day of the Tiles', which caught everyone's attention. Like the rest of France, Grenoble was suffering financially; a poor harvest made things worse, as did the refusal by the upper classes to relinquish their fiscal privileges. Matters finally came to a head in a Grenoble meeting of judges on 7 June when an attempt was made to abolish the Parlements because they refused to enact a new tax that would deal with France's unmanageable public debt.

The Duke of Clermont-Tonnerre was then ordered to remove the magistrates from Grenoble but when he arrived, he found an angry crowd who refused to have their local body of representatives abolished. Around 10 am, the merchants closed their shops and an upset crowd of men and women began to arm themselves. About noon, angry peasants seized the cathedral bells and began to use them to encourage an influx of dissatisfied peasants into the city. As the mob continued to grow, the Royal Navy, which was already in the area, attempted to put down the riot without using firearms.

Unfortunately, things escalated. The soldiers under the Duke of Clermont-Tonnerre then forced angry townspeople off the streets, but in the process a Royal Navy soldier injured a 75-year-old townsman, which further incensed Grenoble residents. Some from the mob then climbed onto roofs and began tossing roof tiles off buildings and hitting the soldiers in the streets below, which thus resulted in the name for the incident.

To avoid being hit, soldiers retreated inside buildings and began to shoot at the threatening crowd, who then rushed them. In addition, four soldiers on patrol fired into the mob that resulted in the death of a civilian and a 12-year-old boy. Rioters then became more furious and attempted to obtain arms from the city's arsenal, thereby forcing soldiers to defend it by opening fire on the crowd.

Hoping to quell rioters, authorities reached City Hall. They tried to reason with the crowd but could not be heard above all the noise, and soon they had to seek refuge with the soldiers as the fuming citizens refused to disperse. In the meantime, buildings were lost to the mob and looting continued. At 6 pm, about 10,000 people forced local representatives to return to the Palace of the Parlement of Dauphiné. They then began to shout, 'Long live parlement' and throughout the remainder of the night, a large bonfire crackled and leapt as the mob danced and sang.

On 10 June, another attempt was made to appease the crowd, but it again proved fruitless. Parlementarians then fled on the morning of 12 June. Order was restored two days later by Marshal Vaux, who replaced the Duke of Clermont-Tonnerre. However, Marshal Vaux found the situation so alarming he refused to allow any more meetings to take place in Grenoble and moved them to another nearby village.

Back in England, Eliza received word from her husband about the riots. Hearing such news made Eliza unsure whether she should return to France. She therefore consulted the French ambassador, who suggested she delay her departure. Brief mentions of the happenings in Grenoble were also published in various papers with the following short snippet appearing in early August. It demonstrated the happenings that Eliza was likely reading and learning about in her adopted country:

> 'The troubles in France are now hastening to a conclusion. The Marechal de Vaux, who has succeeded the Duke de Tonnerre, in the command of Languedoc, notwithstanding the threats he has held out to the people of Grenoble, and the large succours of forces, he has received, still meets with further resistance in every attempt he undertakes to restore the public tranquility.
>
> The nobility and parliament of the province have assembled within ten miles of Grenoble, and have passed several resolutions – one of which is, that they will pay no more money or taxes to Government, till they are satisfied in every point. The Parliament of Bearn and Britanny have done the same. This news has caused the greatest alarm for the seat of government, and the troops are marching from

every quarter for the relief of Paris. It is confidently reported that Government has stopped the payment of interest on their funds.[8]

Eventually, however, news came that things in France had quietened down. It was a huge relief to Eliza. She mentioned that if things had continued to worsen, her husband would have been called to active duty, which meant he would have been forced to perform an 'unpleasant' duty by facing off against his own countrymen.

With tensions ebbing away in France, Eliza knew her departure was imminent and made some last-minute calls to friends. Among them was another trip to see Hastings and his wife at Beaumont Lodge. She had seen her godfather many times since her arrival in England, but she felt one more visit was in order.

This visit also found her godfather busy refurbishing his recently purchased Daylesford estate. Hastings' ancestors first acquired it in the twelfth century, lost it in the fourteenth, and regained it in the fifteenth, only to have his grandfather sell it in 1714 to a merchant. Hastings wanted it back and offered the merchant twice its value but was turned down. Fortunately, success came when he tried again and acquired it from the merchant's son in 1788.

Eliza had also not forgotten about Henry's big crush on her. Because he would not be returning with her to France, she made a special trip to Oxford to see him. She mentioned this visit to Phylly in a letter. Apparently, when Eliza saw Henry, she thought him practically unrecognisable. He had grown much taller since she had last seen him and now appeared much older with his hair powdered and wearing what she termed a 'very tonish style'.

James was also there to greet her. The group undertook tours of the area that included visiting several colleges, museums, and St. John's. It was there that she took a long walk in the garden and imagined what it would be like to be a fellow strolling in the beautiful garden daily and mentioned her delight at the black gown and square cap worn by the fellows.

Eliza and family arrived back in London on Sunday, 17 August. They accomplished their return after travelling through Hounslow Heath in a rain and lightning storm she termed to be the most 'dreadful' she ever experienced. She was later relieved to learn that the storm had been a blessing in disguise. Apparently, two despicable highwaymen had concealed themselves in the trees and were waiting to attack her coach but when the storm broke, they abandoned the idea.

Back in London, Eliza returned to buying 'furniture and fittings' for her French house. It was tiresome work that she had been performing for the past two months and involved picking the right things and getting them properly packed for the move to France. To complicate matters further, amidst all her 'dust, litter, and confusion', the Austens called. She noted their visit in a letter to Phylly and mentioned that she doubted she would be able to leave for France before the first week of September. In addition, she mentioned Hastings Jr.:

> I don't know what other Beaux I can give You a more satisfactory account of unless it is a young Gentleman whom You recollect there was some little scandal about during your stay in Orchard Street, don't be alarmed for I mean your morning visitor little Hastings, He now sports twelve Teeth 8 of which he has acquired since Ramsgate & what is still better he has cut the last without Convulsions, upon the whole I think He is much the better for Sea bathing, he acquires some new Accomplishment every Day & his last is a very elegant one, He doubles his *prodigious* fists & boxes quite in the English style.[9]

Amidst stuffing boxes, packing chests, and filling trunks, Eliza decided to spend a few more days at Tunbridge Wells before she returned home to her husband. She agreed to go partly because she received an invitation from Lady Judith Rous, the daughter of John Bedingfield of Beeston who in 1749 had married John Rous, Suffolk's MP in 1768. Her daughter Louisa-Judith was also there. She was about four years older than Eliza and would eventually marry John Birch, Deputy-Governor of Chandernagore in the East Indies in January 1791.

Chapter 9

The Brink of Revolution

> AT THIS MOMENT ALL PARIS WAS IN CONSTERNATION.
> SAUNDERS'S NEWS-LETTER, AND DAILY ADVERTISER ON
> THE CONDITIONS IN PARIS

Eliza and her mother left London around mid-September 1788 and spent the winter in Paris. If they thought they had no cares, that was quickly dispelled as they found things were still problematic in France. After the horrendous July hailstorm, a severe drought followed. Then came a winter so severe that people remarked it renewed old memories from 1709 when Louis XIV's Bordeaux froze in his goblet. Frenchmen were reporting it was so bitterly cold, thermometers had never registered such lows. Of these freezing times, historian Simon Schama notes:

> Birds were said to be frozen to their perches; wolves to come prowling from their lairs ... poor men in wild places ... to be reduced to boiling tree bark to make gruel. ... Frozen rivers stopped water mills from turning what grain there was into flour, and prevented transportation of emergency supplies to the areas of greatest want. ... In January Mirabeau described Providence as visited by the Exterminating Angel. 'Every scourge has been unloosed. Everywhere I have found men dead of cold and hunger, and that in the midst of wheat for lack of flour, all mills being frozen.'[1]

Eliza was probably not as interested in the weather as she was in hearing news of the shocking elopement of Mrs Austen's distant 18-year-old cousin, Thomas James Twisleton. A liaison began after he met actress Charlotte-Anne Frances Wattrell while performing with her in a London production. The two eloped to Scotland's Gretna Green and six weeks later remarried in London under English law. Yet the disgrace of it all was whispered about for years and in fact, their unorthodox actions perhaps contributed to the stoppage of the private theatrical performances that had been so popular at Steventon. An Austen biographer, George Holbert Tucker surmises:

> Jane Austen's later conviction stressed in *Mansfield Park*, that amateurs are not sufficiently experienced emotionally to cope with the temptations of dilettante performances was not only the result of observations made at the time Steventon rectory was the scene of the provocative performances of *The Wonder*, but was further bolstered by Twisleton's later well-publicised marital difficulties that caused his family and relations additional embarrassment.[2]

Beside the scandalous elopement, there was also the humorous weekly magazine, *The Loiterer*. Brothers James and Henry started it at the end of January 1789 and modelled it on Dr Samuel Johnson's periodicals. It contained articles on university life written by James, Henry, and their undergraduate friends.

Eliza was probably not that interested in *The Loiterer* either as she was now focused on her husband's poor health. He had been extremely ill and sent word that a 'malignant fever' was raging at their estate. He did not want her or her mother to join him there. Instead he told her to stay in Paris and then offered to come there once he recovered.

That was good news for Eliza who thought a season in Paris was always a good thing, even if she too was ill. In Paris, she languished by her fireside to rebuild her strength and wrote to Phylly on 11 February 1789. Eliza informed her that she currently had little to do with the 'gay world' that Paris offered because of her poor health. Moreover, she claimed that her French friends found her boring after her prolonged stay in England, but when it came to her son, she offered up good news.

Besides improving health-wise, Hastings Jr. had greatly bettered his language skills. According to Eliza, he had turned into a chatterbox saying many words in both French and English. She also noted that because of her consistent efforts with him, the next time he saw Phylly, although he probably would not be able to call her by name because it was still too difficult, he would at least greet her as 'cousin' as he could now say the word.

Eliza also described her precious son as 'spoilt'. She maintained that he was 'rude and riotous' but that his grandmother had sworn to her his bad behaviour would end once he could reason and understand more clearly. In fact, Eliza's mother promised her that all his naughtiness would cease once everyone stopped indulging him.

By now Eliza realised that her son would always suffer limitations, and she made it clear that he would be neither 'Alderman' nor 'Lord Mayor'. What he was, she declared, was a good-tempered loving boy. She remarked that this was demonstrated by his desire to share whatever he was munching on, whether it be fruit or pastries, even though she had told him a thousand times that it was inappropriate to do so.

If it appeared that all future news from Eliza and her mother would come from France, that was soon dispelled. Philadelphia sent a letter to Woodman in early February noting that she was planning to return probably around the month of June. However, unlike the women's previous visit to England, this trip would be short as she was coming to transact business and claimed it would last no longer than three weeks and surely no longer than one month.

As the Woodmans had been kind enough on her previous trip to have offered their house in Cleveland Row, Philadelphia asked if it would be possible to stay there if the Woodmans were 'removed' to Ewell. Of course, she didn't want to cause any inconvenience. She also mentioned that if the Count de Feuillide had to rejoin his regiment, then Eliza would accompany her and they would travel as lightly as possible, limiting the entourage to themselves, Hastings Jr. and Philadelphia's maid Rosalie.

Perhaps another reason for Philadelphia wanting to return to England was that tensions in France had increased since their return. Poor harvests and a lack of food was one problem as demonstrated by the villagers of Neuville in north-western France. In early March they decided to do away with rabbits before the animals gnawed away at the measly remainder of their crops. Armed with sickles, sticks, and clubs they descended into the woods to root them out and kill them. In addition, starving peasants smashed the eggs and nests of partridges, pheasants, and woodcocks, and insisted that doves and pigeons either be destroyed or locked up for fifteen days to prevent them from eating their newly-sown crops.

Peasants were so hungry they completely ignored hunting laws and lawlessly poached game from aristocratic estates. There were too

Image of Eliza de Feuillide, year unknown.

Image of Philadelphia Hancock in 1768 by John Smart.

Robert Clive, 1st Baron Clive. Mezzotint by C. Corbutt after T. Gainsborough. (*Courtesy of Wellcome Collection, Wellcome Library no. 644681i https:// wellcomecollection.org/works/ jyukn8gt*)

Warren Hastings in 1772 by Tilly Kettle.

Right: Guards outside the Black Hole of Calcutta where numerous British soldiers died.

Below: Tysoe Hancock's family. Left to right, Tysoe, maid Clarinda, Eliza, and Philadelphia. c.1763–5 by Joshua Reynolds. This painting was originally thought to be of the George Clive family.

Above: Steventon rectory where George Austen and his family lived.

Left: Anna Marie Apollonia Chapuset, who was known as Marian and became Warren Hastings' second wife.

Warren Hastings when he was serving as Governor-General in India.

Edward "Neddy" Austen welcoming his new parents, the Knights, with open arms.

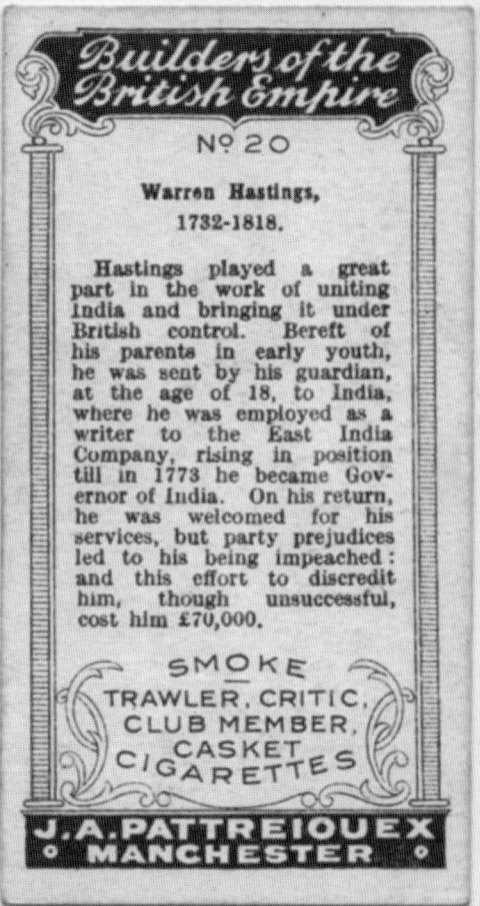

Above: Image of Warren Hastings and India as illustrated on the front and back of a cigarette card.

Left: Sir Philip Francis, who opposed Warren Hastings.

Right: James Austen, Eliza's cousin and Jane Austen's oldest brother.

Below: Tunbridge Wells: entrance to the Pantiles showing the mineral springs. (*Courtesy of Wellcome Collection https://wellcomecollection.org/works/rnpvp226*)

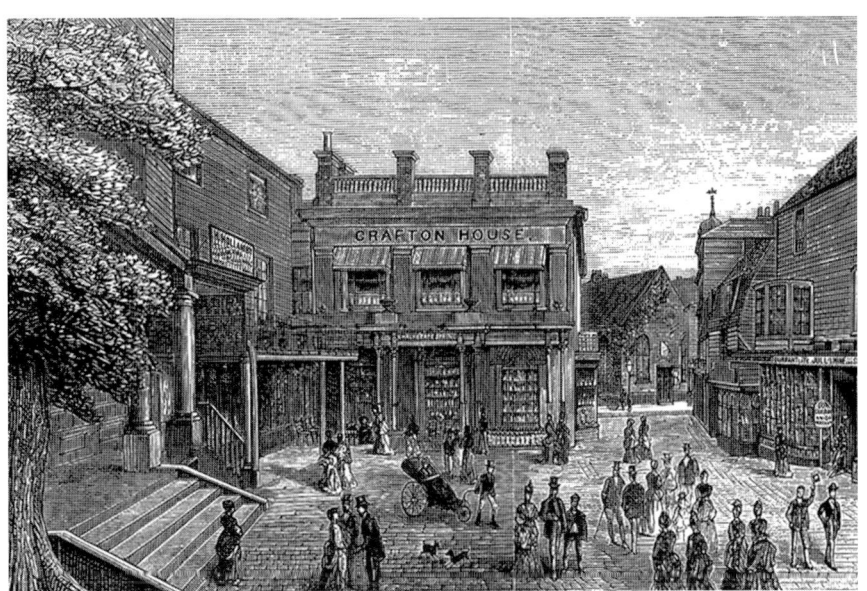

Tuiles Day of the Tiles on 7 June 1788 in Grenoble.

Death of the Princess de Lamballe, 3 September 1792 by Léon-Maxime Faivre.

Right: Henry Austen, Jane Austen's brother and Eliza's second husband.

Below: Jane Austen's own Mr Darcy, Thomas Langlois Lefroy in his later years.

Sir Walter Farquhar, who attended Eliza during part of her battle with breast cancer.

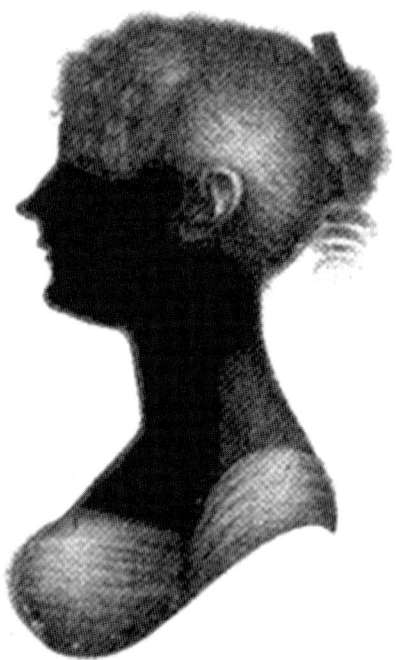

Silhouette of Cassandra Elizabeth Austen of unknown date.

Right: Elizabeth Farren in 1790 by Sir Thomas Lawrence. (*Courtesy of the New York Public Library Digital, NYPL catalog ID b17663494. https://digitalcollections.nypl.org/items/510d47e1-2073-a3d9-e040-e00a18064a99*)

Below: An exact representation of a raft, and its apparatus, as invented by the French for their proposed invasion of England. (From a drawing by a prisoner who made his escape from France.) Published in 1798.

Cassandra Austen's sister-in-law, Jane-Leigh Perrot.

Charles Austen in his Royal Navy uniform.

Right: Watercolour created by Cassandra Elizabeth of her sister Jane Austen from behind.

Below: Chawton cottage where Jane, her mother, and sister Cassandra Elizabeth lived. Now known as Jane Austen's House Museum.

Emmanuel Henri Louis Alexandre de Launay, Count d'Antraigues.

Wife of the Count d'Antraigues, Anne-Antoinette-Cécile Clavel, better known by her stage name Madame Saint-Huberty or Saint-Huberti.

DIED—On Sunday, the 25th inst. in Sloane-street, Elizabeth, the wife of Henry Thomas Austen, Esq.

Death announcement from the *Morning Post* for Eliza.

AUSTEN, MAUNDE and TILSON'S BANK-RUPTCY.—All Persons who intend to prove their debts at the last sitting, on Saturday, the 27th instant, under the Commission of Bankrupt awarded, and now in prosecution against Henry Thomas Austen, Henry Maunde and James Tilson, of Henrietta-street, Covent-garden, in the County of Middlesex, bankers and co-partners, are requested forthwith to transmit to my Chambers, Paper-buildings, Temple, the securities they hold, with instructions for the proof of their debts, distinctly stating the particulars of each claim, with the Christian and Surname at length, and the address and designation of every person interested, and in the case of a partnership, mentioning which of the partners will attend at Guildhall to make the deposition, in order to their accounts being checked, and that their proofs and exhibits may be previously prepared.

WILLIAM VARLO HELLYER,
April 16, 1816.   Solicitor to the Commission.

Publication of Henry Austen and his partners' bankruptcy from the *Morning Chronicle*.

Various plaques located in England related to places associated with Jane Austen during her lifetime.

Statue of Jane Austen in the churchyard at St Nicholas Church, Chawton, near Alton, Hampshire.

many unruly peasants for authorities to stop them even when they tried. The poachers also brazenly hung what they had stolen on poles, sometimes boldly parading with their ill-gotten booty through their village and justifying their wrongful actions crying:

> [It is] the general will of the Nation that game should be destroyed since it carries off a third of the subsistence of citizens and this is the intention of our good King who watches over the common good of his people and who loves them.[3]

Next came the Réveillon riot that happened in April in the Paris suburb of Faubourg Saint-Antoine located east of the Bastille. Jean-Baptiste Réveillon, the self-made capitalist and owner of the Réveillon wallpaper factory, suggested deregulating bread distribution. His suggestion was misinterpreted by Parisians who erroneously believed he wanted to lower their wages.

As most people could barely survive on their meagre wages, it did not take long for a mob to form. It happened across the river in Saint-Marcel on 27 April. Cries of 'Death to the rich' or 'Death to aristocrats' soon reverberated in the streets. The crowd then marched towards Faubourg Saint-Antoine, growing from a few hundred to five hundred and reaching around three thousand by the time they arrived at the place de Grève. However, before they reached Réveillon's factory, their way was barred and they dispersed.

The next day another crowd assembled. This time they were egged on to finish what they had started the day before. As the mob grew, they became bolder and more boisterous until it had swelled to as many as 10,000. They then attacked Réveillon's mansion and factory, and pillaged his wine cellar, consuming 2,000 bottles of wine.

Réveillon and his family luckily escaped to the safety of the Bastille. In the meantime, military troops were called out to quash the disturbance. Their appearance infuriated the crowd and further intensified their anger. A bloody melee ensued that resulted in varying death tolls ranging in reports from 25 to 900. In addition, there was also this account:

> At this moment all Paris was in consternation, though the disturbances were confined to the quarter of St. Antoine,

the rest of the city being perfectly tranquil. Every mode of persuasion and gentleness was at first employed to arrest the disorder and avoid coming to the last extremity with a crowd of half naked wretches, who exhibited nothing but a picture of misery, fury, and drunkenness; yet all proved ineffectual, and it became necessary to have recourse to the grand remedy. Fourteen or fifteen hundred made themselves masters of the large and fine house of the Sieur Reveillon, and intrenched themselves as it were in his garden; others, mounted on the neighbouring roofs, sent down showers of tiles, bricks, stones, rafters, and in a word, every thing that came to hand, on the troops assembled to disperse them. Several of the soldiers were wounded, but none of them killed. At length the enraged military attacked the house, and after a long resistance carried it. The massacre then commenced, and a considerable number were killed on the spot in the garden: The military, however, were too late to save any thing; all was consumed in the flames, or broken to pieces. After this the firing was continued, at different intervals, for an hour and half, to dislodge such as had mounted the tops of adjoining houses, a great many of whom were taken down by the musket shots, and a number killed also in the windows of the upper stories and garrets where they had placed themselves to throw stones and timber at the troops with great security. Notwithstanding the vast number of killed and wounded on the part of the populace, those desperate persons held out obstinately, and some pieces of ordnance were ordered to be brought; happily it was not found necessary to use them; night having come on the rioters dispersed, and the military at last became possessed of the field of battles, after much carnage and infinite trouble. From the most probable calculation, the number of killed and wounded amounted to 300 or 350; the greater part of the latter died since.[4]

The approach of great social unrest in France was even clearer by May 1789. That is when the Estates General met for the first time since 1614. It was a representative and consultative body formed from three classes – First Estate (nobility), Second Estate (clergy), and Third Estate (common people or bourgeoisie) – that had not met since 1614. They were, however, summoned by a royal edict dated 24 January 1789 to meet in May. King Louis XVI had called them hoping to solve the fiscal crisis plaguing France, but the leaders from the three Estates had deep and conflicting interests.

The problems stemmed in part from the system of taxation. Although the French people paid fewer taxes than the British at the time, there were major iniquities within the French tax system. There also existed many exemptions for the privileged classes. Tax reformation had been attempted in earlier years, but those efforts failed to shift more of the tax burden onto the wealthier classes. In the meantime, France's financial problems continued to grow, which also increased the country's debt.

The same rituals that had opened the 1614 Estates General opened the one in May. First, there was a procession that occurred on Monday, 4 May. At the front was a religious processional cross followed by the First Estate decked out in black and white satin with plumed caps. The Second Estate came next, resplendent in purple. The Third Estate brought up the rear, and, in contrast to the finery and sumptuousness of the First and Second Estates, they were unadorned in black with a black and gold overcoat. Royalty closed the procession with King Louis wearing his coronation mantle and on his head, the Regent Diamond. Marie Antoinette was dressed in silver and gold.

Rain had attempted to dampen spirits, but as dawn broke, the rain ceased. Members of the procession travelled from one church to another in serpentine fashion. The three-hour procession moved from Notre-Dame across the Place d'Armes to the Church of Saint-Louis. Nearly everyone carried a lighted candle, and by the time the head of procession reached Saint-Louis, the tail had hardly left Notre Dame.

At the church, the three Estates sat in importance with the First at the front and the Third at the back. There, they listened to a two-hour long sermon by the Bishop of Nancy who 'mentioned the barbarities of tax collectors, the extravagance of Queen Marie Antoinette, the iniquity of the writings of the philosophes, such as the late Voltaire … the necessity for religion as the continuing basis of the national life, and the need for voluntary renunciation of exemptions from taxation'.[5] He also rebuked the court for their appalling luxury and received enthusiastic applause.

The following day, the Estates General met in a temporary hall near the Palace of Versailles. It was on the Avenue de Paris behind the Hotel of Menus Plaisirs and was a rectangular chamber spacious enough to hold 1,200 deputies and numerous spectators. At one end was a platform under a canopy of gold fringe that was splendidly decorated and held the king and queen's thrones. Tiered seating formed the remainder of the seats. To the right of the monarchial thrones were the seats for the Second Estate and to the left, the seats for the First Estate. In front of the thrones at the far end sat the Third Estate.

Strict protocol ensued at the Estates General. The First and Second Estates sat first while the Third Estate stood standing and waiting outside. About an hour and half later, the Third Estate was seated. After the three Estates were seated, the king entered with his entourage. He was followed by the ill-at-ease queen and her respective entourage.

Louis XVI presided over the meeting. He opened with his speech, presented some reforms, and declared himself a friend of the people. He was followed by the Keeper of the Seal, who gave a tedious speech. The King's finance minister, Jacques Necker, spoke next on France's economic situation and weakened his reputation with the people by talking for hours without offering any ideas about how to save the nation. Instead, he gave them financial data, which suggested to the people that he thought the Estates General was simply an administrative function, rather than a new government.

When the Estates General next met, their meeting quickly turned from finances into a debate about how to vote. The Third Estate was less powerful than the First or Second, but they had twice as many delegates and represented the majority. Therefore, the Third Estate wanted to vote based on headcount, not power. As the First and Second Estates had the power, they did not want any change. Necker supported doubling the representation of the Third Estate, but he and the king let the argument go on too long, and by the time they conceded, the Third Estate felt their concession was not very magnanimous.

The three Estates then continued to meet but found themselves unable to reach a substantive agreement. Amid all the discussions, on 4 June, 7-year-old Louis Joseph Xavier François, Dauphin of France died and his 4-year-old brother, Louis-Charles, Duke of Normandy, became the new Dauphin. As Louis XVI and Marie Antoinette

✂ DISCOVER MORE ABOUT PEN & SWORD BOOKS

Pen & Sword Books have over 4000 books currently available, our imprints include: Aviation, Naval, Military, Archaeology, Transport, Frontline, Seaforth and the Battleground series, and we cover all periods of history on land, sea and air.

Can we stay in touch? From time to time we'd like to send you our latest catalogues, promotions and special offers by post. If you would prefer not to receive these, please tick this box. ❏

We also think you'd enjoy some of the latest products and offers by post from our trusted partners: companies operating in the clothing, collectables, food & wine, gardening, gadgets & entertainment, health & beauty, household goods, and home interiors categories. If you would like to receive these by post, please tick this box. ❏

We respect your privacy. We use personal information you provide us with to send you information about our products, maintain records and for marketing purposes. For more information explaining how we use your information please see our privacy policy at www.pen-and-sword.co.uk/privacy. You can opt out of our mailing list at any time via our website or by calling 01226 734222.

Mr/Mrs/Ms ....

Address...

Postcode................................ Email address..

Website: www.pen-and-sword.co.uk Email: enquiries@pen-and-sword.co.uk
Telephone: 01226 734555 Fax: 01226 734438
Stay in touch: facebook.com/penandswordbooks or follow us on Twitter @penswordbooks

Freepost Plus RTKE-RGRJ-KTTX
Pen & Sword Books Ltd
47 Church Street
BARNSLEY
S70 2AS

mourned the loss of their eldest son, the Third Estate decided to pass its own resolutions. On around 17 June, they began calling themselves the National Assembly. They also elected an astronomer, mathematician, and freemason named Jean-Sylvain Bailly as their first president. Then, because the new Assembly had the most delegates, they decided to solve the financial crisis.

In the meantime, Louis, under the influence of his privy council, decided he would dictate reforms and hold a meeting on 22 June to finalise them. On 20 June, when the National Assembly went to meet at the hall in the Hôtel des Menus Plaisirs, they found the door closed and barred. Historians have long debated why. The next scheduled meeting was 22 June, so was it a royal tactic or was it an accident? Nonetheless, when the Assembly learned they were locked out, they were furious. They believed that the king had barred them on purpose and that he would try to force them to disband. So, they moved their meeting to a nearby tennis court, which was, in fact, where Louis played tennis, and there they decided to take an oath refusing to disband until a new constitution was produced.

The oath was a revolutionary act. It was the first time that French citizens stood up to their king. The oath also reflected the Assembly's desires, as its preamble closely resembled America's famous Declaration of Independence that Benjamin Franklin had helped conceive, along with America's other Founding Fathers like Thomas Jefferson, John Adams, Robert R. Livingston, and Roger Sherman. Moreover, the oath inspired future revolutionary activity and reasserted the power that the Assembly had claimed.

When Louis learned of the oath, he personally addressed the Estates General, invalidated the National Assembly's decisions, and instructed the three Estates to continue to meet separately. The Third Estate was incensed and even though a few days later, Louis relented and instructed the First and Second Estates to meet with the Third, tensions continued to build, and Parisians increasingly became more dissatisfied.

Likely due to tumult in Paris, Eliza and Philadelphia began planning to return to England. They had to be aware of what was happening in France. French newspapers reported daily on the contentious events happening within the government and any friends the women had were likely talking about the unrest. Although there was little mention of the trouble brewing in France by either James or Henry in their *Loiterer,* on Saturday, 4 April 1789 James did state:

> [A] Frenchman entertains an opinion, that an Englishman is a rough, ferocious, and uncivilized animal, just one degree above an Ouran Outang, and is most deplorably ignorant of the *agréments* of society, as he can neither fiddle, dance, or laugh, and consequently, *qui ne vaut rien auprès des Dames.* While on the other side, a British subject will tell you, the *Monseers* are all poor, half-starved, lousy devils; that they wear wooden shoes, and ruffles without shirts; and that they have nothing to eat but soup meagre, and fricasseed frogs; of the truth of which heavy accusation he is in his own mind fully convinced, and to which he adds the charge of weakness and effeminacy, it being, he avers, a well-known fact, that one Englishman can at any time *lick three French.*[6]

By early July, Eliza and Philadelphia had barely made it back to England when French revolutionaries took matters into their own hands by storming the Bastille in Paris, a hated prison that represented everything wrong with the monarchy. The fall of the Bastille heralded the collapse of the House of Bourbon that had survived in power for some five centuries, starting with the marriage of the youngest son of King Louis IX to the heiress of the Lord of Bourbon. The French Revolution had begun.

Chapter 10

Philadelphia

> I DISCOVERED THEM TO BE THE MANGLED HEADS OF
> THE GOVERNOR AND COMMANDANT.
> *NORFOLK CHRONICLE* ON THE FRENCH REVOLUTION

When news of a revolution reached Eliza and her mother, they quickly realised they would be staying in England much longer than planned. Moreover, the Count de Feuillide, whom Eliza herself described as a 'strong Aristocrate,' was a military officer and could not feasibly leave France to join them during such turbulent times. Eliza was certainly aware that the French Revolution was a problem for her and her royalist husband. She stated in her letters that she could not be 'wholly unconcerned' in relation to the events unfolding there, as they would ultimately influence her 'future destiny'. Consequently, Eliza and Philadelphia had no choice but to settle in for a time at the Woodmans' house.

Eliza mentioned little else about her or her mother's perspective on the French Revolution. But, tales about the French and their desire for freedom found their way into London newspapers amidst the Estates General meetings. Moreover, two days before the fall of the Bastille on 14 July 1789, wax heads created by Madame Tussaud and Curtius were carried by revolutionaries through Parisian streets after journalist and politician Camille Desmoulins whipped up the crowd: 'Listen, listen to Paris and Lyon, Rouen and Bordeaux, Calais and Marseille; from one end of France to the other, the same cry, a universal cry is heard. ... All want to be free.'[1]

After the fall of the Bastille, some journalists expressed the idea that the revolution in America had laid a foundation for a revolution in France. It seemed possible when real heads on pikes replaced the earlier wax ones. The first of these real heads atop a pike belonged to Bernard-Réne de Launay, governor of the Bastille, and the second was a French official named Jacques de Flesselles. Of this spectacle, one eyewitness wrote:

> A most uncommon shout hurried us all into the street, where thousands of the citizens were passing by in triumphant procession from the conquest of the Bastile. I saw at the moment two miserable figures raised above the crowd. I supposed them to be some of the wretched victims who had pined for years in the Bastile; but upon a nearer approach I discovered them to be the mangled heads of the Governor and comandant. The sight made me squeamish in the stomach, and I hastened to my lodgings. The darkness now approached, and to thousands of minds terror and alarm found a very easy access.[2]

Nine days later, two more heads were plunged atop pikes. This time they were those of public servant Louis Bénigne François Bertier de Sauvigny and his father-in-law, Joseph-François Foullon de Doué, who also has the ignominious distinction of being the first recorded person to have been lynched *à la lanterne*. One anonymous European traveller wrote a letter to his uncle and remarked on the revolutionary spectacles he observed while in the French capital:

> Paris was a scene of action which, to a mind whose first anxieties are for the general rights of men, must render all the subsequent objects of my transcient survey very flat and insipid. The capital of the first empire in the world all in arms for liberty! A King dragged in submissive triumph by his conquering subjects! The Bastile in ruins, and every monument of slavery in flames! These are appearances of grandeur which seldom rise in the prospect of human affairs, and which, during the remainder of my life, I shall think of with wonder and gratification.[3]

Twenty-one-year-old François-René, vicomte de Chateaubriand who was visiting Paris at the time was more direct about what he saw:

In the midst of these murders the people abandoned themselves to orgies similar to those carried on during the trouble of Rome under Otho and Vitellius. The conquerors of the Bastille, heroes of the tavern, rode along in hired carriages, in drunken happiness; low women and sans-culottes began to reign, and formed their escort. The passers-by uncovered their heads with the respect of fear to these heroes.[4]

At the port city of Brest, France, on 11 August, the appearance of an English squadron at the mouth of the Channel raised fears among the French locals. They worried that the 'disorder' happening in France might encourage their English enemies to take advantage of the situation. Therefore, local inhabitants and dockyard men devised a plan to burn Brest if necessary, and, in addition, 'two ships of the line were removed, for the better security of the harbour, to a station where they might lie with springs on their cables, in case of an enemy's approach!'[5]

Despite the fears expressed in Brest, an extract from a letter of a visitor in France dated 18 August downplayed what was happening:

We travelled through 600 miles of the kingdom, and within the limits of every league we were saluted with the shouts of free peasants and free citizens. Down with the Nobles and the Priests was the language of all the villages and towns through which we passed. Arms were in the hands of thousands, and amidst all the tumult we saw not one instance of riot, cruelty, or devastation. At Sens, Dizon, Chalon, Macon, Aix, Marseilles, and Lyons, the Bourgeois were regularly disciplined, and acted at the same time as destroyers of tyranny and the promoters of public peace. I have read the English papers with astonishment. One would think from their account that France is one continued scene of ruins; nay, the rumours of Paris itself give a similar representation. But distant terrors are the most prolific parents of lies. Dauphin and Franche Compre have been specified as theatres of blood and plunder. We travelled through 150 miles of the former province, and we have been so near the latter as to know with certainty that the disturbances ascribed to both are alike imaginary. ... I question whether this grand Revolution will cost the community more than 100 lives. ... At Marseilles appearances bore the greatest resemblance to tumult; but I was assured by a merchant that at night all ended with song and the dance. As soon as we left France, we were constantly trading in the steps of the flying Noblesse. At Geneva we saw several chambers thronged with them; and I learn that the Compte d'Artois and the Duchesse de Polignac are now at Bern; their day is over.[6]

In England, Philadelphia soon contacted her lawyer. She questioned him about the trust because the Count was seeking to gain control of it. Philadelphia learned that would be impossible and that her son-in-law could make no further claims against it. He was only entitled to the interest on the £10,000 and could not get more until the death of Mrs Hancock, Eliza, and Hastings Jr.

Eventually, Philadelphia and Eliza realised they could not indefinitely take advantage of the hospitality offered by the Woodmans. So, they set out to stay temporarily with a series of friends and relatives. Steventon was probably among the places they stayed because sometime after Jane Austen finished her juvenile fiction titled *Love and Freindship*, she dedicated it to her continental cousin Eliza: '*To Madame la Comtesse De Feuillide this Novel is inscribed by her obliged Humble Servant The Author*'.[7]

Philadelphia and Eliza also probably visited James again. He had left Oxford in March 1790 to become the curate at Overton where he took up residence in the tiny vicarage house. Life seemed good for him as he wined, dined, and hunted. Also, while living there, he met General Edward Mathew and his wife Lady Jane Bertie whose daughter Anne would eventually become his wife. Anne was described in a letter as having a 'good deal of nose' despite also being elegant, thin boned, and pale with amazing large, dark eyes.

Although Eliza might have grown closer with Jane and maintained good relations with James, Eliza's relationship with Henry was not so good. She noted that a 'coolness' existed between the two. No longer a boy, the 19-year-old man had grown to 6-foot tall. Perhaps the coolness had to do with Eliza's appearances and disappearances. Her absences forced him to turn on and off his romantic feelings for her. Moreover, Henry also had to face the fact that despite her flirtatious nature, the outlandish and enchanting Eliza was still married, even if her marriage had none of the passion or yearning she might desire.

Eliza's rocky relationship with Henry was not the only problem she faced in 1790. After having made a quick trip to France (leaving the morning of 24 February and arriving back in London on 25 May), Eliza observed that Hastings Jr. was once again having health problems. Always the caregiver, Eliza decided to take the family to Margate, a seaside resort in Kent at the northern extremity of the Isle of Thanet about fifteen miles north-east of Canterbury. The resort was favoured by the rich and the English court because of its sea-bathing benefits. It was detailed as follows in 1820:

> 'The salubrity of the air of the Isle of Thanet, and the longevity of its inhabitants, speak likewise not a little in favour of Margate. There are now living in that town many healthy people from eighty to ninety years of age. The soil of the island is of the purest and whitest chalk, covered with a surface from two to four and five feet thick of mould, as fine as that of a garden, and so fruitful in corn, that no waste or common, but a little of fallow land are to be seen. In short, this island is generally allowed by travellers who have visited it, to be the very garden spot of England; and being an open champaign [level] country, it enjoys all the beauties of fine prospects and clear healthy air.'[8]

Although Eliza wrote a letter to Phylly in 1790, it remains missing and what happened next in Eliza's life was relayed to Phylly in a letter dated 7 January 1791. Eliza had heard that one month of sea-bathing during the winter was 'more efficacious' than six months at any other time. Therefore, because she was an 'exemplary parent' and because Margate offered unprecedented health benefits for her son, she decided not to spend the Christmas holidays with the Austens. She would therefore miss the fun at Steventon and stay in Margate, despite its cold climate and dismal January skies.

Another reason for staying in Margate during the holidays was that she thought it too disruptive to uproot her family. Perhaps her strained relationship with Henry also played a part. She decided that the 'jaunting' she so loved must be put off for another year, even if staying put meant she would be enjoying no balls or plays at the time. Because most visitors were heading home for the holidays, these pleasantries were being dispensed with even though they were the usual activities enjoyed at Margate.

Luckily a small circle of friends remained in the sea-bathing town with whom Eliza could associate. To prevent undue tedium, besides visiting friends and the daily ritual of sea-bathing, her days were filled with reading, playing music, or drawing. To ensure Hastings Jr.'s trip was worthwhile, she also decided to delay her return to the 'Metropolis' for an extra month and announced to Phylly that she would not be back in London until the end of February.

In her letter, Eliza also referred to the Count de Feuillide. Her husband had taken refuge in Piedmont with other royalist supporters, and he was visiting Turin where the Count d'Artois (the future Charles X) had fled. The Count d'Artois would eventually assemble royalist supporters and organise a counter-revolutionary invasion hoping to place the Bourbons back in power. Unfortunately, this invasion would fail, and the Count d'Artois would be forced to seek asylum in England until his triumphant return to France in 1814 when he accompanied his wheelchair-bound brother, Louis XVIII, to Paris.

While at Margate, Eliza received a visit from Neddy, who was now calling himself Edward. After he returned from his Grand Tour in 1790, he had moved in with his adoptive parents. Eliza mentioned Edward's return and his visit to Margate, even though it lasted but a few days. Perhaps it was short because he was not accompanied by his 'beloved', a woman named Elizabeth Bridges, whom he had begun courting and to whom he would propose marriage in March.

Along with her comments on the Revolution, her future destiny, and Edward, Eliza also mentioned that Hastings Jr. was lisping English 'tolerably well'. He had also learned his letters from his grandmother, who appeared to be in good health as she was no longer complaining about rheumatism. Thus, everything seemed perfect when on 28 February, Eliza and her household returned to London on Orchard Street near Portman Square, but things would soon change.

When Phylly visited Eliza from March to April, it was evident that Philadelphia was showing initial signs of breast cancer, although the women may have been unaware that her on-and-off symptoms indicated such a diagnosis. However, Philadelphia's health problems were serious enough for her to seek medical care and Eliza demonstrated in a letter to Phylly dated 23 June 1791 that both women had positive feelings about the expected results:

> Dear Cousin, I fear You have thought me very remiss, but besides my having been much hurried, I wished to have it in my power to inform You of some change for the better; My Dear Mother's general health continues, Thank God, pretty good and her Breast I trust is in a more promising state than when You quitted Town. You know She had just then put herself under the care of a person who then gave and still continues to give us the most flattering hopes of a perfect cure. She however always declared her remedy would be slow in its operations nor did She expect any visible effect from it in less than three weeks. About a fortnight has now elapsed, and I think both her swelling and hardness is some degree abated so that having already reaped more benefit than we had been taught to expect in so short a time, I venture to indulge great hopes that I shall at length have the unspeakable happiness of seeing my beloved parent restored to health. … what I have suffered for this last month beggars all description and has convinced me that tho' I thought I had met with many troubles before, they were all trifles compared to this last heavy affliction. Never will the Year 1791 be effaced from my memory for from the first Month of its commencement to the present period my feelings have constantly been exposed to some fresh trial.[9]

Scottish physician William Nisbet in his 1795 book on 'scrophula' and cancer, *An Inquiry Into the History, Nature, Causes, and Different Modes of Treatment*, stated that there were two forms of cancers found in the breast. The first was a small round swelling in the glandular substance of the breast and the second was called 'Mammary Cancer'. The first was slow and took a long time to progress to an ulcerated state while the second was rapid and passed through the stages quickly because it was a more 'rooted' or an 'obstinate' form of cancer.

Treatments at the time varied but usually included some method of reducing the swelling in the breast by applying a topical application such as 'extract of Saturn', which was applied in the form of a warm poultice, or applications of old linen moistened with a solution of 'Sulphate of Iron' applied over a patient's clothes. There were also internal remedies taken, such as 'Carbonate of Iron' that was administered in any varying number of grains.

Philadelphia must have known the dangers of breast cancer and hoped that she would be cured, as did Eliza, who became her mother's constant companion, doing everything she could to 'amuse' her and take her mind off her illness. Eliza wrote to Phylly again on 1 August stating that her mother did not appear to be worse since the last time Phylly saw her. Moreover, Philadelphia had in fact experienced a softening of the swelling and now found herself completely free from inflammation, although she still occasionally complained of 'acute pain'.

Thoughts of Philadelphia's mortality were almost too stressful for Eliza to manage. She was in a constant state of 'melancholy' over her mother's illness, and both women were trying to remain strong for each other. Hoping for sympathy, Eliza wrote to Phylly about her mother's health at the end of August and again in September. This information Phylly duly forwarded to her brother:

> Poor Eliza is compleatly miserable and has the hard task of being forced to appear cheerful when her heart is ready to burst with grief and vexation. My aunt privately exprest to me how much she felt for her, & that she endeavoured to stifle her pains to avoid her the concern of seeing her mother's sufferings.[10]

Amidst all the news of Philadelphia's poor health, Eliza also provided a tidbit about 5-year-old Hastings Jr. She had decided he needed to present a 'manly appearance' and reported that it could only be accomplished if he stood erect and upright. She decided that for him to do so, he needed to refrain from wearing his 'feminine Garb' and get rid of the 'terrible incumbrances' that she called petticoats. Thus, the new style she had him adopt consisted of jackets and 'trowsers'.

While Hastings Jr. was discarding old clothes for new, Philadelphia continued to suffer health difficulties. A letter in October from Eliza to

Phylly chronicled her unstable physical condition. By now Philadelphia was under the care of a surgeon named Rooss and although there appeared to be no change in the tumour, she had recovered her strength, was free from fever, and appeared to have found relief from the 'agonizing pain' that she had been constantly suffering. This pleased Eliza, but because Philadelphia had been experiencing some bleeding, Rooss now had strict orders that she was not to be agitated and kept as 'quiet as possible'.

Approximately three weeks later, things had worsened for Philadelphia. Eliza became so concerned she called a Dr Austin to come and attend to her mother. He agreed with Rooss that Philadelphia's condition was dire, and for three days everyone feared from second to second, minute to minute, and hour to hour that she might not survive. Fortunately, she pulled through, much to Eliza's relief. She noted shortly thereafter that portions of Philadelphia's swellings were 'detaching' thereby making her hopeful that the whole tumour might be 'removed' and her health restored.

Rooss was a quiet man who never ventured an opinion. However, after the danger had passed, he remarked that he too was hopeful that Philadelphia might be on the mend if her bleeding did not return. Unsurprisingly, Eliza's moods coincided with her mother's health difficulties, and she maintained that she should pay better attention to herself if she was to continue as a positive supporter to 'the dear sufferer'.

On 14 December, Philadelphia made out her will. £6500 was due from the Count de Feuillide, which was to be held in trust by Hastings and Edward Baber of London as they were serving as her executors and trustees. However, Philadelphia also noted that the Count's debt was not to be repaid unless Hastings and Baber deemed it 'proper'.

Apparently, Philadelphia prepared her will just in time because less than two weeks later, she was so ill Eliza was devoting all her time to her mother's care. In fact, Eliza had been so busy taking care of her mother over the past three months, she had not left the house. Her letter to Phylly, sent a few days before Edward and Elizabeth's nuptials on 27 December (of which she would not attend), again mentioned her mother's ill health.

There was no improvement. The tumour stubbornly remained in the same state. Philadelphia also continued to suffer from excruciating pain at times and often had no appetite. Eliza tried everything to get her to eat, but she noted that despite her best efforts the quantity she ate hardly provided enough 'sustenance' to support anyone, let alone her sick mother. However, despite all Philadelphia's sufferings, she remained in a good mood.

Eliza mentioned that she thought her mother's happy disposition was a front and that the only reason she remained so chipper was to keep Eliza's spirits up. Nevertheless, Eliza also admitted that her mother continued to believe that with time and patience she might be rewarded and restored to perfect health. Indicative of this positive hope was Philadelphia's remark that she planned to visit her niece Phylly next summer at Seal.

Unfortunately, Philadelphia had another attack of 'imminent danger' on 20 January 1792. Eliza responded by taking her to Hampstead, hoping for some miraculous treatment that might stop the inevitable progression of her disease. It did not work. Philadelphia continued her slow march towards death.

The Count de Feuillide was finally able to travel to England around late February, just in time to be with his wife as her mother was dying. When she passed away on the last Sunday of February, it had been less than a year since her breast problems first appeared. She was buried in the churchyard of St John-at-Hampstead, London NW3 with the following inscription on her tombstone:

> In memory of Philadelphia Wife of Tysoe Saul Hancock whose moral excellence united the practice of every Christian virtue she bore with pious resignation the severest trials of a tedious and painful malady and expired on the 26th day of February 1792 aged 61.[11]

Chapter 11

Reign of Terror

> ALONG THE ROUTE TO THE SCAFFOLD, ALL OF PARIS WAS THERE.
> GERI WALTON ON THE DEATH OF MARIE ANTOINETTE

The Count de Feuillide took Eliza to Bath, hoping to buoy up her spirits after her mother's death, but the trip did not relieve her melancholy. She derived 'little amusement' as all she could think of was the loss of her dear mother. Although de Feuillide had planned to stay for some time in England, that changed after they returned to London. In a letter from Eliza to Phylly dated 7 June 1792, Eliza wrote that her husband had received word from concerned parties in France that he must return immediately. They feared that if he did not, he would be considered an emigrant, and his fortune and property would automatically be forfeited to the new government. Thus, de Feuillide decided he had no choice but to hurry home.

Before leaving, he promised Eliza that he would return as soon as everything was resolved. However, that would prove difficult under the circumstances. French soldiers were already having great trouble obtaining leave for any reason, and as the Revolution pushed forward, it would become even more problematic to be granted a leave of absence.

Eliza did not realise she was pregnant when her husband left England for France. She had conceived sometime during his visit, and whether it was planned or an accident it wouldn't have made a difference or prevented her husband's departure. Certainly, she was still sad about the loss of her mother and she expressed her thoughts about how she must go on when she wrote to Phylly:

> I [am] once more a very solitary Being, the Acquaintance & Connexions however whom I have here are very kind and attentive to me and I endeavor on my part as much as

possible to struggle with the melancholy which has taken deep root in my mind but which I know was I to give way to it would render me totally incapable of every Duty I have yet to fulfil.[1]

As Eliza mourned her mother and soldiered on, she also mentioned to Phylly that she was hoping to take a trip to Surrey and to visit the Austens at Steventon. Such a trip she thought would go far in restoring her spirits as her health was not just affected by her mother's death. Apparently, she had also been a victim of an unexpected and regretful disturbance that happened on Mount Street.

According to newspapers, about forty or fifty servants assembled at the Pitt's-head public house on Monday, 4 June, and made too much 'merry' when celebrating King George III's birthday. A justice learned of the commotion, ordered constables and patrols be gathered from Hyde Park, and had them sent to the public house where all those involved were arrested, including the landlord and a fiddler. The prisoners then spent a quiet night in jail.

The following morning, locals heard about the arrests and became upset that anyone would be arrested for heartily celebrating the King's birth. An angry mob soon formed opposite the watch-house. They demanded that the prisoners be released and accordingly:

> The constables presented their pistols; this irritating the mob they soon became really riotous, attacked the watch-house with a volley of stones that broke many of the windows, then breaking into the house, heaved out part of the furniture into the street, and would have demolished the whole of the premises, had not several magistrates interfered, who, after reading the riot act, were necessitated to call in the military. Horse and Foot Guard were instantly under arms, and kept a continual fire for near an hour, by which, doubtless, some of the mob were killed, and many wounded.[2]

Amid this disturbance, Eliza was heading home, driven by her coachman. Unexpectedly she found her coach surrounded by the unruly mob, hell-bent on destroying some houses in the immediate area. Some from the mob were also contending nearby with mounted guards on horseback, and there was sporadic gun-fire up and down the street. Then a brick was thrown that nearly killed Eliza's coachman. With bravery and skill, he manoeuvred the coach from the scene and she was delivered home safely, but the fright she experienced from being caught up in the unexpected altercation so affected her that she immediately fell ill.

As Eliza was suffering, soldiers using 'drawn swords' and 'pointed bayonets' were trying to control the riotous situation. The riot spilled over into the next day and with Eliza's residence nearby, she heard the noises associated with the rioters and observed soldiers constantly parading up and down the streets. Eliza and others also feared that should the rioters set fire to any house in the area, the whole city might be set ablaze and that would cause 'serious Consequences' for everyone in London.

Meanwhile, Eliza complained of a violent fever and then for three days, suffered from intense pain in her head before some 'violent eruptions' appeared. Her physician finally diagnosed her with smallpox, but she insisted it wasn't, and she was right. What she had was chicken pox severe enough that everyone who saw her thought she would be forever scarred. Fortunately, when the malady subsided the only remnant that remained on her beautiful complexion was a lone pox mark on her forehead.

The dissipation of the chicken pox did not, however, end Eliza's health problems. She remained unwell even after the chicken pox cleared up. Moreover, apparently at some point, likely before the Mount Street riot, she had a miscarriage, which she obliquely referred to using the traditional euphemism of an 'accidental occurrence'. Because she remained unwell after the chicken pox and the miscarriage, she blamed her continuing ill-health on the fact that she had never fully recovered from the fright associated with the Mount Street riot, and also maintained that all these misfortunes so close together was the reason she had turned into such a 'poor creature' in the first place.

With all her physical problems, she decided the best way to restore herself to perfect health was to have a change of air and thus left London. It happened around mid-July when she visited the Woodmans at their 'charming' house situated between Epsom and Ewell in Surrey. That was about the same time that Phylly travelled to London, and so the two cousins missed each other. Eliza was then expected to travel to Hampshire in August where she intended to remain for the rest of the year.

Unfortunately, things got worse for Eliza while she was staying with the Austens at Steventon. That is when France erupted in violence. The Reign of Terror, consisting of suspicions, domiciliary visits, denunciations, arrests, mass imprisonment, and constant guillotining, commenced with the September Massacres in 1792. This series of brutal murders happened because Parisians feared they would be wiped out by the invading army marching towards them. Rumours had been swirling for some time that if the Austrian and Prussian forces reached Paris, they would free all the prisoners, and Parisians believed these prisoners, along with non-juring priests and others who opposed the Revolution, would kill those supporting it.

Revolutionaries were most worried about those who had been accused of supporting the monarchy and its royal cause. They therefore termed these supporters their 'worst foes'. In consequence, the first attacks by revolutionaries happened against twenty-four priests being transferred to the Abbey of Saint-Germain-des-Prés. This was followed by attacks on hundreds more people, which included several 'aristocrats', who were reputedly roasted alive at the Place Dauphin. Another horrific incident involved a Swiss soldier who was forced to dress the hair of a Swiss officer. The soldier was then ordered to take off the officer's head. When he refused, the soldier was 'cut to pieces and two women sawed the officer's head from his body'.[3] A mob also found a countess and her two daughters, reputedly stripped them, washed them in oil, and roasted them alive.

Among the more well-known of the victims at this time whom Eliza knew was the Princess de Lamballe. She was among the first casualties during the September Massacres. Her 'death sentence was carried out by a mob of men, women, and children, who supposedly rushed forward with great enthusiasm to … "strike, hack, tear with any kind of weapon at the helpless victim till [she] … fell, pierced and torn, upon a heap of naked mutilated corpses."'[4]

After the French royal family had been captured in Varennes and returned under guard to Paris, they were confined at the Tuileries Palace. This escape attempt by King Louis XVI made him more unpopular than ever. So, by the summer of 1792, nearly every Parisian was against him and the royal family, and almost everyone in France wanted him deposed.

If Eliza knew the Princess de Lamballe had died, Louis was deposed, or what was happening to her husband in France, she didn't mention anything in her letter to Phylly written from Steventon in October. However, she did mention that her Uncle George was dearer to her than ever. Having lost her mother, she noted that she often traced her mother's features in her handsome uncle's face. She also mentioned that both Cassandra Elizabeth and Jane had grown tall and that the latter was now taller than her. Of the two Austen sisters who were so close, it was once stated:

> They were not exactly alike. Cassandra's was the colder and calmer disposition; she was always prudent and well-judging, but with less outward demonstration of feeling and less sunniness of temper than Jane possessed. It was remarked in the family that "Cassandra had the *merit* of having her temper always under command, but that Jane had the *happiness* of a temper which never required to be commanded".[5]

As for James and Henry, there were mentions that Eliza's relationships with them had changed. A month or so after Philadelphia's death, James married Anne Mathew on 27 March at Laverstoke. The newlyweds then rented the Court House in Overton before moving to the parsonage at Deane around June. Moreover, Eliza had also recently learned that both James's wife and Edward's wife were now in the 'encreasing way' as both were pregnant.

As far as Henry was concerned, the coolness that had existed between them had dissipated, and Eliza noted in her letter that they were currently on 'very proper' terms. However, there was complete silence about her husband, the Count, who remained stuck in France and unable to leave. There was also no mention of the happenings in France, such as the National Convention replacing the Legislative Assembly on 20 September or that a bitter division now existed between the political parties of the Jacobins on the left and the Girondins on the right.

Nonetheless, Eliza made sure to note the sociality at Steventon and to mention her son. She claimed his bubbly personality made him a popular plaything for everyone. He was also doing well physically and had improved in 'Health & Strength'. Eliza attributed this healthy phase to their pleasant visit at Steventon.

Local society was also discussed. Dancing was always something that Eliza found delightful, even though Phylly was disinclined towards it.

Eliza mentioned two dances, neither of which she attended because she was suffering from a 'feverish Attack'. One was a 'Club Ball' held in nearby Basingstoke and another in the local neighbourhood. Both Jane and Cassandra Elizabeth attended, remarking that both dances were 'very agreeable'. Another dance was slated for 4 November, and Eliza hoped to be well enough to attend but also noted that even if she went, she would not dance.

There is also one extremely odd thing about Eliza's letter dated 26 October 1792. Although it contains nothing shocking, explosive, or insincere, Eliza's last line asked Phylly to burn it. Exactly why she may have requested such a thing seems to be a mystery and there appears to be no reason to have the letter destroyed. Phylly must have thought so too because she didn't bother to follow Eliza's request.

After this letter from Eliza to Phylly, there seems to be no indication as to what Eliza did or where she went, and, in fact, there was no real news about her for about an eighteen-month period. However, during that time there were two shocking events that happened in France. The first was the execution of Louis XVI on 21 January 1793 at the Place de la Concorde, and the second was the execution of Marie Antoinette, a particularly poignant event that happened on 16 October 1793.

Two days after Louis' execution, a baby girl, christened Fanny-Catherine, was born to Edward and Elizabeth. It was the first child that made the newly 17-year-old Jane Austen an aunt. She would honour Fanny-Catherine by writing *Scraps*, humorous letters that she dedicated to her new niece on the conduct of young women. Three months later in April, a second niece, Jane Anna Elizabeth, daughter of James and Anne, would appear. She would also receive instructive tidbits about life from her Aunt Jane:

> One morsel instructed her in such pretty diversions as flinging stones at ducks, and putting brickbats into people's beds. The other coached her in the art of exhibiting an affecting style of permanent indisposition, sighing, fainting, keeping to her bed and only resisting the temptation to think of dying by contriving never to think at all.[6]

However humorous Jane's morsels, things were not so humorous when it came to Britain and France. On 1 February 1793, France's new republic declared war on Britain. It had long been expected and was supposedly based on grounds that the British King had persistently shown he was 'ill-disposed' towards the French nation. Among the litany of complaints given by the French was that George III was supportive of the coalition, provided refuge and protection for French emigrants, augmented his naval and military forces, recalled his ambassador from Paris, and several other similar complaints.

British citizens generally thought that the reason France declared war was because they were eager to do so and because they feared the British would declare war first. True or not, the British response was a vigorous shout of defiance. The whole country hastened to arm themselves, including Henry who left his studies and enlisted, receiving his commission as a Lieutenant in the Oxfordshire Militia in April. Shortly thereafter, Henry joined his regiment in Southampton and two months after that, the Oxfordshire Militia was posted to Brighton Downs in Sussex where fourteen regiments gathered in expectation of an attempted invasion by France.

Eliza had mentioned months earlier that the 'little Sailor' was expected home, and in June 1793 Frank received official word from the Lords of the Admiralty and left the HMS *Despatch* to sail home aboard an EIC ship. His duties in the Far East had not only been military but also involved him trading on behalf of the EIC, so when he returned, they defrayed their costs by charging him for his return trip and by hauling lucrative cargo that could be sold back in England.

Frank set foot on English soil on 13 November 1793 and the following day headed home to Steventon. While on leave, he and Henry attended several balls and house parties where they served as escorts to their sisters Cassandra Elizabeth and Jane. Frank did not return to active duty until March 1794, when he joined the 16-gun sloop HMS *Lark*.

The Count de Feuillide had not been able to visit England since leaving Eliza after their Bath trip in 1792. Unbeknownst to Eliza, his return had been hampered by a disastrous turn of events starting from when he travelled to their restored property in Gabarret to find that neighbouring sentiment had gone against them. The local peasants had found that his reclamation works of draining the marshlands, establishing crops, and stocking his fields with cattle greatly reduced their supply of fish and waterfowl. Angry peasants then began attacking the Count and his workers, and the hostilities caused him to flee to Paris.

Chapter 12

The Count's Fate

DEAR BADDY.
ELIZA'S NICKNAME FOR ONE OF HER ADMIRERS

The Count de Feuillide arrived in Paris in September 1792, the same month that the monarchy was abolished and a new republic declared. Once there, he had made a deal with the widow of his previous commander, Jacques Auger, Marquis de Marbeuf. His widow was Henriette-Françoise Michel, Marquise de Marbeuf and the Count's agreement with her allowed him to obtain money and finance gambling at a gaming house in the Palais-Royal. At the time, such gambling sites functioned as outlets for counterfeit assignats and provided the means to launder huge sums of money from ambiguous sources.

The gaming house that the Count financed was managed by a Swiss woman named Comtesse de Linières. She was mistress to a man named Jean-Baptiste Romney, who was also Swiss. He was a revolutionary supporter and an 'unofficial' member of the Committee of General Security; this organisation acted as a policing agency during the Reign of Terror by investigating reports of treason and referring suspects to the Revolutionary Tribunal for trial and possible execution. However, Romney proved to be disingenuous.

Besides supporting the new Republic, he also began supporting counter-revolutionaries. This meant that he befriended both revolutionaries and counter-revolutionaries. In addition, counter-revolutionaries soon discovered the best way to end the Terror was to create an economic crisis, but to do that meant increasing the Terror.

Because the new Republic needed money to finance itself, it sought to obtain funds from wealthy individuals. Thus, many rich nobles and wealthy bourgeois were arrested, condemned, and their property seized by the state. The Terror and the arrests played into the scheme

THE COUNT'S FATE

of the Committee of General Security to acquire money for the state. It thus became Romney's goal to 'inherit' the property and estates of wealthy individuals who feared they might be executed. Unfortunately, Romney ultimately set his sights on obtaining the wealth of the Count de Feuillide, part of which he had acquired from the loans given him by the 55-year-old Marquise de Marbeuf.

The Marquise had accrued her wealth from her husband inheriting the Champs castle north-east of Paris and her ownership of the Gournay farm that sold dairy produce to Parisians. To manufacture these products, she had converted a large portion of her land from corn and wheat to alfalfa, grass, and clover so that she could feed her cattle. Furthermore, she had transformed her property into one of the largest and most profitable farms in the region thanks to her estate manager, 49-year-old Jean-Joseph Payen, who may also have been her lover.

By the late 1780s, years of bad weather and food distribution problems created food shortages throughout France and resulted in many starving peasants and Parisians. Farmers competing against the Marquise soon accused her of purposely trying to create famine, alleging that instead of growing food for the starving people she was growing feed for cattle. She and Payen were then arrested for conspiring against the safety of the French people, causing disturbances in the commune, 'denaturing' the land, desiring the arrival of the Prussian and Austrian armies, and keeping 'considerable' provision at her house at Champs-sur-Marne for these expected enemies.

Because of his financial relationship with the Marquise, when she was arrested, de Feuillide interceded by bribing the secretary of the Committee of General Security, a man named Morel, who accepted 15,000 livres for the Marquise's release. However, instead of paying Morel directly, the Count decided to pay him through an intermediary named Cordier. Morel and Cordier met at a café in the Palais Royal, but Morel refused to take the money and insisted that he have a face-to-face meeting with the Count.

When the Count and Morel met, Morel then insisted that 15,000 livres was insufficient, and so the Count offered him 20,000 livres. Morel rejected that offer and a final amount of 24,000 livres was accepted. The Count and Morel then visited the Marquise's business manager, 39 year-old Louis-Dominique-Augustin Prédicant, who paid Morel 10,000 livres. Prédicant, Morel, and the Count met again the following day, and this time Morel was given another 4,000 livres and told that the remainder would be paid upon the Marquise's release.

Unbeknownst to de Feuillide, Morel was surreptitiously reporting the bribery to members of the Committee of Public Safety, who worked in conjunction with members of the Committee of General Security. Thus, the Count was arrested one evening at midnight, the usual time for the Tribunal to conduct their raids and arrests. He was taken from his residence at the Rue Grenelle and St. Honoré, and as the Republic believed the 'labouring' poor were the only trustworthy and loyal parties, they left the Count's black maidservant, *citoyenne* Rose Clarisse, in charge of the house and its contents. In addition, they conducted a thorough search of the house for incriminating evidence and accordingly, a receipt was discovered made out by the Count de Feuillide and signed by Morel for 14,000 livres.

When the Count went before the Tribunal, an Austen legend states that he attempted to save himself by declaring he had killed the Count, assumed his identity, and was in truth the Count's valet. No court transcripts state such a thing, so if it was true, the Tribunal must have thought his statement so ludicrous they didn't record it. What is recorded is that the Count's mistress, *citoyenne* Grandville, and his housekeeper, *citoyenne* Joubert, both testified against him. Clarisse was not called because she was illiterate.

As was usual for Tribunal proceedings, almost everyone accused was condemned. The first person found guilty was the wealthy Marquise and her estate manager Payen. They were convicted of conspiring against the state on the 17th of Pluviôse II (5 February 1794). Supposedly, on the way to the guillotine and before they reached the beheading machine, the Marquise exhorted a fearful Payen to die undaunted with bravery and courage.

The Count de Feuillide was executed by guillotine within hours of being convicted of bribery and attempting to corrupt *citoyen* Morel. Alongside him was Nicolas Martin, convicted of consorting with the enemy, and two counterfeiters – a coachman named Nicolas Mangin, and his nephew Clément. The executions took place on the 3rd of Ventose II (22 February 1794).

Prédicant was likewise accused by *citoyen* Morel of bribery. In his case he was detained for fifteen days before he faced the Tribunal. Like the Marquise, Payen, and de Feuillide, Prédicant was convicted of crimes

THE COUNT'S FATE

against the state. He was found to have conspired with the Marquise and to have bribed Morel, and was executed a day after the Count.

Eliza had been married for twelve years when her husband was executed. She apparently had received word within a month of his execution because Hastings visited her on 15 March 1794, and she showed him a report that her husband had been condemned. After de Feuillide's execution, his property was sequestrated, including his estate in Gabarret, which was quickly returned to its original state. The furniture Eliza had so carefully purchased in England, along with their family belongings, were also confiscated. These items were then sold without any consideration for her claim or the claims of her son.

With the death of her husband, just two years after the death of her mother, Eliza was suddenly more alone in the world than she had ever been. While she still had a basic level of support from her trust fund, tragedy had taken the two closest sources of stability in her life. To perhaps find a way to grieve, she soon vanished from London.

Eliza had left London with Hastings Jr. to visit her friends, Reverend Charles Egerton and his wife. They were living in Durham county in northeast England in Washington, a town that has a connection to America's first president, George Washington. Apparently, the Old Hall in that town was the family home of Washington's ancestors, having been built by William de Hertburn after he moved there in 1183. As was customary, Hertburn took the name of his new estates and became William de Wessyngton. The family moved by the mid-sixteenth century but by then their spelling had changed from Wessyngton to Washington.

Although visiting the Egertons allowed Eliza an escape from her problems, she was probably feeling confused and lonely. She might have also viewed the Egertons' home as the best place to find comfort while she adjusted to the conditions of her new life. No longer did she have her loyalty to her mother or her husband to guide her life choices. She would have to care for her son alone. Although she had previously asserted that she did not want a husband, she had been encouraged to take one by her mother, which meant up to that point she had enjoyed an aristocratic lifestyle. With the death of the Count and the loss of their French estate, that dream was shattered.

While Eliza was staying with the Egertons, Hastings forwarded her a letter accompanied by another note that contained a foreign postmark. The foreign note was nothing important but rather came from someone

Eliza described as 'almost a stranger'. She noted in her September reply to Hastings that the stranger was requesting help in getting an English passport. She also reported that she was feeling better, a condition she credited to the fresh 'Northern Air' and mentioned that she had been planning to return home in October, but the Egertons had insisted she remain with them through the Christmas holidays. So, she ultimately reappeared in London during January 1795.

Meanwhile, Henry Austen was granted two months' leave from his regiment to return to St. John's college at Oxford and study for his MA degree. Besides his academic topics, he had also learned that his childhood love-interest, Eliza, was suddenly available. This, no doubt, set him to planning how to reconnect with her and see what might happen.

The weather that February was bitterly cold. In fact, it was so cold a planned ball in Basingstoke was cancelled due to the severe weather. But the weather suddenly warmed and the cold, frosty snows that had been building all winter quickly began to thaw. Throughout February and March, great floods ensued. Newspapers reported on the damages caused by the waters and a neighbour of the Austens wrote to her friend noting the flooding problem in their immediate area of Oakley Hill, just west of Basingstoke:

> [A]s you live on the top of a hill, I will not ask you how you like floating on the Waters, & as we live on the Side of a one, I cannot tell you from Experience, but our neighbours say they rather like the Ground floor than the upper apartments, Mr. Austens family did not descend for two days, Mr. James Austen lost 2 fat pigs, one poor farmer had but 60 Ewes, & above 20 were drownd, Corn carried out of the Barns, & numberless Accidents did the sudden thaw create.[1]

Besides worrying about the flooding, the Austen family and Englishmen in general were concerned about the marriage of the Prince of Wales. A year earlier, he had agreed to marry his cousin, Caroline of Brunswick, and had become engaged without having met her. He was heavily in debt and his engagement to an eligible princess meant Parliament would increase his allowance, which is why he agreed to the marriage.

On 28 March 1795, his future bride left Germany and, despite bad weather, arrived on England's shores at Greenwich on 5 April.

THE COUNT'S FATE

They married three days later at the Chapel Royal, St. James's Palace in London. The wedding was less than splendid. The groom was drunk and considered his new wife unattractive and unhygienic while she thought him grossly fat.

Within months of their wedding, gossip was circulating that the royal marriage was in trouble. That was partly because the prince had already secretly married Maria Fitzherbert, which violated the Royal Marriages Act of 1772 and made his marriage to her invalid. Things got worse when his new legal wife Caroline became popular with the public. That meant he was less popular than ever and now trapped in a loveless marriage.

In the meantime, while Henry continued studying at Oxford, the Oxfordshire Militia at the Blatchington barracks decided to mutiny. The militia took up arms on Thursday, 16 April, and marched with their bayonets into Seaford because provisions were scarce and prices too high. Once there, they seized flour and other provisions and sold them at reduced prices. What followed next was reported in an extract from a letter by an unnamed source at the scene:

> The next morning ... they marched in the same manner, in number about 500, to Newhaven, and to the Tide Mill, near that town, where they found a very large quantity of flour. That they seized the horses of the farmers, and of the artillery, with which they were carrying it away. They also seized a vessel in the river laden with flour and corn, on which they placed a guard of twenty men.[2]

Henry was recalled to duty to help with the disturbance, but he sent a medical certificate stating that he was sick. Fortunately, his absence was no problem because the instigators of the mutiny were quickly ferreted out and imprisoned. The next report thus stated: 'All is now quiet, and it is mentioned with much pleasure, that not a single countryman joined the militia'.[3]

A few days after the militia conflict ended, Hastings' court case finished. It was 24 April and the case had been dragging on for seven long years, which included the House sitting to consider it over a total period of 148 days. The suit had cost Hastings a great deal of money and, in fact, he claimed it had nearly bankrupted him. He, Eliza, and the Austen family found it a relief when he was acquitted on all charges and subsequently compensated by the EIC with 4,000 pounds sterling annually.

Henry sent Hastings a congratulatory note on his win. Apparently, Hastings had shown him many kindnesses and Henry was inclined to return the favour. Henry's note stated:

> An humble and hitherto a silent spectator of national concerns, permit me at the present interesting moment to transgress the strictness of propriety, and though without permission, I hope without offence to offer you the arm and respectful congratulations of a heart deeply impressed with a sense of all you have done & suffered. Permit me to congratulate my country & myself as an Englishman.[4]

By June, as the ringleaders of the Oxfordshire Militia riots were being punished, Henry travelled with his regiment to the Sheerness Camp in Kent, leaving him little opportunity to reconnect with Eliza. Then, as it turned out, his older brother James's wife, Anne, suddenly died. She had sat down to dinner on 3 May 1795 and was unexpectedly stricken, passing away within a few hours. Perhaps the cold winter had weakened her constitution, although the doctor maintained her liver had mysteriously ruptured. She was buried on Monday, 11 May 1795 at Steventon. Not long after her death, James took their child, Anna, to Steventon where she could be cared for by his mother and aunts. Now a widower, it would not be long before he too set his sights on Eliza.

Henry remained with his regiment over the summer until October, when he obtained another leave of absence. Around then, he seems to have met Eliza and proposed to her. Although she was flattered, she refused. It is unclear why. They did seem to enjoy each other's company and have a similar, ambitious outlook on life. Perhaps she thought he was too young or did not meet her criteria for the type of man she was seeking. But, more likely, as she had previously stated, she was simply not interested in having a husband at all. Thus rejected, Henry went on with his military life and apparently gave up on his desire for Eliza.

Eliza seemed to get on well as a widow. Her rejection of Henry's proposal was not even mentioned when she wrote a light-hearted note to Phylly. She did note that she had arrived safely in Tunbridge Wells

THE COUNT'S FATE

without running into any highwaymen or suffering a single 'mishap'. She also revealed she had spent time with an unknown admirer she nicknamed 'dear Baddy' and although his identity remains a mystery to this day, 'Baddy' says it all of his character.

Eliza appeared to be content to live on her inheritance and enjoy time with friends. She reported that she gambled at the local casino and promptly lost all her money. Friends then invited her to attend the local Coronation Ball, an event held annually in every town to commemorate George III's 1761 coronation. Nonetheless, she initially resisted but then decided to go and gave the reason for her attendance as being a way for her to avoid any further gambling temptations.

She ended her letter with news that a party, tea drinking, and ball were to be held at the 'desire' of the Duchess of Gordon. She was a Scottish Tory political hostess who began to entertain on an increasingly lavish scale and became the sole arbitress of fashion in Edinburgh before moving to London in 1787. According to Eliza, the Duchess's events were supposed to be well-attended, and, of course, the extrovert Eliza planned to be there with what she called 'my squad'.

Chapter 13

Flirtations

> I AM ALMOST AFRAID TO TELL YOU HOW MY IRISH FRIEND AND I BEHAVED.
> JANE AUSTEN ON TOM LEFROY

Eliza's cousin James seems to have fared better than his brother Henry in pursuing Eliza, at least initially. While Henry's marriage proposal was rejected, James began courting Eliza in 1795. As both he and she were widowed, a relationship probably seemed to make sense. He had a small daughter and she a son, therefore he likely thought about how both children would benefit with a replacement parent.

Phylly teased Eliza about cousin James's interest and thought the situation funny. Of course, Eliza enjoyed being wooed by him but she did not want to give up her 'liberty', and she could not imagine herself as the wife of a boring country clergyman, confined to a parsonage, tending children, and taking tea with local wives. Her time was being spent at Tunbridge Wells, Brighton, or London, which was much more exciting than living in the countryside. In those places, she could still behave flirtatiously, dress in the latest styles, and take an airing on the arm of one of her many ardent admirers. Thus, when James also proposed marriage, she rejected him as well.

James was not bothered by Eliza's marriage rebuff for long. Another woman was available, and he found her practically under his nose. It was Mary Lloyd, the younger sister of Martha Lloyd. The Lloyds had moved into the Deane parsonage with their mother when her husband, the Reverend Nowys Lloyd, died on 28 January 1789. Martha and Mary then became friends with Cassandra Elizabeth and Jane.

The Lloyds had since moved to Ibthorpe but when Mary was invited to stay at Steventon, she accepted. After seeing her again, James realised she was a perfect candidate for marriage because of her pragmatic sensibility and good humour. Thus, shortly after Eliza spurned him, he found himself engaged to Mary, someone his mother found much more suitable and someone she considered would comfort her in her old age.

Henry was similarly still open to marriage, even if not with Eliza. By early 1796, he was engaged to Mary Pearson, daughter of Sir Richard Pearson, a British naval officer who was captain of the ship HMS *Serapis* during the American Revolution and later captain of Greenwich Hospital. A miniature of Mary was obtained by Henry, who then proudly presented it to his family. Although Eliza did not see the miniature and had not met Mary in person, she offered a curiously critical assessment of his fiancée:

> Our Cousin Henry Austen has been in Town he looks thin & ill – I hear his late intended is a most intolerable Flirt, and reckoned to give herself great Airs – The person who mentioned this to me says She is a pretty wicked looking Girl with bright Black Eyes which pierce thro' & thro'. No wonder the poor young Man's heart could not withstand them.[1]

The harsh assessment by Eliza of Henry's fiancée Mary may have been due to pride and jealousy. Although Eliza may not have wanted to marry Henry at the time, she probably secretly hoped he would pine over her. When it didn't happen, she may have thought that perhaps her charms were not as mesmerising as she had hoped.

Jane Austen also had a flirtation around the same time as her brother Henry. In Jane's case it was with an Irish nephew of her old friend, Madam Lefroy. His name was Thomas Langlois Lefroy and he was attending law school in London, preparing for the bar in Ireland.

Jane was smitten by him and it has been suggested that Jane and Tom's personalities were the models for Elizabeth Bennet and Mr Darcy in *Pride and Prejudice*. For instance, both Jane and Elizabeth were witty, intelligent, and independent women who believed in marrying for love, but were encouraged to marry for financial security. Jane had initially disliked Tom Lefroy just as Elizabeth disliked Mr Darcy, whom she initially perceived to be pretentious and cold. Ultimately, however, just as Jane fell for Tom Lefroy, so too did Elizabeth fall for Mr Darcy.

Tom and Jane had plenty of opportunities to see one another and that included when Madam Lefroy organised a ball which both Jane and Tom attended. Jane mentioned her feelings for him in two letters written to her sister Cassandra Elizabeth. In the first one she stated:

> I am almost afraid to tell you how my Irish friend and I behaved. Imagine to yourself everything most profligate and shocking in the way of dancing and sitting down together. I can expose myself however, only once more, because he leaves the country soon after next Friday, on which day we are to have a dance at Ashe after all. He is a very gentlemanlike, good-looking, pleasant young man, I assure you.[2]

Jane appears to have been optimistic that an attachment would form or that a proposal might be forthcoming from him, but it never happened. Speculation is that Madam Lefroy learned a relationship was forming between the two and discouraged it by promptly packing Tom up and sending him back to London. Having resigned herself to the fact the relationship was no more, Jane sadly wrote:

> At length the Day is come on which I am to flirt my last with Tom Lefroy, & when you receive this it will be over—My tears flow as I write, at the melancholy idea. ... There is a report that Tom is going to be married to a Litchfield Lass.[3]

Another story about Jane's love life that did result in a marriage proposal some years later involves Harris Bigg-Wither. He was the son of Lovelace Bigg, 'a genial widower – even his jowls and squat, stubby nose under a bulbous brow fringed with downy white hair gave him an aristocratic look – as though, his tenants might have said, a horse had sat upon a very fine face'.[4] Lovelace Bigg had inherited the Manydown estate in 1789 after the last Wither died. It was then that he and his two sons changed their surnames to Bigg-Wither.

Lovelace also had seven daughters. Two of them, Catherine and Alethea, became great childhood friends with Jane and her sister. The Bigg-Wither girls were pleasant, cheerful, and lively, and in late November 1802, Jane and Cassandra Elizabeth were planning to stay with them for two to three weeks at the Manydown mansion, an illustrious old residence with a square courtyard and a green park filled with beeches and cedars.

Also in residence at the mansion was 21-year-old Harris, named after his maternal grandmother Jane Harris. He was tall, clumsy, and loved to play practical jokes on his sisters. Unlike his older sisters he was taciturn and silent in public, perhaps because of his stammer. He was also not one to embrace learning, having never done well in school or completed a degree, which likely made him even less appealing to someone like Jane. Nonetheless, he had become heir to Manydown after his older brother died.

The details of Harris's proposal were destroyed with Jane's letters, but one thing is for certain, she did not love him. However, when his proposal came on 2 December 1802 the nearly 27-year-old Jane, who was likely worried about being a spinster, decided to accept. Perhaps she did so because of the practicalities of life: marriage to Harris meant she would become the mistress of a splendid estate and she may have imagined the possibilities of changing him to make him more acceptable. He seemed to have great affection for her, and certainly, she must have decided that she could like him and that there was also the possibility that after marriage, love might grow.

Having a sleepless night to think about marriage to Harris made her come full circle by morning. Whatever induced her to accept his proposal was no longer a consideration with dawn's light and she regretted having agreed. Unlike her cousin Eliza, who had entered a loveless marriage with the Count de Feuillide, Jane found that she could not follow through and marry a man she did not love. Neither could Jane's character Emma in *The Watsons*, who declared:

> To be so bent on marriage - to pursue a man merely for the sake of situation - is a sort of thing that shocks me; I cannot understand it. Poverty is a great evil; but to a woman of education and feeling it ought not, it cannot be, the greatest. I would rather be a teacher at a school ... than marry a man I did not like.[5]

Two years after Jane's refusal, Harris married Anne Howe Frith, daughter of Bedding Bramley and Jane Frith. Harris and Anne had ten children and Harris led the life of a country squire, much respected and beloved by his family. Years later, Jane's niece, Caroline, the daughter of James Austen and Mary Lloyd, mentioned Harris's proposal and noted:

> Mr. Wither was very plain in person – awkward, & even uncouth in manner – nothing but his size to recommend him – he was a fine big man – but one need not look about for secret reason to account for a young lady's not loving him – a great many would have taken him *without* love – & I believe the wife he did get was very fond of him, & that they were a happy couple – He had sense in plenty & went through life very respectable, as a country gentleman – I *conjecture* that the advantages he could offer, & her gratitude for his love, & her long friendship with the family, induced my Aunt to decide that she would marry him *when* he should ask her – but that having accepted him she found she was miserable & that the place & fortune which would certainly be *his* could not alter the man.[6]

The following morning on 3 December, Jane gave her retraction to Harris and then she and Cassandra Elizabeth quickly bolted from Manydown. First, they went to James's house in Steventon and the following day, Jane forced James to take them home. The extra distance probably ensured that there would be no further appeal from Harris or that she would reconsider the proposal. She was also lucky because had her family determined that breaking off the engagement with Harris was improper, she might have indeed become his wife.

Supposedly, although Mary Lloyd regretted Jane's decision, believing they would make a good couple, Jane did not. She even once referred in a letter to her overnight engagement as a mistake. According to Frank Austen's fourth daughter, Catherine, who saw the letter before it was destroyed:

> [I]t was in a momentary fit of self-delusion that Aunt Jane accepted Mr. Wither's proposal, and that when it was all settled eventually, and the negative decisively given she was much relieved. I think the affair vexed her a good deal, but I am sure she had no attachment to him.[7]

As Eliza was planning to leave Tunbridge Wells and head to Brighton in October 1796, she had no such concerns about men or marriage. She had invited Phylly to go with her but had to delay her departure from Tunbridge Wells because Hastings Jr. was benefiting from its healthy waters. Still Eliza wanted to see and spend time with Phylly in Brighton, and she mentioned that Phylly's mother could not possibly object to her going as she would surely obtain numerous health benefits from sea-bathing there. Fortunately, Phylly was ultimately able to accompany her.

The trip, though, took an ominous turn when Eliza fell ill with a breast complaint that was either an abscess or a cyst. In fact, she felt so unwell and was so worried about her health that she decided to cut her holiday short and returned to London where she sought immediate medical attention.

On 17 October from her residence near Portman Square at 3 Durweston Street, Eliza wrote to Phylly. She apologised for the delay in writing and mentioned that she was hoping to provide some detailed news on her health. Unfortunately, she had nothing specific to say about her condition other than that she thought the swelling in her breast had been reduced.

The remainder of her letter focused on the latest gossip. First there was William Dowton, a famed actor at the Tunbridge Wells theatre, who had recently made his first appearance in a comedy at the Drury Theatre. His performance was received with thunderous applause and now he was considered a huge success in London. Politician James Harris, Earl of Malmesbury was also mentioned. He had left London for Paris to negotiate peace with the French Directory. Lastly, Eliza mentioned a pug that she was trying desperately to obtain and that she had so far failed to acquire.

In November Eliza wrote another letter to Phylly, again mentioning her breast problems. By now she claimed to be 'thoroughly disheartened' as she found herself feeling worse each day. It was beginning to seem as if it was a replay of Philadelphia's breast problems. Hoping it was not, Eliza arranged another appointment with Sir Walter Farquhar, 1st Baronet. He was a prominent Scottish physician of the late eighteenth and early nineteenth centuries whose clientele included many of the leading figures of the day.

Eliza noted that when she entered his office at 42 Great Marlborough Street, two young men became focused on her. It wasn't just her rustling skirts or fashionable parasol that drew their attention. She had travelled there unaccompanied, something women seldom did at the time and so when they saw her, she claimed their eyes were as big as 'Barn Doors'. She was so uncomfortable from their stares that she asked to be placed in another room, and subsequently found herself waiting in a chilly study.

There she lingered with no fire for about two hours. Bored, she picked up the doctor's medical books and read several 'shocking' stories. She soon noticed two large cases and, like the character Catherine Morland in Jane Austen's Gothic novel *Northanger Abbey*, her imagination took over. Eliza became convinced that inside the cases she would find skeletons or something more horrid. Instead when she flung open the doors, she was relieved. There were 'crooked scissors', 'formidable Surgical Instruments', and 'Embryos in Spirits'.

About the time she had worked herself into a fearful state was about the same time Farquhar appeared, and she noted that his grave demeanour alarmed her. Nevertheless, she composed herself. After the usual niceties and a few questions on the state of her health, Farquhar decided the mercurial oil earlier prescribed was to be immediately discontinued as it apparently did not agree with her. To her horror, he then prescribed four leeches be applied to her breast that very evening. He also gave her a prescription for 'draughts' that were to be taken both morning and night.

When she left, she headed to the apothecary in Pall Mall as instructed and obtained her medication and leeches. The whole idea of four slimy creatures being applied to her breast terrified her. However, she overcame her aversion and for approximately two hours, they remained attached before she removed them. When she visited Farquhar the next day, he was pleased with the results, but she later claimed to Phylly that she saw no change and thought there was absolutely no reduction in the swelling.

Farquhar then instructed her to continue taking her medicine and ordered her to apply another round of leeches for a longer time-period. When they were removed, severe swelling ran from her neck to her ear and she was so alarmed, she sent an immediate dispatch to Farquhar. His reply reassured her everything was fine as he stated that such swelling was a common occurrence and she had no reason to worry.

He then prescribed a bread and milk poultice to be applied to reduce the swelling. This application essentially confined her to the house and prevented friends from visiting. Eliza was also told to continue her course of medication with Farquhar promising her that within a month or so, her problem would be resolved. Nonetheless, she complained to Phylly that she saw little improvement, but because she had hope of a permanent cure, she continued to follow Farquhar's instructions.

Eliza sent another letter to Phylly in mid-December. She had been busy 'house hunting' because her present lodgings had what she described as too many 'inconveniences'. She maintained that her health made it impossible for her to leave London and so she sought a residence within the capital that had greater 'commodious habitation'. Luckily, she found one that fit her requirements.

It was in an area where many other rich French émigrés resided and where she had once lived too. The location was 33 Manchester Street on the opposite side of the road from her previous residence. It was also while residing on Manchester Street that she hired two housekeepers, Madame Bigeon and her daughter Madame Perigord, as well as a lady's maid named Manon.

Eliza also mentioned that she was continuing to follow Farquhar's orders by continually applying a bread and milk poultice to her breast. Unfortunately, although she had been doing it for over a month, she grumbled that it still had not produced improvements, although she also noted that she maintained hope the tumour might be 'broken'. In addition, she stated that Farquhar's orders were inconvenient and socially ostracising. They prevented visitors from calling and they made it impossible for her to go anywhere; she further complained that she had no idea how long she would be saddled with applying the poultice.

Although her breast issues remained, she had at least solved one problem since her last letter to Phylly. She had finally achieved her goal of purchasing a pug. Unfortunately, the male puppy she bought seemed to suffer from 'weakness' in one of its hind legs and hoping to improve his situation, Eliza reported that she had consulted the doctor. She was therefore busily administering the 'Vapour Baths' he prescribed. In addition, Phylly must have previously reported on her abilities to get Eliza a pug because Eliza wrote that she would be willing to take as many of the 'bewitching' animals as Phylly could procure.

Five days after Christmas, on 30 December, Eliza wrote again to her cousin about her breast issues. With no improvement from the poultice, Eliza had agreed to have the affected breast lanced. She had long dreaded that it might come to this and had tried everything to avoid it, but now she felt she had no choice. It had to be done. Fortunately, the lancing miraculously reduced the tumour to the size of 'a Pea' and what was left of it was to be removed with a 'caustic' application, a painful remedy that would take about a week.

Eliza had also been given permission to resume her social life during the caustic application. She was thrilled. She was so tired of staying home and not receiving visitors that she would have immediately performed social calls if bad weather had not struck. However, she was soon invited to celebrate the first day of 1797 supping and dining with a large circle of friends. She had every intention of ringing in the new year by attending the party, and she had great hope that 1797 would prove to be much better than 1796.

Chapter 14

Henry

> FLIRTATION'S A CHARMING THING, IT MAKES THE BLOOD CIRCULATED.
> ELIZA TO PHYLLY

While Henry was stationed at Norwich, Eliza's other unsuccessful suitor, James, married homely Mary Lloyd on a cold winter's day in January at Hurstbourne Tarrant, Hampshire. Shortly thereafter, there was some sad news about Cassandra Elizabeth's fiancé, Reverend Tom Fowle. She had got engaged to him in 1792 but, for financial reasons, they had not married. In 1796 he had travelled to the West Indies serving as Chaplain to his cousin, Lord Craven, who had been sent there with his regiment to defend British interests. Unfortunately, around the time Fowle was expected to leave, he contracted yellow fever and died. Of this tragedy, Eliza wrote to Phylly on 3 May 1797 noting how much the Austen clan was suffering:

> Mr. Tom Fowle, the Gentleman to whom our Cousin Cassandra was engaged – He was expected home this Month … but Alas instead of his arrival news were received of his Death. This is a very severe stroke to the whole family, and particularly to poor Cassandra for whom I feel more than I can express – Indeed I am most sincerely grieved at this Event & the Pain which it must occasion our worthy Relations – Jane says that her Sister behaves with a degree of resolution & propriety which no common mind could evince in so trying a situation.[1]

Although Cassandra Elizabeth was not married to Fowle, she might as well have been his wife. Unlike Eliza who claimed to be immune to love, Cassandra Elizabeth maintained that she would never fall in love again.

That one-time love she had supposedly found in Fowle, he had returned by leaving her a thousand pounds in his will. Though not nearly enough to live on, it did help make Cassandra Elizabeth less dependent upon her parents.

Fowle's death also resulted in her keeping her promise of loving but once. She had been strangely calm after his death, and as time passed, she maintained she had no wish to marry and thereafter remained a spinster. Her life included being a devoted godmother and a beloved aunt to her many nieces and nephews.

While Cassandra Elizabeth was mourning the death of Fowle, Londoners and the rest of England were busy discussing the latest marriage between Edward Smith-Stanley, 12th Earl of Derby, and Elizabeth Farren, an Irish stage actress, who appeared one night in the role disguised as Dick Rattler. When she appeared in breeches, she was declared to have 'no prominence either before or behind – all is one straight line from head to foot; and for her legs, they are shaped like a sugar loaf'.[2] Her lack of shapeliness did not bother the Earl because, although his previous wife had been dead but six weeks, he wed Farren by special license on 1 May 1797.

Eliza was thoroughly annoyed by the new bride and mentioned her in a letter to Phylly of 3 May 1797, noting that Farren was a spendthrift with thirty muslin dresses, each costlier and lovelier than the next. Perhaps Eliza had a twinge of envy over Farren's sudden meteoric rise from actress to Countess. Whatever the reason, Eliza commented that she had no patience for the new bride's extravagance and stated that Farren had transformed herself from a mere public servant into the second peeress in England.

Although Eliza may have been displeased with Farren, the royal court seemed to accept her without question. Introductions of the new Countess of Derby to the royal court were conducted as courteously as expected. Moreover, due to the public's great interest, details of this meeting were published in the *Ipswich Journal* soon after the event:

> Wednesday's Drawing room at St. James's was the most brilliant that has been known this season. The Princess Royal displayed on her left breast the Russian order of St. Catharine, with which she had been invested that morning. His Royal Highness the Duke of Wirtemberg,

accompanied by the Duke of York, make his entrance at 3 in a blue embroidered dress. ... The Countess of Derby, *ci-devant* Miss Farren, was presented to her Majesty on her recent marriage, and was very graciously received, ... The ceremonial, which naturally excited the curiosity of the courtly circle, was conducted on the part of the Countess, with an elegance of demeanor equally free from affectation and embarrassment. After the Queen had conversed with her some time, and retired, she received the marked attention of the principal nobility, &c. present. She was simply dressed, in a white Chamberry gause, and white beugles, and her head ornamented only with a single small white feather and spray, and a narrow bandeau of white beugles on her hair, which was lightly powdered. The Countess went to St. James's in the plain family coach; attended by two footmen in their usual liveries; indeed the whole appearance was void of ostentation or parade. The Earl of Derby himself appeared in mourning.[3]

The marriage of Farren and Lord Derby was not the only nuptials being noticed by fashionable Londoners. Eliza also mentioned the upcoming wedding of the Princess Royal, Charlotte-Augusta-Matilda, to the extremely fat Frederick, Hereditary Prince of Württemberg and heir apparent, who would become Frederick I of Württemberg on 22 December 1797. Their marriage took place at the Chapel Royal, St James's Palace with the bride attired in an embroidery of white and silver with the body of her dress and her train in silver tissue and trimmed with silver fringe.

Great preparations had been undertaken and all the pomp and circumstance associated with the royal marriage was reported by the press. Music preceded the ceremony and after the procession into the chapel, the groom and bride advanced to the altar. George III then came forward to bestow his eldest daughter's hand in marriage. Apparently, the ceremony greatly affected the royal family, who became emotional upon realising they were losing an 'amiable' and 'virtuous' person. The *Kentish Gazette* reported:

> The Princess Mary, in particular, appeared to suffer so much from the apprehension of her sister's absence, that she hid

her face, bathed in tears, in her bosom, unable to look up; till the Duchess of York, who saw her distress, with the most amiable attention presented her with a handkerchief. Their majesties were not less affected: and indeed, the whole of the company present seemed to sympathize in the feelings of the Royal Family.[4]

Another noteworthy item in Eliza's letter to Phylly was the mention of another actress, Mrs Sarah Siddons. She was a Welsh-born English thespian and perhaps the best-known tragedienne of the eighteenth century. As Eliza was a theatregoer, it was no surprise that she attended a play with Siddons portraying the role of Mrs Beverly in the *Gamester*, a comedy that satirised the manners, affectations, and standards of society. As to Siddons' on-stage skills, biographer Henry Barton Baker wrote, 'One night Charles Young was playing Beverly to her Mrs. Beverly ... and in the great scene was so overwhelmed by her pathos that he could not speak.'[5]

Eliza, in contrast, still seemed to be doing well after a little over three years of widowhood. She wrote numerous letters about how her dance cards were always full and mentioned several flirtations, even remarking at one point, 'flirtation's a charming thing, it makes the blood circulate'.[6] One cause of such circulation at the time was her ardent admirer, 'Baddy'.

In the meantime, Eliza also decided that it was time for her to take a more active role in her finances and wrote to Woodman requesting that he transfer her the stocks that he had being holding in trust for her. Her Uncle George supported her in this, as well as her request to end the trust and turn over to her whatever sums remained. Woodman appears to have been less enthusiastic about doing so and did not immediately reply.

Two weeks later, she sent a more sharply worded demand, stating that such action be taken without delay. In the meantime, as she waited for word from Woodman, on 3 July 1797 she wrote to Phylly and besides telling her how much she was missed, Eliza also referenced the weather. She described London as having been 'deluged with Rain,' which in turn interrupted various parties that had been planned at Kensington Gardens.

Hastings Jr. was doing well, although Eliza remarked that she was thinking of going to Brighton so that he could obtain the benefits of sea-bathing. The Austens were another topic. Eliza's Uncle George and his youngest son Charles had dined with her and she noted that she thought Charles was a 'fine youth', and that her uncle looked as young and well as he did ten years earlier.

Meanwhile Woodman was still considering Eliza's letter. He had not replied to her and had, in fact, sent off a letter to his brother-in-law, Hastings. Woodman was concerned about what action he should take regarding Eliza's trust. Hastings was very clear with his terse reply dated 6 July 1797:

> You have set a case to me, which I am not qualified to solve; nor can I with propriety take the opinion of Counsel upon it, or take any other steps regarding it. As Mme. de Feuillide is desirous of taking the money, which is now in trust with you and Mr. Austen, into her own hands, you certainly ought to comply with her desire, if you have the power to part with the trust. If you have doubts respecting this, it is your business, not hers, to satisfy them by applying to some able counsel for advice upon it; and this, I think, you ought to do.[7]

Woodman finally sent a note to Eliza around mid-July. He requested that she provide him with a death certificate or some confirmation that her husband had passed away. He noted that his request was necessary to protect the trustees from any future claim should the Count suddenly reappear because if he did, he could force Woodman and George Austen to pay him the funds a second time.

In August, instead of heading to Brighton, Eliza travelled to Cheltenham, located on the edge of the Cotswolds in Gloucestershire. Cheltenham waters had been discovered in the early eighteenth century when a spring bubbled to the surface and its potential healing powers enticed hundreds of pigeons to flock to it. Their arrival alerted its owner that the waters were special and encouraged the local populace to also begin enjoying them. Eventually some improvements were made in the area, but it was not until Dr Thomas Short published his *History of Mineral Waters* in 1734 that Cheltenham was noted to be one of the best sites for healthy spa water.

Although the new year had started off stormy and the summer was wet throughout England and Wales, Eliza described London as 'hot' in July. She claimed that it was the smothering heat and emptiness of

London that hastened her departure to Cheltenham. Arriving at the spa town late in the evening on 21 July, she sent Phylly a note on 4 August.

Because Phylly had been unable to accompany Eliza, Maria Payne had taken her place. Maria was the eldest daughter of the wealthy barrister George Payne, who served as Ambassador to the Emperor of Morocco in 1784. He was also a maternal cousin to the Austens and a good friend to Hastings. In fact, Payne was such a good friend that his daughter Maria had served as a companion to Hastings' wife, Chapuset.

Maria loved pugs, just like Eliza. Pugs at this time looked somewhat different than today. They had fewer facial wrinkles, longer legs, and clipped ears, a practice that was officially banned in England in 1895. Of course, the women decided that they could not leave their amiable pugs behind when they headed to Cheltenham, and, thus, they travelled with them, much to the chagrin of innkeepers who thought the women foolish for the inordinate attention they gave their dogs.

Jane Austen had also observed the women's lavish affection for their precious pets. In fact, she poked fun at them with her reference to Lady Bertram and her pug in *Mansfield Park* that states:

> She was a woman who spent her days in sitting nicely dressed on a sofa, doing some long piece of needle-work of little use and no beauty, thinking more of her pug than her children, but very indulgent to the latter, when it did not put herself to inconvenience.[8]

Eliza and Maria were not the only ones charmed by the adorable black-faced creatures. Eliza mentioned that her lady's maid was completely enamoured by her pug and that she made a constant 'fuss' over him. Plenty of other people did too. Whenever the women walked at Cheltenham with their beloved pets, Eliza reported that others out for a stroll also took great notice of their prancing pups.

Because Phylly had never been to Cheltenham, Eliza thought it her duty to provide a description of the place. She stated that it was one 'long and handsome' main street. A guidebook of 1789 reported that the town ran in almost a straight line for a mile and that the surrounding area was 'well-wooded'. Cheltenham also offered plenty of beautiful walks and drives, and the adjacent Malvern hills offered wonderful views and 'picturesque scenes'.

While staying in Cheltenham, Maria and Eliza had plenty to entertain themselves. There were many other vacationers there, including Eliza's Aunt Cassandra and two of her Leigh relatives. When not visiting friends or relations, the women could also attend one of the plays produced three times a week or they could enjoy the twice-weekly balls. Of these balls, Eliza remarked that at the last one she attended, she received no rest as she danced every dance. She also mentioned a 'little flirtation'. It was an anonymous man who earned between thirty and forty thousand per annum, but she also noted that nothing would come of it as he already had a wife. Still, that did not stop her from making the most of her feminine virtues.

Eliza also commented that her chief 'inducement' for going to Cheltenham was because she had just been to see her 'old Friends' the Hastings, who were staying at their Daylesford estate. Eliza described the estate's park and grounds as a 'paradise'. Gardener John Davenport designed the landscape, creating a formal approach from the village of Daylesford through a 300-acre park that had many mature trees, two lakes, and a walled kitchen garden. He also designed an orangery that was constructed in 1789–90 in Gothic style.

Eliza reported that Hastings' house was as magnificent as the Daylesford grounds. It had been remodelled between 1788 and 1793 with designs created by an EIC architect named Samuel Pepys Cockerell. The new house was neoclassical with features inspired by Indian architecture. The interior was in a classical style with one of three fireplaces having Indian motifs. Moreover, the original decorations contained a lot of gold and crimson to match Hastings' collection of oriental furniture.

While there, Eliza also heard word about Woodman's son, Thomas. This was the same man who had been her young playmate, and whom her parents and the Woodmans had hoped she would one day marry. Thomas had followed in his father's footsteps, becoming a lawyer. However, he had recently given it up for the clergy. Eliza mentioned his employment change as well as a false rumour that he was about to marry a widow with six children. In fact, he would not marry for years and when he did on 22 July 1811, it was to the amiable and good-humoured Louisa Chapuset, Hastings' niece.

Eliza left Cheltenham and arrived back in London around 9 August 1797. She then corresponded with Woodman briefly about settling the trust, but told him to delay his visit because she had some unmentioned business that required her to leave on 22 August. When she returned on the 26th she found Woodman had called and requested that he promptly call again on the 29th. She had also by now lost the company of Maria, someone she declared to be a 'pleasant Companion'.

In early September, the funds in her trust were transferred to her and by 22 September she was writing to Phylly from Lowestoft, a town in Suffolk on the North Sea coast and the most easterly settlement of the United Kingdom. She was listed in the *Norfolk Chronicle* as one of the 'distinguished' persons who had visited, alongside the Duke of Gloucester, Prince William of Gloucester, the Duke of Dorset, Marquis of Salisbury, and several others. Eliza had planned to visit it earlier but had fallen ill with a 'Feverish Complaint' that delayed her departure. Another reason she claimed for her visit was that Farquhar had earlier prescribed sea-bathing as the best cure for Hastings Jr.'s ailments and noted that Lowestoft's 'elevated situation' also provided clear, dry air.

Phylly didn't believe Eliza's reasons for going to Lowestoft. She knew right away that Henry and his regiment were stationed nearby to defend the coast from any possible invasion by Holland. When Phylly suggested this ulterior motive, Eliza pushed back and insisted that Phylly's 'cunning' conclusion could not be further from the truth. She then remarked:

> My dear Friend, You see that the contiguity of Suffolk & Norfolk was not my motive for visiting this place, and indeed had You known that Lowestoffe is no less than 28 Miles from Norwich, You would probably have dismissed all your wicked surmises for You must allow that a Person who cannot absent himself from his Corps for more than a few hours at a time, cannot very conveniently travel 56 Miles to pay a Visit.[9]

Phylly's intuition had been right. In fact, Henry did not need to make the 56-mile trip to the seaside town because Eliza met him halfway at Great Yarmouth. Still, Eliza, apparently wanting to keep the relationship a secret, omitted mentioning the *rendezvous* when writing to Phylly. She did mention that besides reading and 'dipping' in the sea, she had made an occasional trip to Great Yarmouth.

Phylly also mentioned to Eliza that her father, William Hampson Walter, had started acting strangely and his lifelong sweet temperament had been replaced with bitterness. Eliza was supportive of what Phylly and her family were going through and noted how upsetting it must be for her cousin to experience such unkindness. She encouraged Phylly to think of her own health and ensure that she got daily exercise.

Eliza returned to London on 20 October. The next day, she sent a letter to Woodman to conclude the details of her trust. A few weeks later, she received the final dividend payment from him that amounted to £78.12s.3d. Eliza didn't mention any of this in her last letter of 1797 to Phylly dated 11 December. However, she did provide some interesting updates.

She had been planning a trip to northern England but would not be going because Hastings Jr. had suddenly developed convulsive seizures and a high fever. Eliza was sure he would die and was distraught. Fortunately, he recovered but as she had planned to leave him with her housekeeper, Madame Bigeon, she found that was now impossible as he remained weak. She therefore noted that any trip north would have to be delayed until springtime.

Henry and Eliza's clandestine relationship also progressed, such that by the end of December she admitted to everyone what Phylly had so 'cunningly' guessed: she had decided to marry Henry, and she sent word of her decision to her godfather:

> As I flatter myself You still take an interest in my welfare, I think it incumbent on me to acquaint You with a circumstance by which it must be materially influenced. I have consented to an Union with my Cousin Captn Austen who has the honor of being known to You. – He has been for some time in Possession of a comfortable Income, and the excellence of his Heart, Temper, & Understanding, together with his steady attachment to me, his Affection for my little Boy, and disinterested concurrence in the disposal of my Property, in favor of this latter, have at length induced me to an acquiescence which I have withheld for more than two years. – Need I say, My dear Sir, that I most earnestly wish for your approbation on this occasion, and that it is with the sincerest attachment I shall ever remain, Your much obliged and affectionate God-daughter, Elizabeth de Feuillide.'[10]

Chapter 15

The Re-Married Life

> LIKE A WISE MAN, HE HAS NO WILL BUT MINE.
> ELIZA ON HER NEW HUSBAND

Eliza's change of heart about marriage and Henry might have arisen due to several factors. Firstly, she may have really been in love for the first time. She and Henry shared similar personalities and enjoyed lively fun-filled conversations. Henry also had true affection for her disabled son, and he seemed to have settled her concerns about being controlled by a man. She also thought highly of Henry and considered him the perfect man for her, which she acknowledged when she stated to Phylly:

> Unmixed Felicity is certainly not the Produce of this World, and like other People I shall probably meet with many unpleasant and untoward circumstances but all the Comfort which can result from the tender Affection & Society of a Being who is possessed of an excellent Heart, Understanding, & Temper I have at least ensured – to say nothing of the pleasure of having my own way in everything, for Henry well knows that I have not been much accustomed to control & should probably behave rather awkwardly under it; and therefore, like a wise man, he has no will but mine, which to be sure some people call spoiling me, but I know it is the best of managing me.[1]

Although ten years older than 26-year-old Henry, Eliza probably realised it was a good time for marriage given her life situation. She could have been worried about ageing, signs of failing health, and the need to care for her son. Besides, she had been mostly living a life of socialising for several years and may have wanted more. Henry's relationship with Pearson was also over; he had given up the idea of the clergy, and he was earning £300 per year in officer's pay.

Eliza may have also begun to worry about finances. She claimed that her landlord wanted to raise her house rent by 32 pounds a year, and she had to pay 4 guineas more for her man servants than previously. These additional expenses meant that she would have to leave London and perhaps give up the luxury of her carriage, something that afforded her much independence and status. Her finances could become Henry's problem if he was her husband, and there was always the possibility that if France's old regime was restored, she might regain her husband's property, which Henry would no doubt be willing to help her resolve.

Their marriage took place by special license on the last day of 1797 at the oblong brick building of St. Marylebone Anglican parish church that had been built in April 1742. It was built on the same site as two previous churches and it also hosted several important events. For instance, there was the marriage of Richard Brinsley Sheridan to Elizabeth Ann Linley in 1772. There was also the wedding of diplomat Sir William Hamilton's to Amy Lyon. She later became known as Emma and was the woman who became lover to Admiral Horatio Nelson. In addition, the poet Lord Byron was baptised there in 1788, as was Nelson and Emma's illegitimate love child, a girl named Horatia, in 1801.

If Eliza wrote to Phylly detailing all the particulars of the wedding, the letter was not preserved, and Jane provided no clues as to what happened at their nuptials. However, there are some suggestions that the Austen family thought Henry and Eliza's marriage was inappropriate or unsuitable because they did not marry at the Austens' home. If that was true, why did Eliza's Uncle George give a generous £40 to Henry's regiment for feasting and celebration? In addition, her uncle seemed genuinely proud of her because shortly after their marriage, a local squire remarked, 'Mr. Austen has put a coronet on his carriage ... because of his son's being married to a French countess'.[2]

As for 24-year-old Jane, she seemed rather neutral about the match whereas James's wife, the smallpox-scarred Mary Lloyd, was unhappy that Henry had married Eliza. In fact, Mary was intensely jealous of the flame James once held for his trim, elegant, and magnetic cousin, and this was noted years later by one of her granddaughters who stated:

> I believe the *ci-devant* Countess, who was an extremely pretty woman, was a great flirt, and during her brief widowhood flirted with all of the Steventon cousins, our Grandfather inclusive, which was more than his after wife [Mary Lloyd] could stand or ever forgive ... I can testify that to the last days of her life my Grandmother continued to dislike and speak ill of her.[3]

Eliza may not have been a fan of Mary either. However, Eliza was not the least bit jealous of her and was kinder in her assessment of Mary than Mary was of her. Eliza stated of Mary that although she was not 'rich or handsome', she was at least 'sensible & good-humoured'.

Eliza found that her new marriage to Henry was ideal in many ways. It provided few changes to her lifestyle as she could continue to flirt and have admirers. This was demonstrated in Eliza's letter of mid-February 1798 from Ipswich to Phylly where she mentioned two gentlemen she was interested in, the 'remarkably handsome' Captain Tilson and the married Colonel Lord Charles Spencer, to whom she was greatly attracted because of his charm, mild manner, and superior breeding.

Another advantage to marrying Henry was her countryside residence in Ipswich. It had a nice garden attached to the house and Eliza ensured her son took advantage of it. Despite the chilly February weather, she sent him outdoors for fresh air and exercise. Thus, according to Eliza, between the 'change of Air' and his constant outdoor activities, Hasting Jr.'s health tremendously improved, even more so than if he was taking medicine.

Her Ipswich letter also included other tidbits related to her new life with Henry. Eliza noted that since her arrival, Henry's 'Brother Officers', their wives, and other locals had paid their respects to the newlyweds, partly because she had the impressive title of countess. Besides these friendly visits she had also been invited to numerous 'country hops', parties, and the weekly-held ball. So, with all the constant activities she claimed she barely had time for any leisure activities or rest.

Ipswich also had the usual gossip that Eliza was willing to share. This time it was about a Captain Talbot who had gone 'out of his senses' for a couple of months after his marriage to a young fashionable woman by the last name of Bedingfield. Fortunately, the Captain recovered but Eliza could not resist adding a mention of his young wife's fashion for not wearing stays, something that was extra scandalous in a place like Ipswich. She supposedly wore a thick muslin petticoat with an outrageously thin muslin dress that exposed her bare throat and bosom, and caused Eliza to state that such 'undress' would never be tolerated in London.

The worry that France would attack also remained strong. It increased further when there were reports that Napoleon Bonaparte planned to build a secret weapon called a 'Floating Machine' or 'war machine'. Although these machines varied in size, one was reputedly large enough to carry 60,000 men and 60 cannons. It was to be propelled in the water by four huge windmills that reputedly produced the same effect as oars. Atop it was to be a wooden fortress filled with French soldiers and at each corner, the largest piece of artillery possible, 48-pounder guns to blast the enemy.

The idea of humongous rafts transporting the enemy to England's shores seemed likely because France had appointed Gaspard Monge Minister of the Marine in August 1792. He was supposedly one of Europe's most 'skilful geometricians', which made it highly possible in everyone's mind that he could create such a thing. There were also numerous French print-makers busy producing images of these terrifying rafts, and, in addition, a pamphlet titled *Recherches sur l'usage des Radeaux pour une Descente, &c.* (*Inquiries concerning the Use of Rafts for an Invasion*) had examined the feasibility of rafts. Moreover, reports stated that the pamphlet was 'calculated to dissipate the timidity even of the most timid'.[4]

While some people were terrified by the idea of floating rafts, Eliza thought the whole idea crazy and commented that she was sure they would prove ineffectual once they hit the rough seas. Yet, that did not put a rest to protecting England's shores. Even if the rafts were nothing more than fantastical propaganda, Englishmen wanted to be prepared. They therefore busily shored up the coastline with troops and ensured soldiers were ready to act on a moment's notice to defend their homeland.

Finances also remained a worrisome topic for Eliza. She was thinking of planning a trip to London but was not taking her coach. Instead Henry had committed to driving her as her servants were being sent there by stage. She remarked that by doing so, she would save the costs of the 'Post Horses' and that this was just one of many ways that she was now demonstrating her stinginess, although she also remained fearful that if France did attack, they might try to lay claim to her remaining fortune.

Soon after Phylly received Eliza's Ipswich letter, her father died. He passed away on 6 April 1798 after suffering years of senility and experiencing even more deterioration in his health during the past year. Eliza must have sent her cousin Phylly condolences just like her 22-year-old cousin Jane did, but it cannot be found. However, Jane's condolences arrived two days after her uncle's passing and stated:

> As Cassandra is at present from home, You must accept from my pen our sincere Condolance on the melancholy Event which Mrs. Humphries Letter announced to my Father this morning. – The loss of so kind & affectionate a Parent, must be a very severe affliction to all his Children, to yourself more especially, as your constant residence with him has given you so much the more constant & intimate knowledge of his Virtues. – But the very circumstance which at present enhance your loss, must gradually reconcile you to it the better; – the Goodness which made him valuable on Earth, will make him Blessed in Heaven. ... I will not press you to write before you would otherwise feel equal to it, but when you can do it without pain, I hope we shall receive from you as good an account of my Aunt & Yourself, as can be expected in these early days of Sorrow.[5]

No records survive for an eighteen month period and it is unclear if Phylly and Eliza corresponded. However, during this time, Thomas Twisleton, who had so frivolously eloped to Gretna Green and married Charlotte Wattrell years earlier, divorced his wife. The couple had been separated since 1794 because she wanted to be a professional actress and he had become disinclined to further pursue such a profession. Just as their elopement had been scandalous, so too was everything associated with their divorce, particularly after she had an adulterous relationship with a merchant named John Stein that resulted in her giving birth to his son. Apparently, however, Twisleton had put everything behind him because in June 1798, he married the daughter of Benjamin Ashe.

Jane had also by now completed what would eventually become *Pride and Prejudice* but was at this time titled *First Impressions*. Her father had tried to help her get it published and submitted it to Cadell & Davies, who promptly rejected it and returned it by post. Thus, one of her most famous novels would not be published until January 1813, and, in the meantime, she began writing the prototype for what would become *Northanger Abbey*, a satire on Gothic novels as well as a coming-of-age story about the young and naïve 17-year-old Catherine Morland.

In June a new tax came into effect. It stated that anyone who painted an armorial bearing on their private coach or carriage was to pay a tax of 2 guineas and if the tax was not paid, owners would face a fine of £20. George Austen's new coronet honouring his daughter-in-law meant he was among those liable to pay the new tax. It would never happen. He became so upset at the prospect of the tax that he stored his carriage.

The year 1798 was also the year, around August, that Catherine Knight deeded over Godmersham to Edward and left for her new residence in Canterbury called 'White Friars'. Godmersham was supposed to go to Edward after her death, but Catherine had decided to do it while she was still alive. She had notified him the previous November that she was making the necessary preparations to transfer the deed and at last it happened. This meant that Edward and his family were moving in to Godmersham around the same time that Henry obtained leave from the Oxfordshires.

By 1 September Jane and her parents had arrived at Godmersham to visit. Their happiness was increased in early October when reports appeared about Admiral Horatio Nelson's grand victory over Napoleon's fleet between 1 and 3 August at the Battle of the Nile. With Napoleon's fleet destroyed, the French general now faced a major blow to any ambitions he might have entertained in the east. Moreover, given its strategic importance, some historians consider Nelson's achievement to be the most significant of his career, even greater than what would happen seven years later at the Battle of Trafalgar.

On 10 October another level of happiness was reached when Edward's wife Elizabeth gave birth to their fourth son and fifth child, William. He would grow up to become a reverend and his birth would be followed by six more children, four girls and two boys. Of course, a healthy baby was always a blessed event, and Elizabeth and Edward probably enjoyed the extra help provided by the visit of his mother and sisters.

Cassandra Elizabeth stayed on at Godmersham after Jane and her mother left. Jane provided the details of their return trip home noting that they had travelled through Sittingbourne, Rochester, and Ospringe before arriving in Dartford where they sat down to dine on beef and boiled fowl. Jane also reported that her writing and dressing boxes had been placed on an outboard coach after their arrival and would have been shipped to the West Indies if the mistake had not been almost immediately discovered. Fortunately, a man was dispatched post-haste and rectified it upon finding the offending coach.

The next night, they stayed in Staines. Jane reported her mother was not feeling well, supposedly suffering from fatigue, travel weariness, and a sore throat. Happily, the following day she seemed to travel better than expected, but they stopped in Basingstoke, about nine miles northeast of Steventon, so she could receive medical attention that included broth and a suggestion that she take twelve drops of laudanum at bedtime. She followed the doctor's order and turned in early at Steventon, remaining in bed the following day.

Jane also reported that Mary Lloyd, who was pregnant, was 'uncommonly large' and that James had retrieved her sister Martha from Ibthorpe. In addition, Jane mentioned that although Mary had hired a new scrub girl, James thought she was probably not up to the task and when Jane wrote to Cassandra Elizabeth on Saturday, 17 November, she stated that although Mary's new nurse possessed no charm in 'person or manner', she was touted to be the best nurse in Hurstbourne. Mary apparently needed one because she was plagued by rheumatism and told everyone who visited her that she could hardly wait to deliver. Fortunately, the baby, a healthy boy named James Edward Austen, arrived the next day at 11 pm.

By the end of November, Henry had found a guarantor for £200 that would help him qualify for a promotion to Captain and by early December, he was officially gazetted as Captain in the Oxfordshires. On Christmas Day he was appointed paymaster, and shortly thereafter the Austens received news of Frank's promotion, with Jane writing that 'Frank is made'. He was promoted to commander and appointed to the *Petterel*, a sloop in Gibraltar.

Between 23 and 25 March 1799, Henry marched with ten companies of the Oxfordshires out of Ipswich and Colchester to Gosport and Portsmouth. Their destination was Ireland. By May, when they reached it, Eliza and her son were staying in the countryside of Dorking in Surrey and it was there that she and Hastings Jr. enjoyed a quiet and uneventful summer.

In the meantime, Jane arrived in Bath around mid-May. She was going to visit her mother's wealthy and childless brother, James Leigh-Perrot, and his wife Jane Cholmeley. They often spent their summers in Bath and had invited their niece Jane to visit. At the end of June, as the Leigh-Perrots stayed on in Bath, Jane returned home, only to receive shocking news in August that her wealthy Aunt Jane had been arrested.

Apparently, on Wednesday, 7 August, she went shopping at Gregory's milliner shop on Bath Street and inquired about some black lace. She returned the following day and purchased it. However, after leaving the store some white lace was found to be missing. Aunt Jane, who was in her mid-fifties, was stopped and the 'stolen' lace was discovered in her parcel. She seemed surprised and claimed that the clerk must have put it in there by mistake.

Four days later a constable appeared on Aunt Jane's doorstep at Number 1 Paragon. He was there to arrest her based on the sworn depositions of those at the store that she was a shoplifter. It was a scandalous incident with Aunt Jane and her husband claiming they were being blackmailed.

Ultimately, although Aunt Jane was imprisoned, she was spared from having to wear the yellow and brown striped prison outfit. She was also relieved of being incarcerated at the gaol. Instead she served her time by living with the jailer and his family. That was only a tad better than the Somerset County gaol in Ilchester, where she would have served if she had not been a wealthy gentlewoman.

She remained living with her jailer for months. Fortunately, she was not imprisoned alone because her husband refused to leave her side and despite suffering gout, he remained with her in the jailer's cramped and squalid quarters. If her husband had not done so, Mrs Austen had thought of staying with her, but as she was sick, she offered up her daughters Jane and Cassandra Elizabeth. Fortunately, Mrs Austen's offer was magnanimously declined as their aunt considered the situation too unpleasant for her impressionable nieces.

In October, after months of no word from Phylly, Eliza received a letter from her and sent a response at the end of October. Eliza had nothing to say about Aunt Jane's shoplifting, but she did have something to say about a favour Phylly had requested. She wanted help for her brother that involved Hastings. Eliza told her that many people requested favours from her godfather and that he had previously told her that his interference always seemed to result in 'unpleasant consequences' and so therefore he was disinclined to help anyone. Furthermore, Eliza stated that although she would provide her godfather's address so that Phylly's brother could make his request firsthand, she thought it would be useless to appeal to him and that under no circumstances was he to mention her name.

Eliza also wrote to Phylly about her time in Dorking. She had been there alone with her son as Henry had gone to Dublin with the Oxfordshires. She noted that during his absence she had tried to live as a 'recluse' but that poet and playwright Lady Sophia Burrell (wife to the Bishop of Kildare named Reverend William Clay), Lady Talbot (widow of Sir Charles-Henry Talbot), and a few other neighbours had sought her out, making it impossible for her to completely shun society. She remarked that she would have loved to have been left alone until December when Henry was due to return because she found her books, her harp, and her pianoforte more enjoyable than any Dorking socialites.

Eliza also mentioned her own ill health and that she was sorry to hear that Phylly was having health problems too. Eliza had hoped that Dorking's country life of fresh air, peace, and quiet would bring a noticeable improvement, but she was sorely disappointed and in fact she remarked that she had not felt well for the past two years. Hastings Jr. was also suffering in Dorking's country air. She noted that his 'epileptic' fits had forcefully returned and that his poor health was constant, making his sufferings a continual 'source of grief' to her.

Chapter 16

Life Changes

> I GET MORE & MORE RECONCILED TO THE IDEA OF OUR REMOVAL.
> JANE AUSTEN ABOUT MOVING TO BATH

On 3 November Henry obtained a leave of absence and by 17 January 1800, the majority of the Oxfordshires returned from Ireland and marched to Birmingham. It was there that Henry joined them, despite having second thoughts about a military career. Over the next few months, these thoughts would grow stronger until he began considering what life would be like as a private citizen.

As Eliza remained quietly in Dorking and as Henry contemplated his future, Frank's sloop the *Peterel* captured two French cargo ships and a brig and then drove another two ships into the rocks near Marseilles on 21 March. The news reached London in May and he was promoted to Post Captain, but because it was difficult to relay such news to a ship under active duty, he did not learn of his promotion for months.

In the meantime, Jane Leigh-Perrot's case was heard between 8 am and 3 pm on Thursday, 27 March 1800 at Taunton. She had the best of lawyers, four to be exact. The outcome could be extremely serious because if found guilty, she might be condemned to death or dragged off to serve fourteen years of incarceration in Australia.

Fortunately, she was found 'not guilty' by a jury of her peers and released. She was immediately surrounded by well-wishers and her Bath friends. Yet, despite all the celebrations and happiness she might have experienced at the 'not guilty' verdict, it did not bring an end to the speculation about her possible guilt.

> Richard Austen-Leigh later wrote privately ... that she "did steal the material and probably meant to". It seems that wealthy ladies may become more unreliable than other

> women, [her lawyer] Jekyll blandly supposed: "Mrs. L.P."
> was like other rich ladies "who frequent bazaars and mistake
> other people's property for their own … It was the blunder
> of my client, Mrs. Leigh Perrot."[1]

Jane Austen also doubted her aunt's innocence. In fact, she mentioned her aunt's 'sad nature' that encompassed meanness, discontentedness and covetousness, and in her novels *Northanger Abbey* and *Persuasion*, Jane hinted at the truth. Author David Nokes also maintains that rumours about Aunt Jane's guilt continued to run rampant after the verdict.

> Mrs. Leigh-Perrot soon found … her enemies … not
> entirely done with her. An anonymous letter repeated the
> threat of printing the "parrot's bill" lampoon unless the
> Leigh-Perrots paid a hundred guineas to the city's general
> hospital. A newspaper claimed that the trial jury had never
> come to a verdict; that Mrs. Leigh-Perrot had staged a faint
> and had been carried out of court; and that when she was
> brought back to court she was tried "by a fresh jury which
> had all been bribed with a guinea each".[2]

Amidst all the continual rumours about Aunt Jane's guilt, besides a ball here and there and Henry's Oxfordshires marching from place to place, life crawled at a monotonous pace with little to report about Eliza or Henry. However, when Henry went on leave in September, he also presumably began making plans to resign his commission so that he could form a partnership with his army friend, Henry Maunde. The men had plans to set up their office at the distinguished address of Cleveland Court, St. James's.

Henry had plans to not only become a banker but also to serve as an army agent. Such a position meant he would function as a middleman between the Paymaster General's office and the regimental paymaster. All financial transactions of the regiment passed through the army agent's hands. These positions could either be purchased or the agent appointed by a colonel. Exactly how an army agent earned his money follows:

> [The army agent] profited by the pay of one "warrant man"
> per company … at sixpence a day; and by twopence in

the pound deducted from the whole regimental payroll. There were other ways by which an agent could profit; he became the private banker of the officers, and he could become a half-pay agent. Half pay, for the inactive officers of the army or navy, was paid out in London semiannually. To avoid the inconvenience of travelling to London, an officer could appoint a half-pay agent to collect his money for him, the agent receiving sixpence in the pound for his trouble (two-and-a-half percent). But the best way for an agent to make money was illicit; it involved the backdoor buying and selling of commissions. Much more than the standard fee would be paid for a desired position, or an attractive regiment, even though an affidavit of denial had to be signed.[3]

At the end of October 1800, Jane sent a letter to her sister and then another letter four or five days later. She mentioned her attendance at one of the latest balls, stating:

> Did you think of our Ball on Thursday evening, & did you suppose me at it? – You might very safely for there I was. On Wednesday morning it was settled that Mrs Harwood, Mary & I should go together, & shortly afterwards a very civil note of invitation for me came from Mrs Bramston, who wrote I believe as soon as she knew of the Ball. I might likewise have gone with Mrs Lefroy, & therefore with three methods of going, I must have been more at the Ball than anybody else. – I dined & slept at Deane. – Charlotte & I did my hair, which I fancy looked very indifferent; nobody abused it however, & I retired delighted with my success. – It was a pleasant Ball, & still more good than pleasant, for there were nearly 60 people, & sometimes we had 17 couple. – The Portsmouths, Dorchesters, Boltons, Portals & Clerks were there, & all the meaner & more usual &c. &c.'s. – There was a scarcity of Men in general, & a still greater scarcity of any that were good for much. – I danced nine dances out of ten, five with Stephen Terry,

> T. Chute & James Digweed & four with Catherine. – There was commonly a couple of ladies standing up together, but not often any so amiable as ourselves.[4]

Near the end of November, Jane wrote another note to her sister. She reported on another dance that she had attended, this time with her brother Charles who had arrived for a visit on 19 November. Henry was also expected to visit and probably stayed Saturday night, 22 November. As Henry's leave expired the next day, he and Charles were expected to leave together. In addition, Jane and Martha Lloyd travelled to Ibthorpe and on the way they stopped in Andover where Jane purchased some 'figured cambric muslin' to make James's now 2-year-old son a frock.

The trip proved pleasant and so it was even more unsettling when Jane returned home to some shocking news. Her father had suddenly decided during her absence to retire, leave the rectory, and move to Bath, a spot popular among clergymen for retirement. Apparently, 'Mr. Austen "was always rapid both in forming his resolutions and in acting on them".'[5] Some people claim that Jane was extremely upset about the decision to leave Steventon but if that was true, she quickly became accepting of the idea because on 3 January 1801, she wrote:

> I get more & more reconciled to the idea of our removal. We have lived long enough in this Neighbourhood, the Basingstoke Balls are certainly on the decline, there is something interesting in the bustle of going away, & the prospect of spending future summers by the Sea or in Wales is very delightful. ... It must not be generally known however that I am not sacrificing a great deal in quitting the Country — or I can expect to inspire no tenderness, no interest in those we leave behind.[6]

On 6 December Jane's father gave his last baptismal service and by 3 January 1801, plans were under way for the Austens to move to Bath. Jane wrote that they had decided to avoid settling at the Axford buildings or on Trim Street. The places they found acceptable included the Westgate Buildings, Charles Street, Laura Place, Pulteney Street, Gay Street, or Chapel Row. Furthermore, Bath was an expensive place and so George Austen was busy trying to raise his tithes and obtain revenue from every available source.

Jane Leigh-Perrot was still hazarding regular visits during the summer to Bath, despite the ordeal she had been through and the supposed shop villains who tried to take advantage of naïve customers. When Aunt Jane heard that the Austen family was relocating to Bath, she was reputedly among the first to congratulate them. Jane said that their aunt couldn't have been happier about their proposed move and that her note expressed 'the greatest pleasure' at the thought of the Austen clan settling there.

The Austens were not the only ones in need of congratulations. Major changes were also on the horizon for Henry and Eliza. Henry performed his last paymaster duties for the Oxfordshires on 24 January 1801 and resigned his commission. By now Henry and Eliza were living at a new address, a lease located at number 24 Upper Berkeley Street in a newly-built terrace off Portman Square, north of Oxford Street. Although they were not living in luxury or splendour, they were living in style. Eliza, dressed in the most fashionable finery, had a carriage to pay visits to her friends and added a chef, a Monsieur Halavant. He was helping Eliza's other domestics, Madame Bigeon and her daughter.

The third week of January was also when Jane decided to provide an update to her sister about Eliza's health, who had become ill in December. Although Jane reported that she was doing 'quite well' now, Eliza appeared not to have completely recovered from her most recent illness as Jane noted:

> [S]he is thinner than we saw her last, & not in very good looks. ... She cuts her hair too short over her forehead, & does not wear her cap far enough upon her head – in spite of these many disadvantages however, I can still admire her beauty.[7]

Despite not feeling her best, the extroverted Eliza continued to keep up a hectic schedule of socialising. Like her mother, she enjoyed making calls on friends. She also enjoyed attending social functions such as the one where she had recently seen Lord Craven, whom she cited as 'pleasing' even though Jane noted that there was also the 'unpleasing circumstance' of him living with his celebrated mistress, Miss Harriet Wilson, at Ashdown Park.

Eliza also enjoyed receiving visitors and she and Henry had plans to play hostess to his sister Cassandra Elizabeth. She had been staying with Edward and his family at Godmersham but would be leaving to spend three weeks in London. Jane sounded envious when she imagined all the pleasures her sister would find in London:

> I hope you will see everything worthy of notice, from the Opera House to Henry's office in Cleveland Court; and I shall expect you to lay in a stock of intelligence that may procure me amusement for a twelvemonth to come. You will have a turkey from Steventon while you are there, and pray note down how many full courses of exquisite dishes M. Halavant converts it into.[8]

Around the same time that Cassandra Elizabeth arrived in London, the planning stages of the Austen family's move turned from talk to action. The rectory was suddenly transformed with things being packaged and boxed. Certain items that were not being taken were being prepared for auction with the Winchester auctioneer making an inventory list. Moreover, every time a neighbour came to express his or her regrets at the Austens' imminent departure, one of them found themselves sidelined into bargaining for furnishings or other household treasures.

Jane's father had also decided that the sensible thing to do was to allow his son James to take over at the Steventon rectory, so he had been busy trying to find someone else to replace him at Deane. As Mary and James would be moving in to Steventon, Mary seemed especially eager to help her in-laws be on their way to Bath. In fact, she hurried them out and watched as her father-in-law sold off his belongings, one by one, including an extensive library of about 500 volumes and Jane's beloved pianoforte.

Although Mary's behaviour was bad enough, Jane was more displeased by the actions of her brother James. First, many of the family possessions that were not being sold would become his property upon their departure, and second, he seemed intent on acting like he already owned the place. She indicated this when she complained in early January of James's eagerness:

> My father's old Ministers are already deserting him to pay their court to his Son; the brown Mare, which as well as the

black was to devolve on James at our removal, has not had patience to wait for that, & has settled herself even now at Deane.[9]

In early May, the Austens left the Steventon rectory for a final time. George Austen travelled to London and then was off to see friends. Mrs Austen and Jane set off to Ibthorpe before heading onward to Bath via Ludgershall, Everley (Everleigh), and Devizes. The Leigh-Perrots had insisted that the Austen family stay with them in Paragon, which the women did, although they found their hostess suffering a 'violent cough' upon their arrival on 4 May.

As Jane and her mother were acclimatising to Bath, Phylly visited Henry and Eliza in London. She wrote a letter to her brother dated 4 June and noted the location of their new residence in Upper Berkeley Street. Furthermore, she wrote that Eliza and Henry seemed discontent because when Eliza spoke of retiring to Wales and 'resigning the world', Henry seemed 'ready to agree' and willing to go.

At the end of May, George Austen left Godmersham for Bath. Along the way he picked up Cassandra Elizabeth in Kintbury. By June the Austen family was once again together in Bath and shortly thereafter, they took a tenancy at 4 Sydney Place, near the Sydney Gardens, after one of them saw an advertisement that ran on 21 May stating:

> TO BE DISPOSED OF, THE LEASE of No. 4, SYDNEY-PLACE, three years and a quarter of which are unexpired at Midsummer. — The situation is desirable, the Rent very low, and the Landlord is bound by covenant to paint the two first floors this summer. — A premium will therefore be expected.
> For particulars apply to Messrs. Watts and Forman, Cornwall-buildings, Bath.[10]

As the landlord got started fulfilling the promised improvements, the family set off on holiday. Before arriving in Bath, Jane had been anticipating a visit with the Bullers at Dawlish and had even stated, 'we greatly prefer the sea to all our relations'.[11] That had happened so now she was hoping a seaside visit was in store. There had been rumours that the Austens were going to Sidmouth, which was later confirmed by Eliza in a note to Phylly, and so the Austens spent a pleasant summer in Devonshire.

The next big news was the birth of Edward Austen's third daughter, Marianne. She was born on 15 September at Godmersham. Although there may have been correspondence about her birth, all letters that Jane wrote between 26 May 1801 and September 1804 were destroyed. There were also other gaps in correspondence by Jane. Caroline Austen, Jane's niece and James's daughter by his second wife Mary Lloyd, noted this lost correspondence: 'My Aunt [Cassandra] looked them over and burnt the greater part (as she told me), 2 or 3 years before her own death – She left, or gave some as legacies to the Nieces – but of those I have, several had portions cut out.'[12]

In addition, there are also no letters that survive between Henry, Eliza, and Jane, despite it being obvious that they would have regularly corresponded. Everything that is known about Eliza comes primarily from the letters she wrote to her cousin Phylly. Thus, it is supposed that Henry destroyed his wife's letters as he was the person who had access to them.

Exactly why Eliza's letters were destroyed is debated. Author Nicholas Ennos makes an explosive argument that the reason was because Eliza was the author of the books that Jane Austen is given credit for writing. He maintains this, despite as he notes, there being 'no direct evidence that Eliza was an author of any poem or story at all'.[13] Along with some other historians, Ennos also points out that Eliza's letters are energetic and amusing, and read like one of Jane Austen's novels whereas Jane's letters are tedious, rambling, and boring:

> The learned editor of the Dictionary of National Biography and father of Virginia Woolf, Leslie Stephen, considered the letters of Jane Austen, when published in Lord Brabourne's 1884 edition, as trivial. Authors of the twentieth century have also been less than impressed by them. Susan J. Wolfson of Princeton University, in her article *Boxing Emma; or the Reader's Dilemma at the Box Hill Games* sums up excellently the reaction of educated readers to the appearance in print of the letters of Jane Austen, comparing them to the tedious ramblings of the impoverished spinster, Miss Bates. ... Even the best of

the modern biographers of Jane Austen, Claire Tomalin, agrees that the letters of Jane Austen are, in the main, disappointing.[14]

Despite the criticism, Austen supporters maintain that in Jane's unguarded letters she reveals more about society than she did in any of her novels, and that her letters were destroyed because Cassandra Elizabeth and Henry wanted to safeguard the memory of their sister. They claim her siblings wanted to ensure that she was perceived as a good, sweet, and loving person, exactly as James portrayed her with his inscription that marks her grave. Moreover, Austen supporters also maintain that the Austen family probably never imagined at the time of Jane's death that years later, her writing would gain such a following; nor could they have thought that the world would accept the real Jane Austen with her laser-focused satirical wit that at times is utterly merciless in attacking the social structure, the religious, or the pompous.

The destruction of Jane's letters was not a consideration or thought in October 1801 because everyone was mourning the loss of Hastings Jr. News of his demise appeared in London's *Morning Post* where a single line acknowledged the death of the poor, sickly, long-suffering 15-year-old at his home on Friday, 9 October. The only letter and the last surviving piece of correspondence that gives a hint as to Eliza's feelings related to her son was what she sent to Phylly on 29 October, related to the condolence her cousin had expressed:

> My dear Philadelphia, I will not lose the opportunity which You afford me of thanking You for your kind letter ... I am much obliged by your kind participation in an event which though, as You justly consider it, a desirable release has greatly affected my spirits. So awful a dissolution of a near & tender tie must ever be a severe shock, and my mind was already weakened by witnessing the sad variety and long series of pain which the dear sufferer underwent – but deeply impressed as I am with the heart rending scenes I have ever beheld I am most thankful for their termination, and the exchange which I humbly hope my dear Child has made of a most painful existence for a blissful immortality.[15]

A sorrowful Eliza buried her beloved son on Wednesday, 14 October. He was laid to rest with her mother at the churchyard of St John-at-Hampstead, London, NW3. However, it seemed that Eliza had little time to mourn her son's loss because she was also extremely worried about the health of her husband Henry.

She claimed he had been suffering constantly for the past five months and noted his symptoms to be a cough and 'hectic pain' that she attributed to consumption. He had been under the care of Dr Matthew Baillie, a popular physician in London who would later serve as a medical advisor to the Prince Regent.

Henry had, of course, followed Baillie's instructions. He had also taken a variety of medications prescribed by him, all to no avail. Finally, however, Baillie wrote a prescription that Eliza said helped with some of Henry's symptoms and having done that, Eliza reported that her husband suddenly began to heal. In fact, within a few weeks of Hasting Jr.'s passing, Eliza pronounced her husband to be nearly as fit as he had been before his mysterious illness began.

Chapter 17

Treaty of Amiens

> HER PERFECT COMMAND OF FRENCH ... DISARMED ALL SUSPICION.
> JOHN F. HUBBACK ON ELIZA'S FRENCH-SPEAKING ABILITY

Almost a year earlier, Frank had arrived home. He and Henry were to become financial partners in Austen & Co. and were also to work as navy agents. In addition, Henry had signed a secret agreement with Maunde and Charles James, a military writer, confidential agent, and businessman who was a chameleon and who reinvented himself to suit his circumstances. Henry's prospects of great riches appeared to be on track until the Treaty of Amiens happened.

The treaty meant that war was coming to an end and although people wanted peace, it also meant there might be other problems. Peace meant that the patriotic, charitable, and commemorative goods so popular during war would no longer be desired and those selling them would no longer make a living doing so. People like Henry would not be able to profit from war, nor would Frank and Charles be in line for any prizes or promotions from the navy. Recruitment of soldiers to protect England would also no longer be needed. In fact, it would likely mean that unnecessary soldiers and sailors would drift home, flood the labour market, and bring unrest.

The peace treaty was brokered between France and the United Kingdom, and signed in the city of Amiens on 25 March 1802. When the preliminary agreement was announced, it was greeted with immense joy and huge celebrations broke out throughout Europe. Besides the joyous pamphlets, poems, and odes published in French, English, and German, there were plays, vaudeville acts, and stage productions related to the signing of the treaty.

Celebrations also erupted throughout Great Britain that included dancing, parading, drinking to the King's health, firing cannon volleys, distributing money to the poor, ringing church bells, and illuminating the night skies with brilliant fireworks. These celebrations were publicised in most newspapers. For instance, the *Ipswich Journal* reported:

> The inhabitants of Sudbury and Ballingdon testified their joy at the Preliminary Treaty being signed. Several hundred pieces of crape, the different manufactures of those towns, were displayed across the streets, with flags, &c. which had a very pretty effect. Meat, beer, &c to the value of 12gs. raised by subscription was given to the poor of Ballingdon, and a fat lamb was roasted whole at the King's head Inn, of which many gentlemen partook. In the evening the Sudbury Loyal Volunteers paraded, and fired vollies at different parts of the towns. These two places were elegantly illuminated, and a variety of transparencies and devices were exhibited. The town of Clare was illuminated the same evening.[1]

The Treaty of Amiens would provide a fourteen-month interlude of uneasy peace. During this illusionary peace, many people quickly took advantage of it because no one expected it to last. For instance, Madame Tussaud arrived with her wax figures in London having joined in partnership with phantasmagoria showman Paul de Philipstal. The balloonist André-Jacques Garnerin also travelled to London with his wife Jeanne Geneviève. There they staged various balloon displays. In addition, Garnerin made a balloon ascent on 5 July 1802 and travelled seventeen miles in just over fifteen minutes; in case he should crash-land, he was also carrying a letter of introduction signed by the Prince Regent.

Another visitor to England was the famed French socialite Madame Récamier. She was married to one of the richest men in France and when she appeared in London, Englishmen had heard so much about her beauty that she was mobbed. One particularly interesting story at the time involves her and her mother visiting Kensington Gardens. Both women were dressed in white and carried violet-coloured parasols. Within a turn and a half around the garden, Madame Récamier was recognised beneath her white veil. Word of her being at the gardens passed from one person to the next with buzzing excitement, and resulted in the *Caledonian Mercury* later sharing her appearance with its readers:

> They [the crowd] pressed on all sides upon her. Men kneeled down before her to peep up under her veil. Some absolutely seemed disposed to uncover her face. There was nothing but crowding, tumults, and squeezing – the delicacy of the fair objects felt this conduct an insult, and … they left the garden. Their situation outside was not less painful. Grooms and footmen with most insolent curiosity crowded around them. Gentlemen on horseback left the ride and rode up to join the admiring mob. The ladies became alarmed, and feared every moment that they should be crushed to death or trampled down by horses. Their servants could not penetrate the crowd to apprize them of the place where their carriage was in waiting. At length they reached it with great difficulty, but fortunately without receiving any other injury than a terrible fright.[2]

While crowds were mobbing Madame Récamier, many upper-class British citizens also had the desire to cross the border and visit France. William Herschel, a German-born British astronomer, composer, and brother of fellow astronomer Caroline Herschel, took the opportunity to confer with his colleagues at the Paris Observatoire. The prominent British Whig statesman Charles James Fox also travelled to Paris and received a personal tour of the Louvre from one of Napoleon's ministers. The English essayist William Hazlitt arrived in France's capital on 16 October 1802 having been commissioned to travel there and copy several artworks hanging in the Louvre, and thus he spent three months' studying and copying the old Italian masters.

Also deciding it was time to visit France were Eliza and Henry. Eliza still hoped to recover the estate of her late husband and there was no better time to visit, as delaying any longer might further jeopardise her claim. Henry also thought that it was a good time to visit France. It was highly possible that he might be able to make some French connections related to the wine trade. Of course, any such trade agreements would last only as long a peace ruled because during war, French wine was not allowed in England and the only way it came in was if it was smuggled.

To make the trip to France, the couple needed a passport as it was dangerous to travel without one. Lord Spencer recommended Henry and

Eliza and on 28 June 1802, Henry paid the Foreign Office £2.2s.6d. for a joint passport. It was numbered 319.

Exactly when they departed for France remains unclear although it is believed they left in July or August, and that their friend, Mrs Marriott, likely a relative of Randall Marriott from the Hancocks' days in India, went with them. Unfortunately, their trip did not result in Henry or Eliza obtaining anything.

Furthermore, Napoleon revoked the treaty and ordered all foreigners to be detained. His decree of 23 May 1803 meant that every British citizen in France or in any territory held by France could be arrested and interned. This also included the British spouse of any French citizen.

No one seems to know the exact count of British citizens arrested and interned after Napoleon's order, only that it was in the thousands, and that most remained imprisoned until Napoleon's downfall in 1814. Many of those imprisoned also remained just a name on a list, although some warranted files. This included John Cobham Pennie who begged to be released because of his failing health; John Synge Blount who had a friendship with actor John Philip Kemble and thought this relationship would result in his release; and hatmaker Richard Gutch who believed his millinery skills would permit him to work outside the prison.

The story of Eliza and Henry's visit to France supposedly became known when John F. Hubback, son of Catherine Anne Hubback, the eighth child and fourth daughter of Jane's brother Frank, mentioned it. Although several slightly different versions exist, according to Hubback, he overheard his mother and his aunt discussing the life and background of their favourite aunt, Jane Austen. During the conversation there was a mention of Eliza and Henry's trip to France during the Peace of Amiens.

Eliza and Henry went to the French authorities to see what needed to be done for Eliza to regain her husband's estate. Unfortunately, the Count had been executed as a confessed criminal. This allowed the state to confiscate his holdings and they determined that Eliza was not entitled to get anything back. If that wasn't bad enough, Hubback maintained that his mother and aunt stated that Eliza and Henry were still in France when Napoleon revoked the treaty.

Being in France at such a time meant that they could be detained and interned for an unknown period. It was a scary prospect and Eliza and Henry supposedly devised a plan to safely return to England. They determined the only way to safely cross the border was if they disguised themselves as honourable and loyal French citizens. The idea already had the advantage that Eliza spoke flawless French, although that was not the case with Henry. He might be gregarious, clever, and have scholarly abilities but if he opened his mouth, it would be clear that he was one hundred percent English. Therefore, to ensure that Henry would not have to speak, he was disguised as an invalid. Of course, both could also rely on their acting skills honed from the Christmas theatricals in the Austens' barn many years earlier.

As there are no letters or any documents detailing exactly what happened next, I have only my imagination to suggest what might have taken place. The deception began when their dusty carriage carrying them slowed to a stop at the French posting station. Inside Henry was curled up in a corner and covered with a patchwork of blankets for warmth. When the posting guard approached, Eliza lowered the window. He saw Eliza tending to a drowsy Henry, spittle languishing at the corner of his mouth as he gave a half-hearted cough.

Eliza introduced herself as the guard made a cursory glance inside. She mentioned her *pauvre cher mari invalide,* who suffered some unknown disease that made him unable to speak. Noticing Henry's precarious state and the inoffensive vaguely medicinal but distinctively herbal-sweet smell of laudanum, the guard relaxed and listened as Eliza answered each question, despite sweaty palms and the rapid beat of her heart.

At some point, she caringly touched Henry's head and gave a tsk, tsk. It was just enough to indicate it was important they be on their way. Eliza mentioned Henry's daily care and his sickly and pale appearance enhanced that perception. She also let it be known in a most subtle way that it was still necessary for them to cross the border and attend to important business.

With the guard finding himself unable to 'detect her [English] nationality; [and with] her perfect command of French … [it] disarmed all suspicion.'[3] Moreover, everything seemed to be in order. Deciding it was just another carriage of legitimate French travellers and noticing the imminent approach of another ramshackle coach, the posting guard gave a dismissive wave and they were on their way.

Arriving in England, Eliza was supposedly cheered by the Austens for getting Henry home safely, but whether my imagining is anywhere close to what happened at the border, one can only guess. The exact details may also not be as important as the fact that the tale of a disguised couple racked by fear of discovery became a colourful story that enhanced Austen history and could be told at kitchen tables on a rainy day, just like the tale of Harris Bigg-Wither's proposal and Jane's ultimate flight.

A month or so before Napoleon revoked the treaty and sent Britain and France back to war, Jane's brother Charles had returned to active service re-enlisting around April 1803 as a First Lieutenant. With renewed hostilities, Henry moved his office to Cannon Row, Parliament Street. His firm soon obtained agency for two new regiments: Nottinghamshire Militia, whose colonel was Edward Thornton Gould, and the North Devon Militia, whose colonel was John Parker, 2nd Lord Boringdon. In addition, Frank also naturally returned to active duty having received orders from the Admiralty.

Sometime earlier he had met Mary Gibson of Ramsgate. She was the eldest daughter of John Gibson and Mary Curling. Frank proposed to her in early February, perhaps when they attended a play at Covent Garden. However, by July 1803, he was back in Ramsgate organising units called Sea Fencibles.

These units were the brainchild of Admiral Sir Home Riggs Popham. They were established to obstruct enemy shipping operations and defend the coast both on shore and off. Sea Fencibles were also divided into thirty-six companies, with each one responsible for patrolling and defending a certain section of the coastline.

Jane was also busy. She made the final edits to her book *Susan* (the original version of *Northanger Abbey*). Her father then attempted to help her get it published but failed. Henry, although once again hopeful about his banking business, then took over and with the aid of his business partner, William Seymour, who was a lawyer, Jane's book was sold to a London publisher, Crosby & Company. Jane received 10 pounds for it and was thrilled because that was about half her annual allowance and a wonderful deal for an unpublished author. Crosby & Company then advertised that *Susan* would be published in 1803 in a brochure called *Flowers of Literature*. Unfortunately, it failed to appear.

By 1804, Henry and Eliza were no longer occupying number 24 Upper Berkeley Street. They had instead moved to Brompton, a semi-rural area that was a collection of market gardens. Their new place was small and located at 16 Michael's Place, having been named for its Italian architect, Michael Novosielski, who had also worked as a scene designer at Drury Lane, the King's Theatre, and Vanbrugh's original theatre.

With the end of peace, that wasn't the only change for Henry. He and Maunde also moved their banking operations. They now took a 97-year lease on 25 March for No. 1 The Courtyard, Albany, Piccadilly.

A few months later, Frank left his Sea Fencible post and on 7 May was appointed captain of the HMS *Leopard*, a 50-gun Portland-class fourth rate vessel serving as flagship to Rear Admiral Thomas Louis. On 22 May the ship set off with orders to patrol the English Channel between Dungeness and the coastal city of Boulogne in northern France.

Chapter 18

George Austen's Death

> HE WENT OFF ALMOST IN HIS SLEEP.
> JANE AUSTEN TO HER BROTHER FRANK

Near the end of June, a month or so after Frank sailed off on the HMS *Leopard*, Henry and Eliza joined the Austens on holiday. George Austen had likely given up the last quarter of the lease on 4 Sydney Place so that he, his wife, and daughters could tour the southern coastline of Devon and Dorset. He was retired and making the most of it.

It is also believed that it was during this trip that Cassandra Elizabeth created the watercolour view of Jane's back as she sat outdoors looking off into the distance. The watercolour was probably done at Lyme Regis, a town in west Dorset that lies at Lyme Bay on the English Channel coast. It is an area noted for numerous fossils that were found in the Jurassic marine fossil beds off its cliffs along the English Channel. In fact, Mary Anning, an English fossil collector, dealer, and paleontologist, became known worldwide for important finds she made in the area as these contributed to significant changes in scientific thinking about prehistoric life and the history of the Earth.

Lyme Regis was also the spot where the travellers separated. Henry, Eliza, and Cassandra Elizabeth headed to Ibthorpe while Jane and her parents went elsewhere in Lyme. Jane was feeling unwell at the time but found Lyme's healing waters helpful:

> I continue quite well, in proof of which I have bathed again this morning. It was absolutely necessary that I should have the little fever & indisposition, which I had;—it has been all the fashion this week in Lyme. Miss Anna Cove was confined for a day or two … and Miss Bonham has been under Mr. Carpenter's care for several days, with a

sort of nervous fever, and tho' she is now well enough to walk abroad, she is still very tall & does not come to the Rooms.—We all of us, attended them.[1]

On 11 September Jane wrote a letter to her sister at Andover, and in another letter three days later, she mentioned Weymouth, one of the first tourist destinations of the 1700s. This was also the seaside town where King George III's brother, the Duke of Gloucester, built his grand residence, the Gloucester Lodge, and where the King often holidayed, once even venturing into the sea in a bathing machine. Yet, for all the interest by royalty, Cassandra Elizabeth expressed her dissatisfaction with the place and Jane responded:

> Your account of Weymouth contains nothing which strikes me so forcibly as there being no Ice in the Town; for every other vexation I was in some measure prepared, & particularly for your disappointment in not seeing the Royal Family go on board on tuesday ... being too late. But for there being no Ice, what could prepare me!—Weymouth is altogether a shocking place I perceive, without recommendation of any kind, & worthy only of being frequented by the inhabitants of Gloucester.—I am really very glad that we did not go there, & that Henry & Eliza saw nothing in it to make them feel differently.[2]

Cassandra Elizabeth would later provide enlightening information about another seaside trip that happened between 1801 and 1804. It involved her sister Jane meeting a man whom she seriously considered marrying. Cassandra Elizabeth told the details to her niece Caroline, probably around 1828. Caroline, in turn, mentioned the incident stating:

> At Newton, Aunt Cassandra was staying with us ... when we made acquaintance ... with a certain Mr Henry Edridge, of the Engineers. He was very pleasing and very good-looking. My aunt was very much struck with him, and I was struck by her commendation; she so rarely admired strangers. Afterwards, at another time ... she spoke of him ... and said that he reminded her strongly of a gentleman whom they

had met one summer when they were by the sea – I think she said Devonshire; I don't think she named the place, and I am sure she did not say Lyme … – that he seemed greatly attracted by my Aunt Jane … and that when they had to part … he was urgent to know where they would be the next summer, implying or perhaps saying that he should be there also, wherever it might be. I can only say that the impression left on Aunt Cassandra was that he had fallen in love with her sister, and was quite in earnest. Soon afterwards they heard of his death. … I am sure she thought he was worthy of her sister, from the way in which she recalled his memory, and also that she did not doubt, either, that he would have been a successful suitor.[3]

When the Austens returned to Bath, they rented a house, number 3 in Green Park Buildings East. It was on the edge of the city and even less appealing and prestigious than 4 Sydney Place. The Austens had, in fact, crossed Green Park off their list of places to live when they first arrived at Bath, as noted by Jane at the time: 'Our views on G. P. Buildings seem all at an end; the observation of the damps still remaining in the offices of an house which has been only vacated a week, with reports of discontented families & putrid fevers, has given the coup de grace.'[4]

Now they were living at Green Park and just as the Austens were settling in, sad news arrived that Madam Lefroy had died. It happened on Jane's birthday when Madam Lefroy and a manservant rode into Overton. There she saw James and mentioned to him the laziness of her horse and that it would barely canter. Caroline Austen recalled:

> My father rode homeward, she staying to do some errands in Overton; next morning the news of her death reached Steventon. After getting to the top of Overton Hill, the horse seemed to be running away – it was not known whether anything had frightened him – the servant, unwisely, rode up to catch the bridle rein – missed his hold and the animal darted off faster. He could not give any clear account, but it was supposed that Mrs. Lefroy in her terror,

threw herself off, and fell heavily on the hard ground. She never spoke afterwards, and she died in a few hours.[5]

Her death warranted just a line in an Oxford paper stating, 'At Ashe, in Hampshire, by a fall from her horse, Mrs. Lefroy, wife of the Rev. G. Lefroy, Rector of Ashe'.[6] However, a longer explanation appeared in the *Hampshire Chronicle*:

> On Sunday morning died, in consequence of a fall from her horse on the day preceding, much lamented by her family and friends, Mrs. Lefroy wife of the Rev George Lefroy, of Ash, in this county. The poor of her neighbourhood in particular have reason to regret the death of this good lady, who at all times made it her study to alleviate their necessities.[7]

Jane did not immediately express how she felt about the loss of her dear friend Madam Lefroy. However, four years later, it was apparent when she honoured her with some verses and 'grieved bitterly'. Jane showed then that her loss was still fresh.

Another loss soon after Madam Lefroy's passing would be even sadder for Jane. This time it was Jane's father, the patriarch of the family, George Austen. He died on Monday, 21 January 1805. According to Jane in a letter sent to her brother Frank, their father had first become ill on Saturday morning and displayed a fever, violent tremors, and feebleness. That same evening, he seemed to get better and the following morning seemed to have almost recovered as he got up, walked around the house and ate breakfast with the family. Nonetheless, as the day advanced, the fever became stronger.

Things took a turn for the worse by Sunday evening. It was at that time that the doctor declared his patient's situation to be 'most alarming'. On Monday morning the doctor appeared around 9 am and determined the situation to be an 'absolutely' lost cause, and, thus, at 10:20 am George Austen quietly took his last breath. Jane stated:

> Being quite insensible of his own state, he was spared all the pain of separation, & he went off almost in his Sleep. —My Mother bears the Shock as well as possible, she was

quite prepared for it, & feels all the blessing of his being spared a long Illness. My Uncle & Aunt have been with us, & shew us every imaginable kindness. And tomorrow we shall I dare say have the comfort of James's presence, as an Express has been sent to him.—We write also of course to Godmersham & Brompton.[8]

James arrived in Bath on Tuesday morning before 8 am. Frank was on his way in the HMS *Leopard* to Portsmouth and Jane sent him a note telling him that the funeral was to be held on Saturday, 26 January at the Walcot Church. Word also reached Edward's family at Godmersham where Henry was staying, and although Edward could not accompany Henry to Bath, Edward's daughter, Fanny Catherine, wrote that her grandfather was dead and that her Uncle Henry had 'went away'.

Eliza must have been extremely sad at her Uncle George's passing. He had always looked out for her and showed how proud he was of her when she married his son. Further, her Uncle George was one of her last connections to her mother and with him gone, she could no longer lovingly trace her mother's features in the lines of his face.

George Austen was buried in the crypt of St Swithin's Churchyard at Bath, the same church where he had married his beloved wife some fifty-one years earlier. In attendance at his funeral were his wife and some of his children. Frank could not be present and, of course, neither could Charles as he had left in November bound for Bermuda aboard the HMS *Cleopatra*.

With the funeral over, the practicalities of finances came into play. Although George had left his wife everything, most of his income was derived from Deane and Steventon, which also meant his wife and daughters would now have to live on a diminished amount. The brothers thus realised they had to figure out how to support the three women.

Frank quickly sent off a missive that he could offer £100 a year, but his mother refused to take more than half. James and Henry each offered a more modest £50. As Charles was far away it was unclear what he could afford, although the brothers expected their brother Edward to provide £100 annually. Jane had nothing to give and between her mother and sister, they could produce only about £210 a year, meaning the three women were expected to live on approximately £460 annually.

GEORGE AUSTEN'S DEATH

The inability of Henry to provide more than £50 shows that Henry and Eliza's fortune had significantly dwindled. They might be able to continue to live in Brompton and enjoy the benefits of a chef, maids, and a carriage, but things were not necessarily looking good for Henry's future as banking was already a scary prospect and a high-risk undertaking.

Amidst all the discussions of finances, in April, a mention of a brooch made or jointly purchased by Jane and Cassandra Elizabeth was given to Henry and Eliza. It was likely some sort of mourning jewellery made in George's memory and may have even included some of his hair as Jane had cut off a piece and wrapped it in paper with a note that it belonged to her father. Acknowledgement of the brooch by the couple, particularly from Eliza, was said to be warm.

A year after his father's death, Henry had business on his mind. It was then that he became partners in three different banks: Austen Gray & Vincent, Austen Blunt & Louch (later Austen Blunt & Clement), and Austen & Louch. In addition, he and Maunde became London correspondents at two banks: the Horwood Well Bank in Wincanton and the Buxton & High Peak Bank in Buxton. Insurance was also in Henry's thoughts because in February he took out a £2000 policy with the Society for Equitable Assurances.

On 24 July 1806 Frank married Mary Gibson at St Lawrence in the Isle of Thanet. Mundane life swallowed up the rest of 1806 and 1807, with one unpleasant event occurring when Jane suffered from whooping cough around the end of 1806. Another health issue involved Mary Lloyd, who took to her sickbed because of a facial abscess in March 1807.

Meanwhile, as Eliza remained cocooned in Brompton, a routine that resulted in a parallel existence between her and Henry, he welcomed 1807 at Godmersham where he joined with Edward's family in their New Year festivities. A few months later, a business venture occupied Henry's time; in an August newspaper notice Henry and his banking firm solicited subscriptions for shares in The Old English Ale Brewery. Although it would prove fruitless, the intended capital was 75,000*l.* and was to be raised with 3,000 shares sold at 25*l.* payable in four instalments, with the first instalment paid on subscribing. The notice in part stated: 'Establishment of a Public Brewery at the West-end of the Metropolis, for supplying the Inhabitants with a wholesome and nutritious Beverage, to be brewed from MALT and HOPS only, and delivered free from Adulteration.'[9]

At the end of August, Edward and Elizabeth, along with their daughter Fanny Catherine, took a coach and drove to Brompton to spend the day with Eliza. A few months later, on 1 October, they saw them again when they dined with them. Afterwards the group went to Drury Lane where they saw two plays, *The School for Scandal* and *A House to be Sold!!*. The following morning, they shopped, and that evening perhaps because Eliza was worn out from all the activity, Henry dined alone with his visitors.

During this period Eliza's godfather Hastings continued to be present in her life. In fact, she sent him a gift of a breakfast cup and saucer that she had painted and gilded in March 1807. Perhaps pursuit of a porcelain hobby was one of the things she did when leading a life separate from her husband Henry. Eliza's gift to Hastings was also later mentioned in his house inventory as having 'black antique figures painted round'.[10]

Eliza and Henry would pay a visit to her godfather about seventeen months later in August 1808 at his Daylesford estate. Although Eliza may have been trying to maintain a close relationship with Hastings, he appears to not have had great concern to stay connected with her because August is notable for being the last time Hastings mentioned her in any of his diaries. With Eliza's correspondence later destroyed, it is difficult to determine exactly why.

Chapter 19

Friendships

> QUEL HORREUR!!
> FANNY CATHERINE KNIGHT

Although Fanny Catherine did not see her Aunt Eliza regularly, when she did, she was impressed by her. To any young girl Eliza probably seemed exotic. She had been born in India, travelled throughout Europe, and lived for a time in France. As a young girl Fanny Catherine probably imagined what it would be like to live such a life, but instead found herself at fifteen functioning as a caregiver to her siblings after the sudden death of her mother.

Elizabeth, Edward's wife and Fanny Catherine's mother, died on the evening of Monday, 10 October 1808, less than two weeks after she had given birth to a boy on 28 September. The 35-year-old had seemed well and had eaten a hearty dinner, but then immediately afterwards became violently ill and died within a half hour. The doctor was stumped as to her sudden demise.

Edward was inconsolable at the unexpected loss of his wife. Jane wrote a letter to her sister remarking on her brother's immeasurable grief and imaging the sad scene:

> I see your mournful party in my minds' eye under every varying circumstance of the day;—& in the Even^g especially, figure to myself its' sad gloom—the efforts to talk—the frequent summons to melancholy orders & cares—& poor Edward restless in Misery going from one room to the other—perhaps not seldom upstairs to see all that remains of his Elizabeth.[1]

Cassandra Elizabeth had arrived to help with the baby's birth and now she found she had to stay to assist Fanny Catherine in her new position of hostess and caregiver for the children, including her newborn brother. Of course, Henry rushed to Godmersham to mourn and comfort the grieving family. Jane also helped by comforting Edward's two older boys. Of this Tomalin wrote:

> She made paper ships with them, to be bombarded with chestnuts, and organized card games and spillikins. She thought up riddles and charades, and best of all went out on the river with them to see a battleship under construction, allowing them to take the oars of the rowing boat for a good part of the way. She knew from her own childhood what boys enjoy, and felt instinctively how much better it was to cheer them up with excursions and games than to insist on mourning.[2]

Amidst all the sorrow, there was also another change. After George Austen's death, Jane, her sister, and their mother rented a house in Southampton, a spot that had become a spa town in 1740 with its port used for military embarkation, including during the eighteenth-century wars Britain fought against the French. The Austen women stayed there until the summer of 1809 and then moved to Chawton to live in a cottage on Edward's Hampshire estate. Why the idea of moving there earlier hadn't occurred to Edward is anyone's guess, but of their new home Honan wrote:

> [The] cottage stands at the very end of its quiet street as an ample-two-storeyed house of good, rosy Hampshire bricks, a high-pitched roof and two attic dormers, all looking rather larger than it is because of an "L"-shape. A long arm of the "L" lies parallel to the road and meets the shorter arm to form two main downstairs chambers. Mrs. Austen's drawing room is at the left as one faces the road, and her dining room to the right of the front door. James Edward [Austen-Leigh] reports that "a good-size entrance and two sitting-rooms formed the length of the house" … One enters a garden door to find oneself in the drawing room with a cosy dining room beyond, both looking out on the London road. Then one climbs six steps to a cheerful landing, eight steps more,

and sees at the left a bedroom which Cassandra and Jane probably shared, ten feet wide and barely more than thirteen deep. A fireplace at one end, and near a window looking on the garden hangs a patchwork counterpane made by Mrs. Austen.[3]

While the Austen women were settling in at Chawton, Eliza and Henry arrived at Godmersham in August 1809 for a temporary stay with Edward and his family. It had been seven years since Eliza had visited there and she perhaps came this time because she and Henry were moving residences. They were leaving 15 Michael's Place in Brompton for a larger house in Chelsea at 64 Sloane Street, a fashionable street that takes its name from Sir Hans Sloane, an Irish physician, naturalist, and collector, who purchased the surrounding area in 1712.

It had been eight months since Fanny Catherine's mother had died. Seeing her Aunt Eliza was probably a relief. It allowed her to be distracted from her daily duties and be regaled by Eliza's exciting stories of France. Fanny Catherine noted her French-speaking aunt's arrival on Wednesday evening on 22 June 1809 and then remarked on her departure of 15 July calling it 'Quel Horreur!!'

In autumn that same year, Fanny Catherine visited Eliza and Henry twice at their Sloane Street residence. Whatever excitement or interest she felt earlier for her Aunt Eliza was missing during these two visits. Apparently, Fanny Catherine no longer found her aunt so interesting and she even called Eliza's older companions dull and boring, and characterised one evening spent with them as 'stupid'.

None of Jane's letters survive for 1810 and the next mention of Eliza happens in the spring of 1811. Jane had received the proof sheets of *Sense and Sensibility* from her publisher Thomas Egerton. She therefore made a visit at Sloane Street to correct them. Eliza and Jane had always been friendly but now their friendship would deepen as Henry was about to leave on business, and Eliza would be the one to ensure the publisher finished printing Jane's book. Thus, the common goal likely drew the women closer.

During Jane's visit she wrote to her sister Cassandra Elizabeth, mentioned seeing a play at the Lyceum, and remarked on Eliza's activities. As usual, the extroverted Eliza was making plans; this time they involved an upcoming party for her and Henry's fashionable London friends. Jane wrote:

> Eliza ... has plenty of business on her hands just now—for the day of the Party is settled, & drawing near;—above 80 people are invited for next tuesday Even^g & there is to be some very good Music, 5 professionals, 3 of them Glee-singers, besides Amateurs ... One of the Hirelings, is a Capital on the harp, from which I expect great pleasure.—The foundation of the party was a dinner to Henry Egerton & Henry Walter—but the latter leaves Town the day before.[4]

Amidst all the party planning, on Sunday, 21 April 1811, Henry, Jane, and Eliza called on one of Eliza's French friends, Emmanuel Henri Louis Alexandre de Launay, Count d'Antraigues. He had an intriguing past and had joined the army at the age of fourteen, eventually becoming a captain. However, he soon found army life dissatisfying and after meeting Enlightenment philosophers Jean-Jacques Rosseau and Voltaire, he resigned his post in 1778.

When the French Revolution broke out some years later in 1789, d'Antraigues initially supported the revolutionaries. Nonetheless, he became disillusioned with their direction after the Palace of Versailles was stormed and the royal family was threatened, removed, and installed in the Tuileries Palace. He then switched sides and became a staunch Bourbon supporter.

Several plots by royalists were then undertaken to help the royal family escape. One such plot, the Favras plot, was engineered by Thomas de Mahy, marquis de Favras. It involved a scheme to save King Louis XVI and end the Revolution. D'Antraigues was pulled into it but once his role was exposed, he found himself in danger and escaped to Lausanne, Switzerland. He was followed there by his mistress, Madame de Saint-Huberty, a celebrated French operatic soprano and one of Marie Antoinette's favourite opera singers.

Saint-Huberty and d'Antraigues soon married, moved to Italy, and had a son named Julien. D'Antraigues then became a secret agent for Louis XVI's Bourbon brother, the Count of Provence, who later became Louis XVIII. Unfortunately, when the French Directory invaded Italy, d'Antraigues and his family were forced to leave, and they found themselves in Milan where Napoleon Bonaparte interrogated him and learned that he had an association with a counter-revolutionary spy.

Napoleon had d'Antraigues and his family placed under house arrest, but they escaped to Austria, where they lived in Graz and Vienna on an allowance provided by Czar Paul I of Russia. Learning of d'Antraigues' escape and fearing that d'Antraigues had betrayed him to Napoleon, the Count of Provence then dismissed him. This dismissal then caused d'Antraigues to become embittered against him.

In 1802, Czar Alexander I of Russia sent d'Antraigues to Dresden as a Russian attaché. While there he published a scorching pamphlet against Napoleon and the French Empire. D'Antraigues was expelled and he and his family then travelled to London where he developed a close friendship with George Canning, the British Foreign Secretary, and the Duke of Kent, one of King George III's sons.

Eliza and Jane were aware that Canning had been replaced as Foreign Secretary in 1809 but they were unaware that d'Antraigues was desperately worried about his future. They also had no knowledge of the 58-year-old d'Antraigues' conspiratorial nature or involvement in plots. Nor did they know that d'Antraigues, who was colossal in stature and had an 'imposing countenance', was hoping to get rid of his wife. It was evident they were oblivious by what Jane wrote:

> Monsieur the old Count, is a very fine looking man, with quiet manners, good enough for an Englishman—& I believe is a Man of great Information & taste. He has some fine Paintings, which delighted Henry as much as the Son's music gratified Eliza ... Count Julien's performance is very wonderful. We met only Mrs Latouche & Miss East—& we are just now engaged to spend next Sunday Even^g at Mrs L.s—& to meet the D'Entraigues;—but M. le Comte must do without Henry. If he w^d but speak English, I would take to him.[5]

Although Jane might have been willing to befriend a French count, she was less willing to meet and associate with those in literary circles. This included such women as Madame de Staël, a French literary lioness, woman of letters, and dear friend to the French socialite Madame Récamier. In fact, Jane once stated to James's daughter Anna, 'I have made up my mind to like no novels really, but Miss Edgeworth's, yours & my own.'[6]

After having spent what seemed to be a wonderful evening at the d'Antraigues, Eliza unfortunately became ill. It happened when the horses jibbed and slipped their collar on a formidable hill that had been freshly gravelled near the Hyde Park gate as they were heading to the d'Antraigues' residence at 27 The Terrace, Barnes. The incident so frightened Eliza that she got out of the carriage and having been subjected too long to the chilly weather, she developed a chest cold.

Still, a cold in her chest was hardly a compelling reason for her to cancel her party, so two days after her visit, despite not feeling well, Eliza held the event as planned on 23 April 1811. It proved to be a success, lasted past midnight, and was mentioned with a single line in the press although the paper misspelled Austen with Austin. Jane enjoyed the party immensely and described it in her next letter to Cassandra Elizabeth, noting that even though there had been great consternation and 'vexations' before the party, everything turned out 'quite right'.

Eliza likely recalled the fashionable and glittering affairs she had attended while living in Paris and so it was no surprise that she turned her evening event into something reminiscent of those given by the *ancien régime*. Decorations included a rented mirror, numerous floral arrangements, and brilliant chimney lights. There was also mahogany furniture situated on a 'planned' carpet.

The musicians arrived about 7:30 pm and a half hour later, Eliza's 'lordly Company' of friends appeared, sixty-six to be exact, minus the d'Antraigues' family who were unable to attend. With such a crowd, it did not take long for the octagonal drawing room to become hot and stuffy. Partyers then flowed into the cooler nearby passageways to listen to the music at a distance, something that Jane also mentioned doing.

Among the songs played were *In peace Love tunes*, *Rosabelle*, *Poor Insect*, *Prike pe Parp in Praise pof Prapela*, and *The Red Cross Knight*, the last of which was written by the eminent English composer, John Wall Callcott. Between the songs were harp or pianoforte solos. Eliza probably ensured there was a harp because it was an instrument well-known to her as she had taken lessons when young. Moreover, it was also an expensive talent that Jane gave to various characters in her novels such as Mary Crawford in *Mansfield Park*, Georgiana Darcy in *Pride and Prejudice*, and the Musgrove sisters in *Persuasion*.

A singer named Miss Davis also performed. Jane described her as bedecked in blue and having a 'very fine' voice. In addition, Jane found herself extremely popular and like Eliza, who once had a full dance card, Jane noted many men 'fancied' her and mentioned that her gentlemanly enthusiasts included Mr Hampton, Mr Seymour, Mr Knatchbull, Mr Guillermarde, Mr Cure, Captain Simpson, brother to Captain Simpson, Mr Walter, and Mr Egerton.

A few months after Eliza's successful party, Eliza's cousin Phylly married a long-time admirer by the name of George Whitaker of Pembury, Kent. Eliza had lost touch with Phylly after her father's death, partly because Phylly remained occupied caring for her ailing and ageing mother, who finally died at the age of 95. Eliza, who had visited Chawton in early August and was in better health than usual, thus sent a congratulatory note to the newlyweds on 18 August 1811 that in part stated:

> My dear Cousin, Your friends at Chawton have been anxiously searching the Papers ever since the beginning of this month for intelligence of you & they have at length had the pleasure of seeing your Marriage announced. I hope you do not need to be assured of our good wishes, I cannot however let the occasion pass without telling you how much we feel interested by an event so important to you nor how sincerely we rejoice in every prospect of goods that attend it. I think I cannot give you a better wish, than that you may be as happy as you deserve & that as a Wife you may meet the reward you so well earned as a Daughter. Mr. Whitaker will of course feel himself included in every good we desire for you; pray assure him it will give us great pleasure to have an opportunity of being introduced to our new relation, and make our best compts. to his Mother & Sister. I shall hope soon to receive from you a very particular account of your new home.[7]

The following month, Henry and Eliza visited Godmersham once again. Fanny Catherine, who had once so admired Eliza, seemed to be even less enchanted with her than she had been during her last visit to Eliza and Henry in London. In fact, she was conceivably even harbouring dislike for her Aunt Eliza because she wrote in her diary that they had 'got on little' and would never be 'intimate'. This can perhaps be attributed to the difference in their personalities: Eliza's disposition was opposite to Fanny Catherine's cautious, matter-of-fact, and homebody spirit.

Chapter 20

A Time to Mourn

A WOMAN OF BRILLIANT GENEROUS AND CULTIVATED MIND.
HENRY ABOUT ELIZA

Eliza began to suffer increasing health problems after the falling out with Fanny Catherine and around the time that Jane began *Mansfield Park*. As breast cancer tends to run in families, it is likely that the disease was what she was suffering from but whether she initially knew it or not is unclear. She became so ill that she stopped dining with visiting relations and was often unable to receive guests. The bright light that had burned so brightly in her youth had been reduced to a flicker and even it was slowly diminishing.

While Eliza was ill, Henry was busy helping Jane. She paid to have her book *Sense and Sensibility* published, giving the publisher a commission on its sales. The cost to publish it was more than a third of the £460 annually that she, her sister, and mother received. Fortunately, the reviews seemed to bode well for the book making a profit. One of the first reviews appeared in February 1812 in *The Critical Review* by an anonymous source who praised it stating:

> "Sense and Sensibility" is one amongst the few, which can claim their fair praise. It is well written; the characters are in genteel life, naturally drawn, and judiciously supported. The incidents are probably, and highly pleasing, and interesting; the conclusion such as the reader must wish it should be, and the whole is just long enough to interest without fatiguing. It reflects honour on the writer, who displays much knowledge of character, and very happily blends a great deal of good sense with the lighter matter of the piece.

> The story may be thought trifling by the readers of novels, who are insatiable after *something new*. But the excellent lesson which it holds up to view, and the useful moral which may be derived from the perusal, are such essential requisites, that the want of *newness* may in this instance be readily overlooked.[1]

Another review followed in May by the *British Critic* that was even more flattering. Nonetheless, neither review raved about the book but were instead highly encouraging. We recognise Jane Austen's novels today to be 'psychologically realistic' and that is likely the reason people still relate to her characters, but the reviews at the time looked at the book's morality and debated the probability of the events occurring.

As Jane was achieving success in her writing, a man by the name of John Bellingham was reaching his limit and about to make a fateful decision. His troubles had begun years earlier when a Russian ship that belonged to Solomon van Brienen and Vassiley Popoff was lost at sea. At the time, the ship was insured through Lloyd's of London. The ship's owners filed a claim to receive restitution for their loss. Unfortunately, Lloyd's of London received an anonymous letter alleging the ship had been sabotaged, so they refused to pay compensation to the owners.

At the time, Bellingham was working in Russia as an export representative but preparing to leave that country. Van Brienen believed Bellingham had sent the letter to Lloyd's of London and, therefore, he and Popoff took retaliatory action by claiming Bellingham owed them a debt of 4,890 rubles. This meant Bellingham could not depart the country because of the accusations. Van Brienen and Popoff then made matters worse by convincing the Governor-General to arrest Bellingham for the debt. He was then sentenced and forced to serve a year in jail. In the meantime, he was writing letters to the British government asking for help but receiving little response.

When Bellingham was released, he attempted to impeach the Governor-General, which upset Russian authorities, and, caused them to re-arrest Bellingham on another charge and re-imprison him. In 1809, Bellingham left Russia for good and once back in England, he began petitioning Parliament for compensation for his wrongful imprisonment. England had unfortunately broken off diplomatic dealings with Russia and determined Bellingham's petition inadmissible.

This did not dissuade Bellingham and he resumed his attempts to gain relief in 1812 but received no help. Finally, bereft of all hope and upset that Prime Minister Spencer Perceval refused to sanction his claims, he was driven to despair and acted. He purchased two .50 calibre pistols, which he sewed inside his coat pockets. Bellingham made his way to the House of Commons, waited for Perceval's arrival, and, to the shock and horror of everyone, shot and killed him. Mary Lloyd was the only Austen to mention it, but it had to be on the minds of everyone.

A few months after Perceval's assassination, as Henry continued to travel for work and as Eliza's health continued to decline, another shocking murder made headlines in England. This murder happened on Wednesday, 22 July and the victims were well-known to Eliza. It was the Count d'Antraigues and his wife. They had been murdered at home by their Italian manservant Lorenzo Stelli.

Reports indicated that the Count had called for his carriage so that he and his wife could take their regular scheduled Wednesday trip to see a friend. While his wife was waiting in the carriage, the Count descended the stairs with his hat and some papers in his hand. Stelli was waiting at the bottom of the staircase and when the Count was about six steps away, Stelli suddenly aimed a pistol and fired at him.

The pistol Stelli used was one he had stolen from d'Antraigues, along with a Turkish dagger, called a poignard or poniard. Stelli's shot missed its target, passing by the Count, who was so shocked he stood frozen. Stelli then rushed forward and stabbed the Count in the shoulder with the stolen poignard. The blow would prove fatal, but not before the Count was able to flee upstairs to his room.

In the meantime, the Count's wife heard the shot and re-entered the house. She then shrieked in disbelief as Stelli turned his attention to her and attacked. He 'plunged, in the most furious manner, the poinard into her breast. She fell … without any groans, saying only, "Lorenzo, Lorenzo!"'[2]

Stelli was not finished. He then rushed to the Count's bedroom and seized one of the guns that d'Antraigues kept at his bedside. Without hesitation, he put the pistol into his own mouth and pulled the trigger. The bullet killed him on the spot, and he fell face down alongside the dying Count.

Initially it was unclear why Stelli killed the Count and the Countess. It appeared as if he had no reason, but investigators soon discovered that the Countess treated her servants badly. They also learned Stelli was going to be let go by the d'Antraigues and conjecture was that he might have learned about his upcoming dismissal and killed them as revenge. Nonetheless, some people believed the killings were politically motivated, either because of the Count's involvement in the Favras plot or because of Napoleon's or the Count of Provence's unhappiness with him.

Although any thoughts Eliza had on the d'Antraigues' murders have been lost to history, another tragedy soon struck that captured the Austen family's attention. On 14 October 1812 at the age of 59, Catherine Knight passed away. There was a long-standing proviso related to Edward's inheritance that any heir who came into possession of the Knight estates had to change their surname to Knight. On Tuesday, 10 November 1812, less than a month after Catherine's death, Edward's surname was officially confirmed. Of this change, author David Nokes states:

> The most obvious consequence of her death was that Edward was now obliged, by the terms of old Mr. Knight's will, to give up the name of Austen and become a Knight himself. "We have reason to suppose the change of name has taken place," Jane wrote in her letter to Martha, "as we have to forward a letter to Edward Knight Esqre from the lawyer who has the management of the business." Fanny [Catherine] seemed quite distraught at the change. "We are therefore all *Knights* instead of dear old *Austens*,' she wrote. "How I hate it!!!!!!"[3]

Around the same time that Edward was officially becoming a Knight, Henry was negotiating on Jane's behalf with the publisher Thomas Egerton. It involved the publication of Jane's second romantic novel *Pride and Prejudice* that used the working title of *First Impressions*. The sale of the copyright was completed by the end of November with Egerton buying it for £110. It also happened around the same time as the *Edinburgh Review* mentioned *Sense and Sensibility* being a recent publication.

At the end of December, Henry was spending time with some of the newly-minted Knights visiting London. They went to Covent Garden and saw two plays that Fanny Catherine termed 'very good'. The following day Henry went shopping with them and the group dined together again that evening. Both times Eliza was absent, and it can only be presumed that she was not feeling well.

In late January 1813 Jane received her first copy of *Pride and Prejudice*. Henry sent it by coach from London. Other copies also arrived, one for Edward and another for Cassandra Elizabeth. However, Jane requested that a fourth and fifth copy be sent as one was to be given to James and the other was for Frank, who was at Portsmouth. Of her latest book Jane wrote:

> I want to tell you that I have got my own darling Child from London;—on Wednesday I received one Copy, sent down by Falknor, with three lines from Henry to say that he had given another to Charles & sent a 3ᵈ by the Coach to Godmersham; just the two Sets which I was least eager for the disposal of. I wrote to him immediately to beg for my two other Sets, unless he would take the trouble of forwarding them at once to Steven & Portsmouth.[4]

The following day, 28 January, Egerton's first advertisement of *Pride and Prejudice* appeared in the *Morning Post*. It appeared on the second page and stated: 'This day is published, in 3 vols, price 18s. boards, Pride and Prejudice; a Novel. — By a LADY, the Author of "Sense and Sensibility." Printed for T. Egerton, near White-hall.'[5]

Pride and Prejudice would become Jane's most popular book and its title is still recognised by many of those who have never read her novels. Perhaps the book's popularity has something to do with its memorable opening line, 'It is a truth universally acknowledged, that a single man in possession of a good fortune, must be in want of a wife.' The first seven words of this phrase are so popular today that they are often used to advertise and promote all sorts of things.

Much praise also followed the publication of *Pride and Prejudice*. In the meantime, Eliza's health continued to worsen. She was likely suffering from the same painful illness that had taken her mother, and like her mother, Eliza would prove to be long-suffering. The chest cold she had developed after visiting the d'Antraigues was probably the first sign that something was seriously wrong. When Eliza understood the cause, she probably could not help but realise what her future held, having watched her mother suffer and die from breast cancer. Such a realisation had to be depressing.

During Eliza's illness she obtained support from her French servants, Madame Bigeon and her daughter Madame Perigord. The Austen family was less supportive. It can only be guessed why. Perhaps they were put off by her Frenchness, her light-hearted attitude towards religion, or unhappy with her and Henry's parallel lifestyles. The distance may have been a factor that made it difficult to help, or she may have declined their help if they offered it.

If there was any news passing amongst the Austen family about Eliza's condition, it has been lost and even when any of the Austens visited London, they remained silent on the topic of her poor health. When Henry was in Oxford in February, he received news that Eliza's end was approaching. It had been nearly two years since she suffered the chest cold and now it appeared as if things were reaching their conclusion.

Henry headed back to London. He stopped along the way at Chawton on 21 April. It was freezing weather and everyone at Chawton was suffering with a cold. He told his siblings of Eliza's failing health, picked up his sister Jane, and took her with him back to London.

Eliza died three days later at Sloane Street with Jane at her bedside. Eliza was buried in the parish churchyard alongside her mother and son in a spot that is today hidden amongst the full bushes and green trees of St John-at-Hampstead. Jane returned home and after her departure, Eliza's funeral was held. It was a small affair with neither James nor Edward attending. Henry added his own thoughtful epitaph to her gravestone and although today it is faded, it once clearly stated:

> Also in memory of Elizabeth wife of H.T. Austen, Esq. formerly widow of the Comt. Feuillide a woman of brilliant generous and cultivated mind just disinterested and charitable she died after long and severe suffering on the 25th April 1813 age 50 much regretted by the wise and good and deeply lamented by the poor.[6]

Chapter 21

Thoughts of a Writer

As delightful a creature as ever appeared in Print.
Jane Austen on her character Elizabeth Bennet in
Pride and Prejudice

Despite Eliza's passing, stories of her survive. She continues to fascinate Jane Austen's readers and is often referred to as saucy, pleasure-loving, or an incurable flirt. Certainly, aspects of her personality lend themselves to such a description. But Eliza was much more complex and real than any fictional or casual caricature.

Eliza was raised to be a successful woman in the times and culture in which she lived. She was smart and accomplished, and no doubt she got a level of satisfaction from being the centre of attention. Perhaps she was somewhat insecure and needed that kind of validation. Or she may have simply enjoyed making people happy and being entertained by the company of others. A person with her kind of personality is often a people-pleaser, and we can see that while she interacted with others a lot, she rarely got into conflict with them and did not push her own aspirations.

She had few close male role models in her life, and this may have contributed to her not really finding love with a man until she married Henry in her late thirties. Urged by her mother, she seems to have at first pursued an aristocratic life, but then later, perhaps due to the many tragedies she faced, gravitated back toward the Austen family. Even then, she lived somewhat independently, with Henry travelling a lot for business. While she still enjoyed flirtation, there is no evidence of any actual dalliances. In fact, she appears to have been quite loyal to her husbands, disabled child, and family.

Henry no doubt grieved over Eliza. She had been his great love from childhood, and they were married for fifteen years. Nonetheless, he was a practical man, and she had been ill for a long time. No doubt he expected her demise, and so once she passed, he set about quickly settling her affairs and planning his future without her. In addition, less than a month after Eliza's death, when Jane returned to help him, she wrote that it was an 'excellent Journey' that she 'thoroughly enjoyed' despite the depressing circumstances of her trip.

Within two months of Eliza's death, Henry seemed to have rebounded. Perhaps he was aided by Jane, who had taken over the role as his confidante. Jane mentioned her brother's happy state on 3 July when she noted that he was getting along well as a widower. Apparently, he had never been one to mope or mourn:

> We are in hopes of another visit from our own true, lawful Henry very soon, he is to be *our* Guest this time.—He is quite well I am happy to say, ... Upon the whole his spirits are very much recovered.—If I may so express myself, his Mind is not a Mind for affliction. He is too Busy, too active, too sanguine.—Sincerely as he was attached to poor Eliza moreover, & excellently as he behaved to her, he was always so used to be away from her at times, that her Loss is not felt as that of many a beloved Wife might be, especially when all the circumstances of her long & dreadful Illness are taken into the account.—He very long knew that she must die, & it was indeed a release at last.[1]

Henry's future without Eliza included a move into a new residence. Madame Perigord and Madame Bigeon helped him relocate above his office at No. 10 Henrietta Street in Covent Garden. After the move though, Eliza's faithful servants would have a diminished role in Henry's new household, despite finding lodgings in Henry's neighbourhood. As Jane noted, they would 'come to him as often as he likes or as they like'.[2] Of course, Madame Bigeon would also continue to do Henry's marketing, although Jane would soon become his housekeeper.

Things were also looking good for Jane as an author. Her *Sense and Sensibility* sold out by July. In addition, it was clear that *Pride and Prejudice* would be a big hit too. Jane was also in the throes of finishing *Mansfield Park*, which meant she had more high hopes on the horizon.

Henry visited Warren Hastings at his Daylesford estate in August, but Henry's visit prompted no consolatory remarks from Hastings about his goddaughter or Henry's loss. This startling lack of condolence was improper if not shocking to Jane and she wrote, 'Mr Hastings never *hinted* at Eliza in the smallest degree'.[3] She might have been even more critical of him if she had realised that he also failed to mention Eliza's death in his diary. Yet, perhaps Hastings' actions were not shocking when one considers he has been characterised in the following fashion:

> [Hastings] in his private life ... [was] a cold, cruel, and selfish man and he unfortunately left a trail of broken lives in the wake of his ambition. ... he was amongst the most corrupt and venal of the employees of the East India Company at the time.[4]

A month or so after Henry's visit, he sent Hastings a copy of Jane's *Pride and Prejudice*, of which Hastings offered great praise. Henry was just as proud of his sister and could not keep silent about the book's author. He was soon spreading the word and among those who discovered Jane's identity was the Prince Regent. He had bought *Sense and Sensibility* for 15 shillings from Becket & Porter on 28 October 1811 (two days before it was publicly advertised), and although he was one of her biggest fans, the feelings she had for him were not mutual as she was put off by his disreputable and immoral ways.

The Prince Regent discovered the identity of the author because of Henry. Around mid-October 1815, after Henry was living at 23 Hans Place, he was not feeling well. He was soon bled twice but it did not help, and he had to cancel plans to go to Oxfordshire. He continued to worsen and on Sunday, 22 October, Jane was concerned enough to send an express on his condition to her family members. She also called in a second doctor, Dr Matthew Baillie, who had attended to Henry before and who was now the Prince Regent's physician.

While under his care, Henry let slip Jane's authorship. The doctor, knowing that the Prince Regent was a fan, relayed this juicy bit of news to him. He promptly invited Jane to visit him and as he was the Prince Regent, she had to go. When it was hinted that she should dedicate *Emma* to him, she had to do that too, but she did it with no pleasure. Jane's favourite nephew James Edward Austen-Leigh related the incident:

> [The doctor] informed her one day that the Prince was a great admirer of her novels; that he read them often, and kept a set in every one of his residences; that he himself therefore had thought it right to inform his Royal Highness that Miss Austen was staying in London, and that the Prince had desired Mr. Clarke, the librarian of Carlton House, saying that he had the Prince's instructions to show her the library and other apartments, and to pay her every possible attention. The invitation was of course accepted, and during the visit to Carlton House Mr. Clarke declared himself commissioned to say that if Miss Austen had any other novel forthcoming she was at liberty to dedicate it to the Prince. According such a dedication was immediately prefixed to 'Emma,' which was at that time in the press.[5]

In April 1814, a year after Eliza's death, the Treaty of Fontainebleau was agreed to between Napoleon Bonaparte and representatives from Russia, Prussia, and the Austrian Empire. The treaty was signed on 11 April in Paris and ratified two days later. It ended Napoleon's rule as emperor of France and sent him into exile on Elba.

Many people were ecstatic about Napoleon's dethronement including the *Cobbett's Weekly Political Register* which noted it with much glee:

> The powers of the continent, having got rid of their dread ... I shall not be at all surprised to hear many others ... regret the fall of Napoleon. ... The alarm is over; The old maiden ladies will sleep in peace ... News will now come from the Continent by post, and to every one who may have a mind to receive it. It will be no longer *treason* to correspond with France, or to shake a Frenchman by the hand. ... There is great good. The *bugbear* is gone: The *hobgoblin* is destroyed: Reason will now resume her sway.[6]

Despite the celebration that Napoleon was no longer a threat, he would return less than a year later and spread fear after escaping from Elba. Fortunately, the fear was short-lived. Arthur Wellesley, 1st Duke of Wellington, ended the spectacular career of Napoleon, along with twenty-three years of persistent conflict between Europe and France, at the Battle of Waterloo; thereafter, Waterloo became a word that today represents insurmountable difficulties and irreversible defeat.

The defeat of Napoleon brought peace, but peace would soon pose economic turmoil for anyone associated with war and that is precisely what happened to Henry. In addition, shortly after Eliza's death, Henry began thinking about taking a new wife. Three possibilities included a Miss Burdett, a chatty Miss Moore, and a Berkshire widow, Mrs Crutchley. But with Napoleon's downfall, Henry found the possibility of marriage must be postponed because a period of financial uncertainty followed. In fact, his banking activities collapsed, which then forced him to declare bankruptcy in March 1816, with *The Times* and the *London Gazette* both reporting on it.

Adaptive as always, Henry seemed hardly fazed by his declaration of bankruptcy and was reportedly as 'cheerful as ever'. In fact, by the end of March he had decided to switch vocations. He then followed James's example by embracing a church role, something that had been expected of Henry before he joined the military. He was thus by December 1816 thundering on Sundays at Chawton, having been ordained a deacon before becoming a curate. Seeing Henry in action in his new profession, Jane wrote to a nephew stating, 'Uncle Henry writes very superior Sermons'.[7]

As Henry was engrossed with his new career in the church, everyone likely expected Jane would enjoy a long career. She was focused on her novels, and people thought that her readership would increase and that she would produce many more books of pleasing entertainment and long-lasting amusement. But this was not the case. Jane soon developed a severe illness that Henry mentioned:

> [T]he symptoms of a decay, deep and incurable, began to show themselves in the commencement of 1816. Her decline was at first deceitfully slow; but in the month of May, 1817, it was found advisable that she should be removed to Winchester for the benefit of constant medical aid, which none, even then, dared to hope would be permanently beneficial.[8]

Resignation of Jane's sad and unfortunate fate occurred over the next two months. Despite it all, her personality remained the same with bouts of temper, cheerfulness, or warmth. She also 'retained her faculties' to the end and one of the last things she mentioned was her gratefulness to her medical attendants. In addition, when asked for a final time if there was anything she wanted, she replied 'I want nothing but death.'[9]

Death came shortly thereafter when she passed away in the arms of her beloved sister on Friday, 18 July 1817. That same month, Jane was buried at Winchester Cathedral surrounded by a grief-stricken family. Henry arranged for her burial in the north aisle of the nave, and her brother James composed the epitaph for the slab that would mark where she would be laid to rest:

> In memory of Jane Austen, youngest daughter of the late Revd. George Austen, formerly Rector of Steventon in this County. She departed this life on July 18, 1817 aged 41, after a long illness, supported with the patience and hope of a Christian. The benevolence of her heart, the sweetness of her temper, and the extraordinary endowments of her mind, obtained the regard of all who knew her, and the warmest love of her immediate connexions. Their grief is in proportion to their affection: they know their loss to be irreparable, but in their deepest affliction they are consoled by a firm, though humble, hope that her charity, devotion, faith, and purity have rendered her soul acceptable in the sight of her Redeemer.[10]

As retrospective diagnoses are difficult to provide, there's no way to know with absolute certainty what caused Jane's death. However, in 1964, Sir Vincent Zachary Cope, an English physician, surgeon, author, historian, and poet, proposed that Jane died from Addison's. This was a disease named for Thomas Addison, a British physician, who described the condition in 1855, noting that it was a long-term endocrine disorder in which the adrenal glands do not produce enough steroid hormone. Although some historians believe Jane suffered with Addison's throughout her life, they claim she didn't die from it. They maintain because of chronic adrenal insufficiency, she developed a secondary infection and died from lymphoma or tuberculosis.

Before Jane died, she appointed Henry her 'literary executor'. He was thus the first to add basic biographical information about her to the posthumously published novels *Northanger Abbey* and *Persuasion* issued in December 1817 but dated 1818. Eventually he also provided much more detailed information in *Sense and Sensibility* under the title of 'Memoir of Miss Austen' published by Richard Bentley in 1833.

A year after Jane's death, Eliza's unacknowledged father, Warren Hastings, died on 22 August 1818. He reportedly died quietly 'without a grunt, a sigh, or the slightest appearance of convulsion'.[11] Interestingly, despite him receiving substantial compensation from the EIC, he overspent just as he had done years earlier and was thus technically insolvent at the time of his death.

The lack of funds apparently did not matter because his funeral was splendid and costly. His remains were attended to by undertaker Goodman Parsons and taken from Daylesford House to Daylesford Church on Sunday, 30 August. It was there that he was interred after receiving what was described as an 'affecting sermon' based on the fourth verse of the 23rd Psalm. The funeral procession to the interment site was also lengthy. It included a carriage for the clergy and pall bearers, one for his surgeons, two mourning coaches, a family carriage, and ten additional carriages for attendants.

Jane's brother James was the next to die. It happened on a frosty, cold Monday on 13 December 1819. He was buried at St Nicholas Church in Steventon five days later. A plaque in his honour can be found in the church. In the later years of his life, his health deteriorated and he suffered many digestive complaints. In fact, he had a severe flare-up on the day of Jane's funeral, could not attend, and sent his son in his place. James also suffered a strain with his family members over how Mary Lloyd treated his first daughter Anna. As she grew and spent more time with her aunts, he distanced himself even further from his siblings.

Jane's mother passed away eight years after James. She was 87 at the time of her death and was buried in the Chawton cemetery. Her daughter, Cassandra Elizabeth, was then left alone. She continued to receive and visit friends and relatives. In 1843, as mentioned, she burned some of Jane's correspondence, but it was also because of her that her nieces and nephews learned of Jane and kept her memory alive.

Cassandra Elizabeth had a stroke in March 1845 while on a trip to see her brother Frank. He was about to depart to take command of the Royal Navy's North American Station when it happened, so she moved in with Henry at his home in Porchester House near Portsmouth. He remained her caregiver until she died on 22 March 1845 at the age of 72. Her body was then returned to Chawton and she was buried alongside her mother at St. Nicholas Church.

Henry was the next to pass away. After Jane's death, he continued to pursue his calling in the church, even becoming 'zealous' in the gospel. He served as the Steventon rector from December 1819 to 1822 and married Eleanor Jackson in 1820. He then served as the Farnham curate in Surrey from 1822 to 1827 and was also curate near Alton in Hampshire from 1824 until 1839. He spent his last years at Colchester, Essex, and Tunbridge Wells, which is where he was buried at the Woodbury Park Cemetery after his sudden death on 12 March 1850.

Charles, who had been shadowed by misfortune and poverty, died at the age of 73 from cholera. It happened on 7 October 1852 while he was commanding the British expedition during the Second Anglo-Burmese War. He had led a distinguished naval career and was given command of the 36-gun frigate HMS *Phoenix* around the time of Napoleon Bonaparte's escape from Elba when he was sent to search for a Neapolitan squadron suspected to be at large at the time. In addition, like his siblings, Charles was a fan of his sister's works, and when *Emma* was published Jane sent him a copy to which he replied: 'Emma arrived in time to a moment. I am delighted with her, more so I think than even with my favourite Pride & Prejudice, & have read it three times in the Passage.'[12]

A little over a month after Charles's death, the well-loved Edward died at the age of 84 on 19 November 1852. He had never remarried and had been looked after by his daughter Fanny Catherine and a sister-in-law. He had always led a healthy life and died peacefully in his sleep. He will be eternally remembered for Jane dedicating her juvenile work, *The Three Sisters*, to him.

The last of Jane's siblings to pass away was Frank. After his first wife died, he got married in 1828 to Jane's dearest friend and confidante Martha Lloyd, Mary Lloyd's sister. Martha died in 1848. Frank survived another seventeen years before he passed away at his home in Portsdown Lodge at Widley in Hampshire on 10 August 1865. He was buried in the churchyard at St Peter and St Paul, Wymering, Portsmouth.

Although Jane Austen is more famous today than she was during her lifetime, there is no question that Eliza inspired her. She could not have written her fascinating characters without Eliza because she embodies many of the characteristics found in Jane's female characters.

For instance, there is Lady Bertram who obsessively loved her pug in *Mansfield Park*, and who can forget the scene in *Northanger Abbey* where Catherine Morland's imagination takes over just like Eliza's did while waiting at Farquhar's office. The harp-playing abilities of Mary Crawford, Georgiana Darcy, or the Musgrove sisters also mirror Eliza's own talented musical abilities.

Everyone also agrees that Eliza was cultured, charming, vivacious, smart, and clever. Many of Jane's characters also possess these characteristics. For instance, there is Elizabeth Bennet in *Pride and Prejudice* who Jane described 'as delightful a creature as ever appeared in print, & how I shall be able to tolerate those who do not like *her* at least, I do not know.'[13]

Although Eliza may not have been as appealing as Elizabeth Bennet, the real Eliza was like Elizabeth in several ways. She was intellectual, intelligent, and quick-witted. Eliza could also verbally spar with anyone and Elizabeth's 'liveliness' of her mind is the reason Mr Darcy fell for her. Elizabeth and Eliza were likewise appealing, beautiful women adept at successfully manoeuvring within the male-dominated power structure of their time.

Eliza has also been described as the consummate coquette and someone who flirted outrageously, a skill that Jane gifted to several of her female characters. For instance, there was Lucy Steele in *Sense and Sensibility,* who captured the hearts of two brothers, much like Eliza did with James and Henry, and there was also the beautiful and charming Mary Crawford of *Mansfield Park*. No reader can forget the flirtatious Lady Susan, who has been described as a sociopath with her vain, self-centred, guiltless, manipulative, and loveless ways. In fact, some people believe Lady Susan was based on Eliza and point to her letters that sometimes reveal a calculating, self-centred, and vain person and someone that even Eliza pointed out liked to maintain the upper hand in her relationships with the opposite sex.

Just like many of Jane's characters, Eliza also showed strong will, graceful deportment, and intellectual abilities. After her first husband's death, she did not want to lose her liberty or give up her freedom to a man. In fact, Eliza wrote at one point about the idea of remarriage:

> I was most highly entertained with your account of Lady Frances B's *modest attempt* on Mr. S. whom She will

certainly carry by Storm, unless you kindly condescend to Chaperon him – Pray let me know how this affair comes on … She certainly pays a great Compliment to the married state by wishing to engage in it a fourth time – I am sure I find it difficult enough to determine on a second. Be satisfied My Dear Phillida that I cannot take amiss any thing that your Friendship may prompt on this subject, and that I am fully sensible of the truth & justice of the observations in your last, but *my impulse* in favour of Liberty & disfavor of a Lord & master, is as irresistible as Mr. Merlin's.[14]

One book often cited as having great parallels with Eliza's life is a piece of juvenilia written by Jane and titled *Henry & Eliza*. It is the tale of a childless couple, Sir George and Lady Harcourt, who discover in their 'Haycock' a 'beautifull little Girl.' They adopt her, name her Eliza, and give her a good education. She is also taught to be virtuous but when she is 18, she is caught stealing a £50 banknote and turned out from Harcourt Hall.

The fictious Eliza's best friend then introduces her to the 'Dutchess of F.' who takes her in as a companion and treats her as she does her own daughter, Lady Harriet. However, just as Lady Harriet is set to marry Henry Cecil, he and Eliza fall in love, secretly marry, and flee to France pursued by 300 armed men hired by the Dutchess of F. to return them at any cost.

Fictional characters Henry and Eliza then spend three years in France, during which time she gives birth to two sons before Henry dies. Unable to survive without her husband, Eliza immediately sets sail for England, but no sooner does she set foot on English soil than she is seized by officers who throw her into a dungeon, a 'snug little Newgate,' built by the Dutchess of F. specifically for her.

Eliza then escapes and returns with her sons to Harcourt Hall where her voice reminds Lady Harcourt that Eliza is her natural daughter. Apparently, Eliza was born while Sir George was away in America and hidden by Lady Harcourt because she was not a boy. Lady Harcourt realises she must tell her husband the truth, and thus Eliza is forgiven for stealing the banknote and she and her two sons return to live at Harcourt Hall.

Then a dramatic ending unfolds. Jane allows Eliza to achieve a heroine's reward. She writes that Eliza 'raised an Army, with which she entirely demolished the Dutchess's Newgate, snug as it was, and by that act, gained the Blessing of thousands, & the Applause of her own Heart.'[15]

The tale of *Henry & Eliza* also seems to further suggest that Eliza was indeed Hastings' child. Moreover, the real Eliza had a life much like that of the fictional Eliza: she lived in France, she married Henry, and she was left to bring up a son alone after de Feuillide's death. However, where the fictional Eliza is acknowledged by her father, Hastings never acknowledged the real Eliza as his daughter and even remained quiet about her death.

According to other historians and writers, including twenty-first century author Nicholas Ennos, there is more than just Jenny's allegations or Clive's remarks to make the case for Hastings fathering Eliza. Hastings was always at the centre of his goddaughter's life and she displayed characteristics shown by Hastings. For instance, she was highly intelligent just like Hastings, who was 'one of the most educated, intelligent and learned people in eighteenth century England and who, on his retirement, devoted himself entirely to reading and writing literature'.[16]

Ennos also points to the fact that Eliza learned the classical languages of Latin and Ancient Greek, which was unusual for females at the time. As Hastings was a great scholar of them, it is contended that he thought it imperative for her to have such knowledge because she was likely his child. Ennos also claims that it would have been a huge embarrassment for the Austen family to have Hastings revealed as Eliza's father and so her illegitimacy was covered up.

To further prove his point, Ennos asserts that Hancock all but verified Hastings was Eliza's biological father in writing. Ennos explains it thus:

> Mr. Hancock ... confirms Warren Hastings' parenthood in a letter dated 11th December 1772 in which he says that Warren Hastings had given 40,000 rupees (approximately £5,000) to him for the benefit of Eliza "under the polite Term of making his God daughter a present". In an earlier letter to his wife of 23rd September 1772 Hancock had written that "Debauchery under the polite name of Gallantry is the Reigning Vice of the Settlement". We can therefore be sure that "polite name" was Hancock's term for

a euphemism, and that the idea that Hastings was Eliza's godfather was merely a polite fiction. In the same letter of 23rd September 1772, Hancock also wrote pointedly to his wife, "You Yourself know how impossible it is for a young Girl to avoid being attached to a Young Handsome Man whose address is agreeable to Her."[17]

As conjecture of Eliza's true biological father continues, Jane's novels have gone on to outlive their author. Her books almost always use an all-knowing narrator to help create lifelike characters and credible events. In addition, she helps readers understand her characters through emotionally- and intellectually-charged dialogue. With her pen she has established herself as the queen of the romantic novel, served as a subtle satirist on life, and offered astute observations on human behaviour. Nonetheless, although Jane Austen may be lauded for writing memorable and realistic stories about life, one can never forget that it was her outlandish and flirtatious cousin, Eliza de Feuillide, who lived life to its fullest and inspired Jane.

Bibliography

Abbott, J.S.C., *Marie Antoinette*, New York: Brunswick Subscription Company, 1917.
Adams, O.F., *The Story of Jane Austen's Life*, Chicago: A.C. McClurg, 1891.
Anon, *A Guide to all the Watering and Sea Bathing Places in England and Wales, with a Description of the Lakes; A Sketch of a Tour in Wales, and Itineraries*, London, 1824.
Arbiter, P., *Memoirs of the Present Countess of Derby, late Miss Farren; Including Ancedotes of Several Distinguished Persons*, London: H. D. Symonds, 1797.
Austen, J., *The Loiterer: A Periodical Work*, Dublin: William Porter, 1792.
Austen, J., *Mansfield Park*, London: Richard Bentley, 1833.
Austen, J., *Sense and Sensibility: A Novel*, London: Richard Bentley, 1833.
Austen, J. and Oulton, L., *The Watsons*, New York: D. Appleton, 1923.
Austen-Leigh, J., 'New Light Thrown on JA's Refusal of Harris Bigg-Wither', *Journal of the Jane Austen Society of North America - Persuasions*, No. 8, 1986 http://www.jasna.org/persuasions/printed/number8/austen-leigh.pdf.
Austen-Leigh, J.E., *A Memoir of Jane Austen: To Which are Added Lady Susan and Fragments of Two Other Unfinished Tales by Miss Austen*, London: Richard Bentley & Son, 1882.
Austen-Leigh, R.A. (ed.), *Austen Papers 1704–1856*, London, 1995.
Austen-Leigh, W. and Austen-Leigh, R.A., *Jane Austen: Her Life and Letters A Family Record*, New York: E.P. Dutton & Company, 1913.
Baker, H.B., *History of the London Stage and Its Famous Players (1576–1903)*, New York: George Routledge and Sons, Limited, 1904.
Bence-Jones, Mark, *Clive of India*, London: St Edmundsbury Press Limited, 1974.
Blaikie, T., *Diary of a Scotch Gardener at the French Court at the End of the Eighteenth Century* (Cambridge: Cambridge University Press, 2012)

BIBLIOGRAPHY

Campbell, R., *The London Tradesman*, London: T. Gardner, 1757.

Chapman, C., 'Jane Austen's Banker Brother: Henry Thomas Austen of Austen & Co., 1801–1816', *Journal of the Jane Austen Society of North America - Persuasions*, No. 20, 1998 http://www.jasna.org/persuasions/printed/number20/caplan.pdf.

Chesterfield, P.D.S., *Genuine Memoirs of Asiaticus: In a series of letters to a friend, during five years residence in different parts of India*, London: G. Kearsley, 1784.

Christie, T., *The Analytical Review, Or History of Literature, Domestic and Foreign, on an Enlarged Plan*, v. 27, London: J. Johnson, 1798.

Claretie, J., *Camille Desmoulins, Lucile Desmoulins: Étude sur les dantonistes*. aris: E. Plon and Cie, 1875.

Clark, J.R., and Motto, A.L., *Satire--that blasted art*, New York: Putnam, 1973.

Cotton, E., *Calcutta, Old and New: A Historical & Descriptive Handbook to the City*, Calcutta: W. Newman, 1907.

Devert, A.M., 'Le Marais de Gabarret et de Barbotan', *Bulletin de la Société de Borda*, No. 340 (1970): 331–50.

Dickens, C., *Household Words: A Weekly Journal*, v. 15, London: Charles Dickens, 1857.

Ennos, N., *Jane Austen: A New Revelation*, Manchester: Senesino Books Limited, 2017.

Forrest, G., *The Life of Lord Clive*, v. 2. London: Cassell, 1918.

Galt, J., *George the Third, His Court and Family*, v. 1. London: H. Colburn, 1821.

Grier, S.C., *The Letters of Warren Hastings to His Wife*, Edinburgh: W. Blackwood and Sons, 1905.

Hastings, W., and Grier, S.C., *The Letters of Warren Hastings to His Wife*, Edinburgh: W. Blackwood, 1905.

Honan, P., *Jane Austen: Her Life*, New York: St. Martin's Press, 1987.

Jackson, C.C., *The French Court and Society: Reign of Louis XVI and First Empire*, 2 vols. v. 1. Boston: L. C. Page and Company, 1897.

Kincaid, D., *British Social Life in India, 1608–1937*, London: George Routledge and Sons, Limited, 1938.

Le Faye, D., 'Jane Austen and Her Hancock Relatives *The Review of English Studies* 30, No. 117 (1979): 12–27. Accessed 22 January 2019. doi:10.1093/res/XXX.117.12. https://academic.oup.com/res/article-pdf/XXX/117/12/9928628/12.pdf.

Le Faye, D., (ed.) *Jane Austen's Letters*, 3rd. Oxford: Oxford University Press, 1997.

Le Faye, D., *Jane Austen's 'Outlandish Cousin': The Life and Letters of Eliza de Feuillide*, London: The British Library, 2002.

Le Faye, D., *Jane Austen: A Family Record*, 2nd ed. Cambridge: Cambridge University Press, 2004.

Malleson, G.B., *Life of Warren Hastings, First Governor-general of India*, London: Chapman & Hall, LD, 1894.

Mitchell, C., and Mitchell, G., 'Passages to India', *The Times Literary Supplement*, Accessed 5 February 2019. https://www.the-tls.co.uk/articles/public/passages-to-india/.

Nokes, D., *Jane Austen: A Life*, Berkeley: University of California Press, 1998.

O'Leary, M.R., *Forging Freedom: The Life of Cerf Berr of Médelsheim*, Bloomington: iUniverse, 2012.

Oulton, W.C., *Picture of Margate and its vicinity*, London: Baldwin, Cradock & Joy, 1820.

Ripley, G., and Dana, C.A., (eds.) *The New American Cyclopædia*, New York: D. Appleton and Company, 1859.

Schama, S., *Citizens: A Chronicle of the French Revolution*, New York: Alfred A. Knopf, 1989.

Schwartz, R.B., *Daily Life in Johnson's London*, Madison: University of Wisconsin Press, 1983.

Sprange, J., *The Tunbridge Wells Guide ... Or, An Account of the Ancient and Present State of that Place: To which is Added a Particular Description of the Towns and Villages*, J. Sprange, 1786.

The Athenæum, London: J. Francis, 1849.

The Critical Review: Or, Annals of Literature, 1. London: W. Simpkin and R. Marshall, 1812.

Tomalin, Claire, *Jane Austen: A Life*, New York: First Vintage Books, 1997.

Tucker, G.H., *Jane Austen the Woman: Some Biographical Insights*, New York: St. Martin's Griffin, 1995.

Walton, G. *Marie Antoinette's Confidante: The Rise and Fall of the Princesse de Lamballe*, London: Pen and Sword Books Ltd, 2016.

Woolsey, S.C., (ed.), *The Letters of Jane Austen*, Boston: Little, Brown, 1905.

Yonge, C.D., *The Life of Marie Antoinette, Queen of France*, New York: Harper & Brothers, 1876.

BIBLIOGRAPHY

Articles in Newspapers

Bath Chronicle and Weekly Gazette, 'To Be Disposed of', 21 May 1801.

Blackwood's Edinburgh Magazine, v. 175. London: William Blackwood, 1904.

Caledonian Mercury, 'Brest, Aug 11', 20 August 1789.

Caledonian Mercury, 'Madame Recamier', 13 May 1802.

Chester Chronicle, 'Riot in Mount-Street', 15 June 1792.

Cobbett's Weekly Political Register, 16 April 1814.

Hampshire Chronicle, 'Winchester', 24 December 1804.

Ipswich Journal, 'Sunday's Post', 20 May 1797.

Ipswich Journal, 'Ipswich, Oct. 24', 24 October 1801.

Kentish Gazette, 'Ceremonial for the Nuptials of Frederick William, Hereditary prince of Wirtemberg, Stutgardt, with Charlotte-Augusta Matilda', 23 May 1797.

Morning Advertiser, 'The Old English Ale Brewery', 26 September 1807.

Norfolk Chronicle, 'Sunday and Tuesday's Post', 9 August 1788.

Norfolk Chronicle, 'Revolution in France', 12 September 1789.

Norfolk Chronicle, 'Revolution in France', 19 September 1789.

Northampton Mercury, 'Sunday and Tuesday's Posts', 25 April 1795.

Oxford Journal, 'Country Fair', 29 December 1804.

Royal Cornwall Gazette, 'Dreadful Murder', 1 August 1812.

Salisbury and Winchester Journal, 'Thursday', 11 February 1788.

Salisbury and Winchester Journal, 'Salisbury', 31 August 1818.

Saunders's News-Letter, and Daily Advertiser, 'Foreign Intelligence', 6 June 1789.

The Morning Post, 28 January 1813.

The Times, 'France: Imprisonment of the King and Queen, and the Late Massacre', 23 September 1792.

Endnotes

Chapter 1 – Aspirations for a Better Life

1. R. Campbell, *The London Tradesman* (London: T. Gardner, 1757), 208
2. Ibid., 208–9
3. D. Nokes, *Jane Austen: A Life* (Berkeley: University of California Press, 1998), 29
4. D. Le Faye, *Jane Austen's 'Outlandish Cousin': The Life and Letters of Eliza de Feuillide* (London: The British Library, 2002), 12–13
5. D. Kincaid, *British Social Life in India, 1608–1937* (London: George Routledge and Sons, Limited, 1938), 82
6. G. Forrest, *The Life of Lord Clive* v. 2 (London: Cassell, 1918), 311
7. E. Cotton, *Calcutta, Old and New: A Historical & Descriptive Handbook to the City* (Calcutta: W. Newman, 1907), 87
8. G. Ripley and C.A. Dana, (eds.), *The New American Cyclopædia* (New York: D. Appleton and Company, 1859), 308

Chapter 2 – Betsy

1. C. Mitchell and G. Mitchell, 'Passages to India', *The Times Literary Supplement*, accessed 5 February 2019, https://www.the-tls.co.uk/articles/public/passages-to-india/
2. Mark Bence-Jones, *Clive of India* (London: St Edmundsbury Press Limited, 1974), 220
3. D. Le Faye, 2002, 18
4. Ibid.
5. *Blackwood's Edinburgh Magazine* v. 175 (London: William Blackwood, 1904), 499
6. J.E. Austen-Leigh, *A Memoir of Jane Austen: To Which are Added Lady Susan and Fragments of Two Other Unfinished Tales by Miss Austen* (London: Richard Bentley & Son, 1882), 7
7. C. Mitchell and G. Mitchell

8. Ibid.
9. R.B. Schwartz, *Daily Life in Johnson's London* (Madison: University of Wisconsin Press, 1983), 52
10. Ibid., 52–53
11. *Blackwood's Edinburgh Magazine*, v. 175, 499
12. D. Le Faye, *Jane Austen: A Family Record*, 2nd ed. (Cambridge: Cambridge University Press, 2004), 35–36
13. D. Le Faye, 2002, 23–24
14. *Blackwood's Edinburgh Magazine*, v. 175, 500
15. Ibid., 501

Chapter 3 – Back in India

1. Ibid., 504
2. N. Ennos, *Jane Austen: A New Revelation* (Manchester: Senesino Books Limited, 2017), 300
3. R.A. Austen-Leigh, (ed.), *Austen Papers 1704–1856* (London, 1995), 25
4. C. Dickens, *Household Words: A Weekly Journal* v. 15 (London: Charles Dickens, 1857), 239
5. J. Galt, *George the Third, His Court and Family* v. 1 (London: H. Colburn, 1821), 368
6. *Blackwood's Edinburgh Magazine*, v. 175, 503
7. D. Nokes, 1998, 30
8. D. Le Faye, 2002, 27
9. *Blackwood's Edinburgh Magazine* v. 175, 504
10. D. Le Faye, 2002, 31
11. Ibid., 33

Chapter 4 – Tysoe Hancock's Last Stand

1. R.A. Austen-Leigh, (ed.), 65–66
2. C.D. Yonge, *The Life of Marie Antoinette, Queen of France* (New York: Harper & Bothers, 1876), 49
3. D. Nokes, 1998, 47
4. D. Le Faye, 2002, 35
5. D. Le Faye, ibid., 36
6. P.D.S. Chesterfield, *Genuine Memoirs of Asiaticus: In a series of letters to a friend, during five years residence in different parts of India* (London: G. Kearsley, 1784), 115–16
7. R.A. Austen-Leigh, ed., 32–33

Chapter 5 – Paris

1. G. Walton, *Marie Antoinette's Confidante: The Rise and Fall of the Princesse de Lamballe* (London: Pen and Sword History, 2016), 59–60
2. C.C. Jackson, *The French Court and Society: Reign of Louis XVI and First Empire,* 2 vols. v. 1 (Boston: L. C. Page and Company, 1897), 17
3. R.A. Austen-Leigh, (ed.), 89–90
4. J.S.C. Abbott, *Marie Antoinette* (New York: Brunswick Subscription Company, 1917), 56–57
5. Ibid., 57
6. D. Le Faye, 2002, 46
7. S.C. Grier, *The Letters of Warren Hastings to His Wife* (Edinburgh: W. Blackwood and Sons, 1905), 397
8. D. Le Faye, 2002, 43–44
9. D. Nokes, 1998, 66
10. D. Le Faye, 2002, 50

Chapter 6 – Becoming a Countess

1. A.M. Devert, 'Le Marais de Gabarret et de Barbotan', *Bulletin de la Société de Borda*, No. 340 (1970): 336
2. R.A. Austen-Leigh, (ed.), 97–98
3. D. Le Faye, 2002, 52–53
4. R.A. Austen-Leigh, (ed.), 98
5. C. Tomalin, *Jane Austen: A Life* (New York: First Vintage Books, 1997), 54
6. W. Hastings and S.C. Grier, *The Letters of Warren Hastings to His Wife* (Edinburgh: W. Blackwood, 1905), 46

Chapter 7 – Hastings, Jr.

1. D. Le Faye. 2002, 68
2. G.B. Malleson, *Life of Warren Hastings, First Governor-general of India* (London: Chapman & Hall, LD., 1894), 445
3. D. Le Faye, 2004, 57
4. Ibid., 59
5. J. Sprange, *The Tunbridge Wells Guide ... Or, An Account of the Ancient and Present State of that Place: To which is Added a Particular Description of the Towns and Villages* (Tunbridge Wells: J. Sprange, 1786), 81
6. Ibid., 95

ENDNOTES

7. Ibid., 96
8. Ibid., 96–97
9. D. Le Faye, 2002, 80

Chapter 8 – The Year of 1788

1. D. Le Faye, 2004, 61
2. J.E. Austen-Leigh, 1882, 25
3. *Salisbury and Winchester Journal,* 'Thursday', 11 February 1788, 3
4. D. Le Faye, 2002, 84–85
5. P. Honan, *Jane Austen: Her Life* (New York: St. Martin's Press, 1987), 50
6. Anon, A *Guide to all the Watering and Sea Bathing Places in England and Wales, with a description of the Lakes; a sketch of a tour in Wales, and Itineraries* (London, 1824), 17
7. T. Blaikie, *Diary of a Scotch Gardener at the French Court at the End of the Eighteenth Century* (Cambridge: Cambridge University Press, 2012), 215–16
8. *Norfolk Chronicle,* "Sunday and Tuesday's Post', 9 August 1788, 1
9. D. Le Faye, 2002, 90

Chapter 9 – The Brink of Revolution

1. S. Schama, *Citzens: A Chronicle of the French Revolution* (New York: Alfred A. Knopf, 1989), 305
2. G.H. Tucker, *Jane Austen the Woman: Some Biographical Insights* (New York: St. Martin's Griffin, 1995), 154
3. S. Schama, 1989, 323
4. *Saunders's News-Letter, and Daily Advertiser,* 'Foreign Intelligence', 6 June 1789, 1
5. M.R. O'Leary, *Forging Freedom: The Life of Cerf Berr of Médelsheim* (Bloomington: iUniverse, 2012), 257
6. J. Austen, *The Loiterer: A Periodical Work* (Dublin: William Porter, 1792), 56–57

Chapter 10 – Philadelphia

1. J. Claretie, *Camille Desmoulins, Lucile Desmoulins: Étude sur les dantonistes* (aris: E. Plon and Cie, 1875), 76
2. *Norfolk Chronicle,* 'Revolution in France', 12 September 1789, 4

3. *Norfolk Chronicle,* 'Revolution in France', 19 September 1789, 4
4. *The Athenæum* (London: J. Francis, 1849), 40
5. *Caledonian Mercury,* 'Brest, Aug 11', 20 August 1789, 2
6. *Norfolk Chronicle,* 4
7. J.R. Clark and A.L. Motto, *Satire--that blasted art* (New York: Putnam, 1973), 325
8. W.C. Oulton, *Picture of Margate and its vicinity* (London: Baldwin, Cradock & Joy, 1820), 29
9. D. Le Faye, 2002, 100
10. N. Ennos, 2017, 53–54
11. D. Le Faye, 'Jane Austen and Her Hancock Relatives', *The Review of English Studies*, 30, no. 117 (1979): 12

Chapter 11 – Reign of Terror

1. D. Le Faye, 2002, 112
2. *Chester Chronicle,* 'Riot in Mount-Street', 15 June 1792, 4
3. *The Times,* 'France: Imprisonment of the King and Queen, and the Late Massacre', 23 September 1792, 2
4. G. Walton, *Marie Antoinette's Confidante: The Rise and Fall of the Princesse de Lamballe* (London: Pen and Sword Books Ltd, 2016), 196
5. W. Austen-Leigh and R.A. Austen-Leigh, *Jane Austen: Her Life and Letters A Family Record* (New York: E.P. Dutton & Company, 1913), 51
6. D. Nokes, 1998, 141

Chapter 12 – The Count's Fate

1. D. Le Faye, 2004, 90
2. *Northampton Mercury,* 'Sunday and Tuesday's Posts', 25 April 1795, 4
3. Ibid.
4. C. Tomalin, 1997, 107

Chapter 13 – Flirtations

1. D. Le Faye, 2002, 129
2. D. Le Faye, (ed.), *Jane Austen's Letters*, 3rd (Oxford: Oxford University Press, 1997), 1
3. Ibid., 4
4. P. Honan, 1987, 188
5. J. Austen and L. Oulton, *The Watsons* (New York: D. Appleton, 1923), 8

6. J. Austen-Leigh, 'New Light Thrown on JA's Refusal of Harris Bigg-Wither', *Journal of the Jane Austen Society of North America - Persuasions*, No.8, 1986 http://www.jasna.org/persuasions/printed/number8/austen-leigh.pdf, 35
7. D. Le Faye, 2004, 138

Chapter 14 – Henry

1. D. Le Faye, 2002, 138
2. P. Arbiter, *Memoirs of the Present Countess of Derby, late Miss Farren; including anecdotes of several distinguished persons* (London: H. D. Symonds, 1797), 20
3. *Ipswich Journal,* 'Sunday's Post', 20 May 1797, 1
4. *Kentish Gazette,* 'Ceremonial for the Nuptials of Frederick William, Hereditary prince of Wirtemberg, Stutgardt, with Charlotte-Augusta Matilda', 23 May 1797, 2
5. H.B. Baker, *History of the London Stage and Its Famous Players (1576–1903)* (New York: George Routledge and Sons, Limited, 1904), 131
6. D. Le Faye, 2002, 103
7. Ibid., 143–44
8. J. Austen, *Mansfield Park* (London: Richard Bentley, 1833), 16
9. D. Le Faye. 2002, 147–48
10. Ibid., 151

Chapter 15 – The Re-Married Life

1. D. Le Faye, 2002, 152–53
2. D. Nokes, 1998, 178
3. D. Le Faye, 2002, 169
4. T. Christie, *The Analytical Review, Or History of Literature, Domestic and Foreign, on an Enlarged Plan* v. 27 (London: J. Johnson, 1798), 321
5. D. Le Faye, (ed.), 13

Chapter 16 – Life Changes

1. P. Honan, 1987, 150–51
2. D. Nokes, 1998, 213
3. C. Chapman, 'Jane Austen's Banker Brother: Henry Thomas Austen of Austen & Co., 1801 1816', *Journal of the Jane Austen Society of North America - Persuasions*, No. 20, 1998 http://www.jasna.org/persuasions/printed/number20/caplan.pdf, 70

4. D. Le Faye, (ed.), 52–53
5. O.F. Adams, *The Story of Jane Austen's Life* (Chicago: A. C. McClurg, 1891), 26
6. D. Le Faye, (ed.), 68–69
7. Ibid., 75
8. Ibid., 78–79
9. Ibid., 71
10. *Bath Chronicle and Weekly Gazette,* 'To Be Disposed of', 21 May 1801, 1
11. D. Le Faye, (ed.), 78
12. N. Ennos, 2017, 194
13. Ibid., 197
14. Ibid., 210–11
15. D. Le Faye, 2002, 159–60

Chapter 17 – Treaty of Amiens

1. *The Ipswich Journal,* 'Ipswich, Oct. 24', 24 October 1801, 3
2. *Caledonian Mercury,* 'Madame Recamier', 13 May 1802, 4
3. P. Honan, 1987, 187

Chapter 18 – George Austen's Death

1. D. Le Faye, (ed.), 92
2. Ibid.
3. D. Le Faye, 2004, 143
4. D. Le Faye, (ed.), 86–87
5. D. Le Faye, 2004, 145
6. *Oxford Journal,* 'Country Fair', 29 December 1804, 4
7. *Hampshire Chronicle,* 'Winchester', 24 December 1804, 4
8. D. Le Faye, (ed.), 96
9. *Morning Advertiser,* 'The Old English Ale Brewery', 26 September 1807, 1
10. D. Le Faye, 2002, 165

Chapter 19 – Friendships

1. D. Le Faye, (ed.), 148
2. C. Tomalin, 1997, 208
3. P. Honan, 1987, 262–63
4. D. Le Faye, (ed.), 180

5. Ibid., 185
6. S.C. Woolsey, (ed.), *The Letters of Jane Austen* (Boston: Little, Brown, 1905), 273
7. D. Le Faye, 2002, 170

Chapter 20 – A Time to Mourn

1. *The Critical Review: Or, Annals of Literature* 1 (London: W. Simpkin and R. Marshall, 1812), 149
2. *Royal Cornwall Gazette,* 'Dreadful Murder', 1 August 1812, 2
3. D. Nokes, 1998, 395
4. D. Le Faye, (ed.), 201
5. *The Morning Post*, 28 January 1813, 2
6. N. Ennos, 2017, 227

Chapter 21 – Thoughts of a Writer

1. D. Le Faye, (ed.), 215
2. Ibid., 230
3. Ibid., 221
4. N. Ennos, 2017, 23
5. J.E. Austen-Leigh, 1882, 111
6. *Cobbett's Weekly Political Register*, 16 April 1814, 491–92
7. D. Le Faye, (ed.), 323
8. J. Austen, *Sense and Sensibility: A Novel* (London: Richard Bentley, 1833), vi
9. Ibid.
10. O.F. Adams. 1891, 220
11. *Salisbury and Winchester Journal,* 'Salisbury', 31 August 1818, 4
12. D. Le Faye, 2004, 230
13. D. Le Faye, (ed.), 201
14. D. Le Faye, 2002, 134
15. N. Ennos, 2017, 173
16. Ibid., 349
17. Ibid., 19

Index

Anning, Mary, 160
Austen, Anne Mathew, 94, 105
Austen, Cassandra Elizabeth,
   29, 34, 52, 105-107, 116, 118,
   120, 140-141, 148-149, 151,
   161, 165, 167, 169, 172,
   178, 186
   death, 186-187
   fiancé, 125-127
   watercolour of Jane Austen, 160
Austen, Cassandra Leigh, 13, 22,
   34-35, 52-53, 57, 62-63, 82,
   141, 149, 168
   death, 186
Austen, Charles, 57, 129, 146,
   153, 164, 178
   death, 187
Austen, Edward, *see* Knight,
   Edward Austen
Austen, Fanny Catherine,
  see Knight, Fanny Catherine
Austen, Francis 'Frank', 1, 34,
   65, 107, 140, 143, 153, 156,
   158-159, 160, 163-165, 178,
   186-187
   death, 187
Austen, George, 1, 13, 22, 34-35,
   57, 63, 105, 135, 139, 147, 149,
   160, 163-165, 185
   as trustee to Eliza, 32,
     49, 128-129
   death, 163
Austen, George Jr., 29, 67, 77
Austen, Henry, 29, 57, 66-67,
   74, 80, 83, 90, 94-96, 105, 107,
   112-114, 116, 132, 139-140,
   142-143, 146-151, 155,
   159-161, 164, 166, 168-171,
   173-174, 177-182, 184-186,
   188, 190
   business dealings, 144, 153,
     158, 165
   death, 187
   engagement to Mary
     Pearson, 117
   escape from France, 156-158
   illness, 152
   marriage to Eliza de Feuillide,
     133-137
Austen, James, 29, 62-65, 73-75,
   80, 90, 94, 105-106, 112, 114,
   120, 136, 140, 148-149, 151,
   162, 164, 178, 185, 188
   death, 186
   Loiterer, 83, 90
   marriage to Anne Mathew, 105
   marriage to Mary Lloyd, 125
   proposal to Eliza de Feuillide, 116

INDEX

Austen, Jane, 1, 35, 46, 62-63, 65-66, 76, 94, 105-107, 116-120, 122, 125, 130, 135, 138-140, 144-151, 158, 160-165, 167-175, 177-182-4, 186-189
   death, 185
   Emma, 46, 183, 187
   Henry & Eliza, 189-190
   illness, 184-185
   Lady Susan, 188
   letters destroyed, 150-151
   Love and Freindship, 94
   Mansfield Park, 83
   Northanger Abbey, 122, 139, 144, 158, 186, 188
   Persuasion, 144, 172, 185
   Pride and Prejudice, 44, 48, 117, 139, 172, 177-178, 180, 181, 182, 188
   Sense and Sensibility, 169
   Susan, 158
   typhus, 52
Austen, Martha Lloyd, 116, 146, 177, 187
Austen, Mary Lloyd, 116, 120, 125, 135-136, 140, 150, 165, 176, 186-187

Baillie, Matthew, 152, 182
balloon flight, 54-56, 154
Basingstoke, 22, 106, 112, 140, 146
Bath, 13, 15, 68, 101, 143, 146-149, 162, 164
Bigeon, Madame, 123, 133, 147, 179, 181
Bigg-Wither, Harris, 118-120, 158
Buchanan, Mary, 9-10

Carnac, John, 11, 14
Cawley, Mrs, 52
Chapuset, Anna Marie Apollonia, 21, 27, 33, 43, 64, 130-131
Christmas theatricals, 73-74
Clarinda, 13, 22, 36-37, 43
Clive, Robert, 5-6, 10-12, 14, 17, 190
Clive, Margaret Maskelyne, 11-12, 14
Cooper, Jane, 52
Covent Garden, 2, 158, 177, 181
Count of Provence, 170-171, 177

Day of the Tiles, 78-79

Estates General, 86-89, 91

Farquhar, Sir Walter, 121-123, 132, 188
Farren, Elizabeth, 126-127
Feuillide, Eliza de, 1, 17-19, 22, 25-34, 36-37, 49-52, 64-68, 76-77, 79-84, 89-91, 94, 102-107, 111-112, 114-117, 121-134, 138, 141-142, 147-150, 152, 155, 160, 164-167, 169-173, 180-184, 186-191
   death, 151
   as party hostess, 172-173
   birth of Hastings Jr., 63
   Christmas in Steventon, 73-75
   death, 179
   disturbance Mount Street, 102-103
   escape from France, 156-158
   health, 122-124, 147, 172, 174, 176, 178

living in France, 38, 40-43,
  45-47, 53-54, 56-57, 61-63
India, 11-13
letters destroyed, 150
meeting Count de Feuillide, 48
marriage to Henry Austen,
  135-137
miscarriage, 60, 103
Orchard Street, 75
reaction to George Austen's
  death, 164
return to England from India, 13
Ramsgate, 76-77
Tunbridge Wells, 68-72, 74-76,
  81, 114, 116, 121
Feuillide, Hastings Jr. de, 63, 67,
  73, 76-77, 81, 83-84, 94-96, 98,
  111, 121, 128, 132-133, 142
Feuillide, Jean-François Capot,
  Count de, 48-50, 58, 60-61, 63,
  65, 84, 91, 94, 96, 99-101,
  107-111, 119, 129, 156
  execution, 110
  Gabarret, 48, 56, 58, 107, 111
  Nérac, 48-49, 51-52
Floating rafts, 137
Fowle, Tom, 125-126
Francis, Sir Philip, 58-59
Franklin, Benjamin, 37, 89

George III, 102, 107, 115, 127
Gibson, Mary, 158, 165
Godmersham, 57, 139-140,
  148-150, 164-165, 168-169,
  173, 178

Hampshire, 13, 22, 34, 103, 125,
  163, 168, 187

Hancock, Elizabeth 'Eliza',
  see Feuillide, Eliza de
Hancock, Philadelphia, 1-5, 7, 10,
  12-14, 16-18, 20, 22-23, 25-40,
  43, 45, 47-50, 52, 64-65, 71, 76,
  84, 89-91, 94, 97-100, 105, 151
  breast cancer, 96-100, 174
  death, 100
  marriage to Tysoe Saul
    Hancock, 4-5
  will, 99
Hancock, Tysoe Saul, 4-5, 7,
  10-14, 16-35, 44, 48, 100,
  190-191
Hastings, Warren, 7-9, 12-14,
  16-19, 21, 23, 26-29, 31-35,
  43, 45, 48-49, 42, 58-59,
  63-64, 75-76, 80, 99, 111-114,
  129-131, 142, 166, 182
  affair with Philadelphia, 10
  Daylesford estate, 80, 131, 166,
    182, 186
  death, 186
  Eliza being his child,
    11, 190-191
  impeachment and trial, 59,
    75-76, 113
  Nandakumar incident, 58-59
  son George, 13
Hubback, John F., 153, 156

Impey, Elijah, 58-59
India, 1, 3-13, 16-19, 21-28, 31,
  33-35, 58-59, 182
  Black Hole, 8-10
  Calcutta, 1, 5-10, 12, 19-22,
    27-28, 31, 33, 44
  Cuddalore, 4, 6

INDEX

Kelsall, Jane 'Jenny', 11-12, 190
Kindersley, Jemima, 1, 6-7
Knight, Catherine Knatchbull, 57-58, 139, 177
Knight, Edward Austen, 57, 65, 96, 99, 106, 139, 148, 164, 166-169, 177-179
   as 'Neddy', 57, 63-64, 96
   death, 187
   name changed from Austen to Knight, 177
Knight, Fanny Catherine, 164, 166-167, 169, 173, 177, 187
Knight, Thomas, 57-58

Lamballe, Princess de, 37, 54, 104
Launay, Emmanuel Henri Louis Alexandre de, Count d'Antraigues, 170-172, 176-178
Lefroy, Anne, Madam, 66, 117-118, 145, 162-163
Lefroy, Thomas Langlois, 116-118
Leigh-Perrot, Jane, 140-141, 144, 147
Lloyd, Martha, *see* Austen, Martha Lloyd
Lloyd, Mary, *see* Austen, Mary Lloyd
Loiterer, 83, 90
Louis XVI, 38, 39, 87-88, 96, 104, 106, 170
Lyme Regis, 160, 162

Marbeuf, Henriette-François Michel, Marquise de, 108-111
Marie Antoinette, 30, 37-38, 41, 46, 54, 87-88, 101, 106, 170
millinery, 2-3, 68, 156

Nandakumar, 58-59, 64
Napoleon Bonaparte, 137, 139, 155-156, 158, 171, 177, 183-184, 187

Paris, 23, 37-38, 40-46, 50-53, 64, 80, 82-83, 85, 88-90, 96, 101, 104, 107-109, 121, 155, 172, 183
Payne, Maria, 130
Prince Regent, 152, 154, 182
pugs, 121, 123, 130, 188

Réveillon riot, 85-86

sea-bathing, 95-96, 128, 132
Siddons, Sarah, 128
Siraj ud-Daulah, 8-9
Steventon, 22, 29, 35, 57, 64, 66, 73, 83, 94-95, 102, 104-105, 107, 114, 116, 120, 140, 146, 148-149, 162, 164, 186

Treaty of Amiens, 153-154
Twisleton, Thomas James, 82-83, 138

Walter, Philadelphia 'Phylly', 40-43, 46-47, 50, 53-54, 60, 62, 65, 67, 71, 73-77, 80-81, 83, 95-103, 105-106, 114, 116, 121-123, 125-126, 128, 130, 132-136, 138, 141-142, 149-151, 173
Woodman, John, 14, 31-33, 49, 52, 64, 84, 128-129, 131-133
Woodman, Thomas, 14, 131